Signs of Light

SIGNS OF LIGHT

French and British Theories of Linguistic Communication, 1648–1789

MATTHEW LAUZON

CORNELL UNIVERSITY PRESS
ITHACA AND LONDON

Copyright © 2010 by Cornell University

All rights reserved. Except for brief quotations in a review, this book, or parts thereof, must not be reproduced in any form without permission in writing from the publisher. For information, address Cornell University Press, Sage House, 512 East State Street, Ithaca, New York 14850.

First published 2010 by Cornell University Press

Printed in the United States of America

Library of Congress Cataloging-in-Publication Data
Lauzon, Matthew, 1972–
  Signs of light : French and British theories of linguistic communication, 1648–1789 / Matthew Lauzon.
    p. cm.
  Includes bibliographical references and index.
  ISBN 978-0-8014-4847-8 (cloth : alk. paper)
  1. Linguistics—France—History—17th century. 2. Linguistics—France—History—18th century. 3. Linguistics—Great Britain—History—17th century. 4. Linguistics—Great Britain—History—18th century. 5. Language and languages—Philosophy—History—17th century. 6. Language and languages—Philosophy—History—18th century. 7. Enlightenment—France. 8. Enlightenment—Great Britain. I. Title.

  P81.F7L38 2010
  410.944'09032—dc22   2009048592

Cornell University Press strives to use environmentally responsible suppliers and materials to the fullest extent possible in the publishing of its books. Such materials include vegetable-based, low-VOC inks and acid-free papers that are recycled, totally chlorine-free, or partly composed of nonwood fibers. For further information, visit our website at www.cornellpress.cornell.edu.

Cloth printing   10 9 8 7 6 5 4 3 2 1

For Karen and Gerald, my parents, from whom I came

Contents

Acknowledgments ix

Introduction 1

Part I. Animal Communication 11

1. Bestial Banter 13

2. *Homo Risus:* Making Light of Animal Language 40

Part II. Savage Eloquence 67

3. Warming Savage Hearts and Heating Eloquent Tongues 69

4. From Savage Orators to Savage Languages 102

Part III. Civilized Tongues 133

5. French Levity 135

6. English Energy 176

Coda: French Levity and English Energy in the Revolutionary Wake 216

Bibliography 231

Index 245

Acknowledgments

I would like to communicate my deep gratitude to the many institutions, teachers, scholars, friends, and relatives who have helped me over the years.

I am grateful to the Department of History and the Department of Philosophy at Carleton University and to the departments of history at The Johns Hopkins University, l'École des Hautes Études en Sciences Sociales, and the University of Hawaii at Manoa. I also thank the librarians at the Interlibrary Loan Department at the University of Hawaii at Manoa for their help. Some material in this book appeared as papers at annual conferences of the American and Canadian Societies for Eighteenth-Century Studies; thanks to those who organized, attended, and participated in the sessions where I presented. I am also deeply grateful to my editor at Cornell University Press, John Ackerman, for shepherding the project through the publication process.

I received a great deal of support and encouragement in Eastern Ontario from Stanley Clarke, Bruce Elliott, Béla Egyed, Naomi Griffiths,

Robert Goheen, Konrad Koerner, and especially Mark Phillips. At The Johns Hopkins University, I was both challenged and helped by Anthony Pagden and David Bell. Roger Chartier did the same for me during my years in Paris. At the University of Hawaii I have been fortunate to find many good colleagues and friends. Although they have all given me something, I especially thank Leonard Andaya, Jerry Bentley, Shana Brown, Arindam Chakrabarti, David Chappell, Marcus Daniel, Edward Davis, David Hanlon, Peter Hoffenberg, Karen Jolly, James Kraft, Vina Lanzona, Paul Lyons, Kieko Matteson, Robert McGlone, Njoroge Njoroge, Richard Rapson, Richard Rath, Suzanna Reiss, Matt Romaniello, John Rosa, Yuma Totani, Giovanni Vitiello, and Wensheng Wang.

I would also like to acknowledge the many engaging conversations about history and even more important things that I have been lucky enough to carry on with other close friends over the years. Among these sociable and witty, though not always light, conversationalists, I especially acknowledge Shane Agin, Patrick Coyne, Carolyn Eastman, François Furstenberg, Eric Henophy, Linda Lierheimer, Mary-Catherine Moran, Neil Safier, Dale Smith, Paul Tonks, Phil Vogt, Craig Yirush, and Giovanni Zanalda.

Above all I am grateful for the affection, patience, concern, and help that people dear to me outside the academic world have demonstrated over the years. My mother spent many years encouraging me and wondering whether I would ever finish school. My father's fascination with etymologies inspired my interest in other people's attitudes to languages. He also read and commented on some of the chapters. My brothers, Philip, Andrew, and Simon, each helped in their own ways. I am especially glad to thank Andrew, who shares my interests in history and linguistics and with whom I traveled to many conferences and libraries. I am happy to thank my wife, Kim, who with unflinching support and love has sustained me. Our baby, Zozo, even though she can't yet speak, has in her own way contributed to this book on the history of ideas about linguistic communication.

Signs of Light

INTRODUCTION

> The philosophy of language is now so well understood by the learned among us, that we know not only what a language is, but what it ought to be.
>
> MONBODDO, *Origin and Progress of Language* (1774)

In 1740, the French literary historian Claude-Pierre Goujet (1697–1767) published the first volume of his massive history of French literature. This volume reviewed a century of controversy over the merits of the French language and defended it from critics like the seventeenth-century magistrate Jean Belot, who "held our language responsible for the errors of recent times, the furors of the Wars of Religion, the seditious opinions that were spreading at that time, and the revolt of the people."[1] Goujet, who insisted that languages and national characters "are so closely tied together that they have the same beginnings, the same progress, and the same revolutions," argued that "the French tongue has all the advantages of other languages, with almost none of their disadvantages."[2] While Belot

---

1. Claude-Pierre Goujet, *Bibliothèque Françoise* (Paris: Chez P. J. Mariette et H.-L. Guerin, 1741), 1:19–20. Goujet's reference was to Jean Belot, *Apologie de la langue Latine* (Paris: Chez François Targa, 1637).
2. Ibid., 5 and 37.

and Goujet disagreed about the French language in particular, some of their near contemporaries, like Thomas Hobbes, blamed all human languages for violent disputes like the English Civil Wars and pointed out that, by contrast, "certain living creatures, as Bees, and Ants," because they do not communicate the way humans do, "live sociably one with another."[3] In Voltaire's *Ingénue* (1766), a story about a Huron who visits France, one of the French characters asked "which of the three languages he liked best, Huron, English, or French?"[4] Questions like this preoccupied Voltaire and many other early modern thinkers who were deeply concerned about the implications of forms of communication. While some bitterly complained that their language was responsible for infelicitous forms of communication by promoting ambiguity, dissimulation, or barbarism, others confidently celebrated their languages as responsible for the virtues of their speech communities. In this respect, although they were all committed to the notion that some languages were better than others, they could not agree on which languages generated the best forms of social communication.

In recent years, historians have drawn attention both to the new ideas and practices of sociability that emerged in the eighteenth century and to changing ideas about language in this period. They have failed, however, to understand many of the vital connections between these two subjects, which they have treated separately. One of the main reasons for this has been a tendency to characterize European thinkers during this period as caught in the grips of a "crisis of representation." As a consequence, discussions of early modern linguistics have privileged those thinkers who blamed existing languages for disputes and who therefore sought either to reform those languages or to invent new kinds of language.

On the one hand, this has contributed to a long-standing tendency—exemplified by Hans Aarsleff—to associate innovations in early modern linguistics principally with two exceptional individuals: John Locke (1632–1704) and his French disciple, the abbé de Condillac (1715–1780). There is no doubt that Lockean linguistics did leave a very deep impression on eighteenth-century ideas about language. In his *De l'homme* (1772), Claude-Adrien Helvétius (1715–1771), for example, followed Locke in

---

3. Thomas Hobbes, *Leviathan* (New York: Penguin, 1968), 225–226.
4. Voltaire, "Ingenuous," in *Voltaire: Candide, Zadig and Selected Stories*, ed. John Iverson (New York and London: Signet Classics, 1961), 258.

blaming interminable disputes in "morality, politics, metaphysics, and theology" on the fact that for different people "the same words do not represent the same ideas."[5] There is no question that Locke's interest in the definitions of words as signs for ideas did contribute crucially to the shaping of a very important discourse on language in the eighteenth century, and in the chapters that follow I am in no way suggesting that Locke's ideas were neither important nor influential. Locke, however, tended to view words "as a sort of private property in the individual's mind."[6] This rather individualistic and introspective focus led Locke and his followers to largely disregard many of the social uses of language for communicative purposes other than the representation of things and ideas.

Recognizing this as a problem, Thomas Sheridan (1719–1788), the British theorist of language and rhetoric, lamented, "What a pity is it that [Locke], this penetrating writer, did not carry his enquiries farther. We might then have had, an accurate knowledge of the whole of language.... But he confined himself entirely to that branch of language, which related to... the human understanding; his only object was, to examine the nature of words, as symbols of our ideas." Sheridan pointed out that what he called "social communication" involved a different, if complementary, set of issues that he set out to study.[7] For many early modern thinkers, like Sheridan, the best languages had something more than precisely defined words. The following chapters are focused on these other discourses about what made certain languages better for communication than others.

A second long-standing tendency resulting from seeing early modern linguistic thinking as a reaction to a crisis of representation and a desire for transparency has been to focus on schemes that were intended not so much to reform existing languages as to invent a new kind of transparent language that would replace them. As the most recent contribution to this tendency has argued, "ever worsening linguistic shortcomings were

---

5. Claude-Adrien Helvétius, *De l'homme* (London: Société typographique, 1773), 40. "Because of Locke," he wrote elsewhere, "the old man is destroyed and a new man who walks according to truth is born." See Helvétius, *Notes de la main d'Helvétius,* ed. Albert Keim (Paris: Félix Alcan, 1907), 5.

6. John Durham Peters, *Speaking into the Air: A History of the Idea of Communication* (Chicago: University of Chicago Press, 1999), 81.

7. Thomas Sheridan, *A Course of Lectures on Elocution: Together with Two Dissertations on Language* (London: Printed by W. Strahan, 1762), 97–98.

seen as a hindrance to the formulation of thoughts (whether of the moral, religious, political or philosophical kind) and their transparent expression. In seventeenth-century England, many people believed that the only plausible curative for this condition—and the only likely prophylactic against further linguistic slippage—was the construction of an artificial language that would exactly map the order of things, and of thought."[8] A number of historians have extended and deepened significantly our understanding of the various early modern European language schemes to invent what John Wilkins called a "real character," a language of signs that could represent things or ideas without any semantic or logical ambiguity.[9]

As important as Locke, his Enlightenment disciples, and the language schemers were in shaping linguistic concerns, historians have tended to focus exclusively on their idealizations of new kinds of language that could transparently represent the order of things by rigidly assigning definitions to words. This tendency generally has led scholars to overlook other important early modern idealizations of language. These other discourses on language had significant implications not just for understandings of semantic and logical representation but also for conceptions of sociable communication. Historians have therefore tended to ignore both the period's tremendous engagement with the broader social implications of different languages that prevailed across the European republic of letters and the ways in which such an engagement involved much more than issues of semantic and logical clarity.

One recent work that stands out as an exception to the tendency to treat separately ideas about language and ideas of sociability in an emerging public sphere is Sophia Rosenfeld's *A Revolution in Language: The Problem of Signs in Late Eighteenth-Century France*.[10] By focusing exclusively on the French interest in developing a "mute" language of signs in the

---

8. Rhodri Lewis, *Language, Mind and Nature: Artificial Languages in England from Bacon to Locke* (Cambridge: Cambridge University Press, 2007), 2.

9. See, among others, Umberto Eco, *The Search for the Perfect Language* (Oxford: Blackwell, 1995); James R. Knowlson, *Universal Language Schemes in England and France, 1600–1800* (Toronto: University of Toronto Press, 1975); Robert Markley, *Fallen Languages: Crises of Representation in Newtonian England 1660–1740* (Ithaca: Cornell University Press, 1993); Sophia Rosenfeld, *A Revolution Language: The Problem of Signs in Late Eighteenth-Century France* (Stanford: Stanford University Press, 2001); and M. M. Slaughter, *Universal Languages and Scientific Taxonomy in the Seventeenth Century* (Cambridge: Cambridge University Press, 1982).

10. Rosenfeld, *A Revolution in Language*.

second half of the eighteenth century, however, Rosenfeld's work explores only one of the many types of communication that engaged early modern thinkers concerned with the linguistic regeneration of society. Not only does Rosenfeld's book largely ignore the many other languages that some French Enlightenment thinkers considered in their attempt to regenerate society by resolving what they took to be the crisis of representation, but it also ignores the important fact that many other French thinkers, from the late seventeenth century well into the Revolution, continued to insist that French already was a perfect language. Consequently, they argued that French not only did not need to be replaced or reformed but was already contributing to intellectual and cultural refinement by becoming a universal language.

This book adopts a comparative approach to analyze how various British and French discourses about language reflected early modern hopes that an ideal speech community that already existed could be protected and promoted. This hope resulted, however, not only in arguments for reforming existing defective languages or replacing them with artificial ones that could guarantee representational clarity. The hope also resulted in arguments that celebrated and encouraged the spread or the emulation of particular languages. The chapters that follow therefore examine early modern discourses about the properties of specific languages that, according to some thinkers, contributed to an ideal speech community.

Each of these discourses championed an already-existing language, such as that of animals or "savages," as well as French or English, for the specific communicational properties that they possessed. The following chapters show that, as strong as the appeal of linguistic clarity was, not all early modern thinkers idealized clarity to the exclusion of other communicational virtues. Significantly, some of these properties contributed not so much to *clear* forms of communication as to *energetic* or *light* forms. In fact, these contrasting linguistic ideals drove early modern thinkers to champion different forms of communication. While some, like Hobbes, did believe that all human languages potentially generated social disorder specifically because they were insufficiently clear, other thinkers believed that particular human languages—American Indian languages, for example—could ensure greater sincerity because they expressed strong emotions better than others did. Also, while British thinkers tended to argue that French promoted frivolous, equivocal, and insincere speech, many French linguists argued throughout this period that important properties particular to that language made French conversations especially brilliant, polite, and amusing, and so they praised their own language for spreading enlightenment by encouraging gallant and sociable exchanges of wit. These contrasting ideals of passionate sincerity and amusing levity played central roles in shaping early modern attitudes to different languages, but historians like Rosenfeld have overlooked their importance by focusing too exclusively on issues of semantic or syntactic transparency.

To highlight the contrasts among these three different attitudes to forms of communication, the material in this book is divided into three pairs of chapters that move from the most abstract communicative types to those that were most particularly familiar to early modern British and French thinkers. The first pair of chapters analyzes discussions about the difference between animal and human communication, the second deals with discussions about savage and civilized languages, and the last section of the book looks at debates about the character of two "cultivated" languages: French and English.

The two chapters about animal communication contrast the ideals of linguistic transparency and levity. Hobbes, writing in the wake of a century of unprecedented civil and religious violence, argued that sociable animals lived peaceably with one another because their languages were free from the ambiguity that inhered in human communication and made it possible for humans to redescribe vices as virtues and virtues as vices. Not everybody who discussed animal communication, however, agreed with Hobbes that unambiguous animal languages were superior to human languages. Jonathan Swift, for example, suggested that what made human communication superior to that of animals was precisely the human ability to use figural language, particularly irony, to say one thing and mean another. He observed that humor, wit, and ridicule could be used to defuse the violence that might result from communicating different points of view.

The second pair of chapters shows how late-seventeenth-century missionary concerns about the sincerity of American Indian conversions generated a particularly positive representation of savage speech. By linking sincerity with the expression of heated emotions, missionaries in both New England and New France developed a representation of savage eloquence that later Enlightenment thinkers attributed to the structures of primitive languages. In 1770, a French author named Nicolas Bricaire de la

Dixmerie (1730–1791) imagined a Pacific Islander speaking to his European interlocutor in the following terms: "Our Island is home to different Nations, directed by different chiefs. Each communicates with all the others without deceptions or errors. They have never known discord, fraud, or the wish to spread confusion, or even the means to harm themselves."[11] Dixmerie used the recently discovered "Tahiti," which he represented as a concert of different nations all living peaceably together, as an allegory for the European past and potential future. In the end, Dixmerie's imaginary Pacific Islander asks his civilized French correspondent to "leave us our Language such as it is, and do not look at all to enrich it."[12] Like Dixmerie, many early modern French and British thinkers, from the Abbé Dubos to Thomas Reid, used this conception of savage eloquence and sincerity to criticize their own overcivilized languages, which tended to facilitate dissimulation and generate social discord.

The last pair of chapters analyzes similar issues: discussions about how the French and English languages reflected and reinforced distinct national practices of enlightened communication. From about 1670, French thinkers began idealizing their language as one that promoted amusing, sociable, and polite communication as well as clear communication. Although Antoine Rivarol (1753–1801) asserted that "what is not clear is not French," his argument that French was destined to be the universal language also rested on his belief that because of his language, "the Frenchman has a spark of gaiety that never leaves him."[13] Such early modern linguistic attitudes contributed to the rise of a myth not only of French clarity but also of French gaiety. While the British took longer than the French to recover their linguistic nerve after a protracted period of unprecedented civil violence, by the early eighteenth century British thinkers were increasingly praising English for facilitating, like savage languages, the expression of strong emotions and therefore characterized English as a guard against what one British thinker called "the assaults of flattery" that plagued French society. These last two chapters also explore the links

---

11. Nicolas Bricaire de la Dixmerie, *Le Sauvage de Taïti aux Français; avec un envoi au philosophe ami des sauvages* (London: Chez Le Jay, 1770), 110.

12. Ibid., 149.

13. Antoine de Rivarol, "L'Universalité de la langue française," in Académie de Berlin, *De l'universalité Européenne de la langue française,* ed. Pierre Pénisson (Paris: Librairie Arthème Fayard, 1995), 162 and 145.

between these linguistic attitudes and contrasting national practices of enlightened communication involving such things as the participation of women in conversation, science as a sociable enterprise, and attitudes toward print and the theater.

Although they had deep roots that could be traced back to classical and early Christian debates, each of the discourses analyzed in the following chapters was revived or reinvigorated in specific contexts during the second half of the seventeenth century. Claims that sociable animals communicated more effectively than humans appeared toward the middle of the seventeenth century as a response to concerns that the ambiguity inherent in human languages had contributed to or even caused the civil and religious violence of the previous decades. The belief that so-called savages in the New World communicated more energetically and therefore more sincerely and more eloquently than Europeans developed in the context of missionary attempts to guarantee the authenticity of Indian conversions in the mid-seventeenth century. Around 1670, the quarrel of the ancients and moderns sparked a renewed interest in the relative merits of certain European languages, and particularly of French and English. The following chapters therefore trace the development of these different but related discourses on languages from the second half of the seventeenth century to the end of the eighteenth. Although these dates correspond very closely with the dates from the publication of the *Port Royal Grammar* (1660), by Antoine Arnauld (1612–1694) and Claude Lancelot (1615–1695), to the French Revolution (c. 1800) or what French historians tend to call *l'âge classique,* I have decided simply to refer to these thinkers, their texts, and their arguments with the less loaded, if more generic, label of "early modern."

Taken together, these six chapters have significant implications for understanding how theories of communication were tied to idealizations of distinct forms of community and sociability during the period that corresponds roughly to the Enlightenment. In 1784, several of the essays that competed for the Berlin Academy's prize for answering the question why French had become the universal language of Europe argued that the French language had played an important role in spreading enlightenment. Etienne Mayet's entry insisted, for example, that "languages are the bond of societies, the vehicle of enlightenment." While he asserted that "Speech is the basis of enlightenment," he shared his contemporaries' belief that some forms of speech are better than others as foundations for this enlightenment.[14] The book therefore also contributes to recent interpretations of eighteenth-century intellectual history by highlighting the fact that different thinkers, while sharing a general concern about forms of communication, subscribed to contrasting idealizations of what enlightened communication and communities should be. Current work on Enlightenment theories of signification tends to assume that an ideal language would simply be one that guarantees representational clarity. While many thinkers did idealize linguistic clarity, others preferred languages that were emotionally expressive and communicated warmth and sincerity. Still others held that the best languages were those that encouraged polite and witty forms of sociability by communicating levity and defusing the dangers associated with fanaticism. In this respect, some thinkers made the communication of energy or levity just as important as clarity. In fact, over the period examined by the book, a general preference for linguistic energy supplanted an earlier tendency to value linguistic levity. Late-seventeenth- and early-eighteenth-century thinkers who complained, for example, about the ranting speech of enthusiasts frequently attacked energetic or heated language. By the mid-eighteenth century, however, Enlightenment thinkers were increasingly complaining that modern communication had become too frivolous and that light languages were responsible for the inability to vehemently persuade the civil community to energetically embrace the public interest. The book's coda traces the shifting place of these contrasting linguistic values by examining their fates in the American and French revolutions, when revolutionaries attacked frivolous aristocratic languages and celebrated energetic republican speech.

This book thus explores some of the important ways in which early modern French and British thinkers developed and deployed discourses that idealized different forms of linguistic communication. Historians have long understood that establishing clarity in communication was a central and constant concern of these early modern thinkers. Although historians have explored this particular concern, the suggestion by some in the seventeenth and eighteenth centuries that animals might communicate more clearly and therefore more effectively has gone entirely unnoticed. The early modern critics of this suggestion have similarly received no scholarly

---

14. Etienne Mayet, "Est Brevitate Opus," in Académie de Berlin, *De l'universalité Européenne de la langue française,* ed. Pierre Pénisson (Paris: Librairie Arthème Fayard, 1995), 73.

attention. This oversight is significant, however, as it shows that clarity, while an important early modern communicative ideal, was not the only one.

Despite the explicit hostility to rhetoric and figural language that some, like Locke, demonstrated, a number of others embraced the way in which human speakers were able to deftly manage certain forms of ambiguity effectively, either to suggest novel but indefinite notions or to communicate propositions without actually saying them. Some early-eighteenth-century French and British writers therefore celebrated this communicative capacity for humor, epigrammatic conceits, and redescriptive wit as one that allowed people to entertain and exchange contrasting and often inconsistent ideas and so learn new things while attenuating the potential for violent dispute. Beginning around 1670, many—French thinkers in particular—began to argue that French, more than any other language, exhibited this characteristically human capacity for managing ambiguity, a capacity that promoted gallantly polite conversation and sociably gay learning. In this way, one set of early modern linguistic discourses contributed to the myth not only of French *clarté* but also of French *légèreté*.

A third, contrasting communicative ideal had its origins in classical and Christian discourses of rhetorical primitivism and migrated into early modern discourses about American Indian oratory and English speech. Not only was this third communicative ideal not inconsistent with notions of representational clarity, but the idea that certain languages communicated emotions more effectively than others actually reinforced the notion that certain speakers, because of the language they spoke, could be trusted to be more sincere than others. Ultimately, as the final two chapters show, these contrasting idealizations of the French and English languages influenced how some thinkers conceived of other communicative issues. For example, the English-speaking William Smellie and the French-speaking Antoine de Rivarol each presented his own language as the best guarantor of future public felicity, commercial success, and imperial strength.

Part I

ANIMAL COMMUNICATION

1

BESTIAL BANTER

> The *taciturnity* of the other animals is a problem to be accounted for, as well as the *loquacity* of man.
>
> JAMES DUNBAR, *Essays on the History of Mankind* (1781)

The idea that clarity is a virtue in communication is hardly unique to the early modern period. The desire to communicate as clearly as possible is no doubt as old as communication itself. Throughout history, however, there have been various motives that have driven people to worry, even to obsess, over how communication might be clarified. Ideas about what forms an ideally clear communication should take, therefore, have a definite history. Concerns about language and communication naturally arise during periods of acute controversy and discord. The unprecedented levels of religious and civil controversies and violence in seventeenth-century Europe no doubt contributed to growing worries about the role that language and communication had played in aggravating or even generating these disputes. The rise of new philosophical systems and scientific ideas as well as the introduction of new technologies of communication such as the printing press also heightened people's interest in the nature of communication. Finally, the European encounters with a growing variety of non-European languages and systems of communication in the sixteenth and seventeenth centuries as well as the European desire to trade with, convert, or otherwise dominate non-European peoples also contributed to a growing sensitivity to communication. The cultural stakes involved in finding ways to clarify linguistic communication were therefore very high.

Historians have made John Locke one of the central figures in their accounts of this early modern search to clarify communication. Indeed, in the "Epistle to the Reader" of his *Essay Concerning Human Understanding* (1690), Locke complained that the "greatest part of the questions and controversies that perplex mankind [depend] on the doubtful and uncertain use of words, or (which is the same) indetermined ideas, which they are made to stand for." For Locke, then, linguistic communication could be clarified only by reforming what he took to be the opaque medium of language itself. Locke therefore insisted that if what he called the "abuse of words" could be corrected, then even moral claims would be just as "capable of demonstration...as mathematics." In order to correct abuses of words, Locke recommended fixing their definitions. "Thereby," he argued, "moral knowledge may be brought to so great clearness and certainty." Locke added that, in fact, "a definition is the only way whereby the precise meaning of moral words can be known; and yet a way whereby their meaning may be known certainly, and without leaving any room for any contest about it."[1]

Despite his having recognized that communication was a communal enterprise, the method for studying and reforming language that Locke recommended was principally solipsistic. Locke believed that what people communicated or made public when they used language was the private contents of their minds. As he put it in his *Essay Concerning Human Understanding,* "words in their primary or immediate signification, stand for nothing, but *the ideas in the mind of him that uses them.*" Locke held that the main problem with linguistic communication was that when "those ideas are collected from the things which they are supposed to represent," the collecting, so to speak, was done either "imperfectly" or "carelessly." Locke thus translated the problem of outward and social communication into a problem of inward and private signification or representation. He

---

1. John Locke, *An Essay concerning Human Understanding,* ed. Alexander Campbell Fraser (New York: Dover, 1959), 1:23; 2:156–157.

then set out to recommend that people attend more closely to the meanings that they assigned to individual words.²

While Locke thus established an influential semantic program for reforming the lexicon and thereby clarifying language, many historians who have studied ideas about language in early modern France and Britain have tended to focus their attention on schemes to invent new kinds of languages that would transparently represent the order of things and thoughts. The assumptions underlying these projects to invent new languages were largely similar to those underlying Locke's project to correct existing languages. In order to communicate more clearly, they believed, it was necessary to represent truth more clearly. John Wilkins (1614–1672), bishop of Chester, for example, argued that his project for inventing a "real character" would

> contribute much to the clearing of some of our Modern differences in *Religion,* by unmasking many wild errors, that shelter themselves under the disguise of affected phrases; which being Philosophically unfolded, and rendered according to the genuine and natural importance of Words, will appear to be inconsistencies and contradictions. And several of those pretended, mysterious, profound notions, expressed in great swelling words, whereby some men set up for reputation, being this way examined, will appear to be, either nonsense, or very flat and jejune.³

The invention of a new language that would be as clear as possible, then, was essentially to put the mind and its contents in order by scrupulously managing the lexicon.

While most studies of early modern fantasies of linguistic clarity have focused on attempts, like Wilkins's, to invent new kinds of languages, some historians have noticed that certain early modern thinkers considered the possibility that such transparent languages might already exist among speakers somewhere in the world. A number of seventeenth-century thinkers took Egyptian hieroglyphs to be an example of a language that could best express the nature of things. Some also similarly took Chinese

---

2. Ibid., 2:9. Throughout, all emphases appearing in quotations are in the original unless otherwise noted.

3. John Wilkins, "The Epistle Dedicatory," in *Essay towards a Real Character and a Philosophical Language* (London: Printed for Sa. Gellibrand, and for John Martyn, 1668), no page no.

character-writing to be a "natural" language.[4] Egyptian hieroglyphs and Chinese ideograms shared what a number of early modern language theorists took to be an important communicative virtue: that of transcending ambiguity and confusion through visual representations of things or ideas. While most recent studies of the quest for a perfect language have focused on projects to invent new systems of communication, and while some attention has focused on the early modern interest in actual languages that used graphic systems of communication, the idea that animals might communicate more effectively than people has received no attention.[5] Yet the fantasy of a perfectly transparent system of communication was so strong in early modern Europe that some important thinkers did in fact consider the possibility that animals might communicate more effectively, because more transparently, than humans. I will examine such claims in this chapter. The next chapter will then show that certain early modern thinkers not only rejected but even ridiculed these fantasies of lexical and representational clarity associated by some with animal communication. For these other thinkers, it was precisely the uniquely human capacity to use words in potentially equivocal ways that made human forms of communication far superior to the less versatile forms of animal communication.

Abstraction and Human Language

One of the concerns shared by most early modern thinkers who worried about ambiguity in human communication and the "abuse of words" was

---

4. James R. Knowlson, *Universal Language Schemes in England and France, 1600–1800* (Toronto: University of Toronto Press, 1975), 22–27. See also Umberto Eco, *The Search for the Perfect Language,* trans. James Fentress (Oxford: Blackwell, 1995), 144–176 and 212–213; and Rhodri Lewis, *Language, Mind and Nature: Artificial Languages in England from Bacon to Locke* (Cambridge: Cambridge University Press, 2007), 12–13.

5. On early modern ideas about animals and animal communication, see George Boas, *The Happy Beast in French Thought of the Seventeenth Century* (Baltimore: Johns Hopkins University Press, 1933); Erica Fudge, *Brutal Reasoning: Animals, Rationality, and Humanity in Early Modern England* (Ithaca: Cornell University Press, 2006); Hester Hastings, *Man and Beast in French Thought of the Eighteenth Century* (Baltimore: Johns Hopkins University Press, 1936); R. W. Serjeantson, "The Passions and Animal Language, 1540–1700," *Journal for the History of Ideas* 62, no. 3 (2001): 425–444; Helmut Weiss, "Animal Language: A Chapter from the Controversy between Rationalism and Sensualism," in *Diversions of Galway: Papers on the History of Linguistics from ICHOLS V,* ed. Anders Ahlqvist (Amsterdam: John Benjamins Press, 1992), 203–212.

what they took to be the danger of abstraction. A recent survey of sixteenth- and seventeenth-century ideas about animal communication notes that "early modern natural philosophers almost universally insisted that only humans were capable of language and speech."[6] Most of those who argued against the possibility that animals used language to communicate agreed on a number of criteria for this judgment. They agreed that animals lacked the anatomical structures required for articulating their sounds, that they did not intentionally make sounds, and finally, that the sounds they did make were merely expressions of their passions rather than of abstract ideas. While most Renaissance thinkers may have agreed that animals could at best communicate only passions and not ideas, from the middle of the seventeenth century, a number of influential thinkers conceded that animals did communicate ideas, but that these could be only particular and not abstract ideas.[7] They generally insisted, however, that because animals could not communicate abstract ideas, they neither communicated as effectively as humans nor could be said to be using language.

Historians of linguistics have rightly argued that Locke, who insisted on the importance of *abstraction* in forming a workable language, influenced the eighteenth-century theories of the origin of language.[8] Most notable among those who were influenced by Locke's emphasis on the linguistic importance of abstraction was Étienne Bonnot, abbé de Condillac (1714–1780), who explicitly presented himself as building on Locke's insights into the mind and language. For Condillac, the capacity to abstract from particular ideas and to form general terms to represent those abstract ideas was the distinguishing mark of humanity. In his *Essai sur l'origine des connoissance humaines* (1746), he remarked that a person without abstract ideas lives in a prelinguistic state and "leads a purely animal existence."[9] In another work dealing specifically with the cognitive characteristics of animals, the *Traité des animaux* (1755), Condillac wrote that "the instinct of beasts does not take notice of more than a small number of properties in objects. It... makes no, or almost no, abstractions.... Virtually everything is

---

6. See Serjeantson, "The Passions and Animal Language," 425.
7. Ibid., 430–433.
8. On Locke's influence see Hans Aarsleff, *From Locke to Saussure: Essays in the Study of Language and Intellectual History* (Minneapolis: University of Minnesota Press, 1982), 146–209.
9. Condillac, *Œuvres completes* (Paris: Lecointe et Durey, 1821–1822), 1:189.

particular for them.... Man, on the contrary, capable of all sorts of abstraction, can compare himself with everything that surrounds him. He enters into himself.... His knowledge multiplies, arts and sciences are born, and are born for him alone."[10] Condillac thus argued that what marked the superiority of humans over beasts was the fact that human languages possessed general terms for abstract ideas that permitted humans to think and communicate more effectively.

Almost two decades later, the Scottish language theorist James Burnett, Lord Monboddo (1714–1799) argued in a very similar fashion that any system of communication made up only of particulars would be too impractical, if not impossible, and could not even properly be called a language. "No language," he wrote, "ever existed, or can be conceived, consisting only of expression of... what is commonly called *proper names*.... What therefore constitutes the essential part of language, and makes it truly deserve that name, is the expression of *generals*."[11] While Monboddo denied that a communicative system composed wholly of terms for particular things could be called language, he and many of his contemporaries agreed that animals did communicate, if only by way of terms for particular ideas. Monboddo allowed that a system of "*inarticulate cries,* by which the brutes signify their appetites and desires" was composed of signs for particular ideas alone and not abstract ideas. He insisted, however, that "the word [language] is used metaphorically, and not as it ought to be used in the style of science."[12] Monboddo noted that "the brute" "has sense and memory as well as we, and, like us, he can distinguish the same from a different object; for who will deny that a dog knows his master, or a horse his keeper?" But then he added, "[N]o farther [do] the brutes accompany us.... But in order to form the *idea,* a *separation* or *discrimination* is necessary of these qualities one from another: And this kind of *abstraction* I hold to be the first act of human intellect and that it is here the road parts betwixt us and the brute."[13] Many of those who attempted to answer the question of how language was first formed and of how it subsequently developed sought

---

10. Condillac, *Traitié des animaux* (Paris: Librairie J. Vrin, 1987), 494–495.
11. James Burnett, Lord Monboddo, *Of the Origin and Progress of Language* (Edinburgh: Printed for J. Balfour and T. Cadell, 1774), 1:5.
12. Ibid., 6.
13. Ibid., 58 and 59–60.

to show that there was in fact a gradual process of abstraction from a first proper noun, from a first particular term, to a fully developed language with abstract or general words. Adam Smith (1723–1790), for example, in his "Considerations concerning the First Formation of Languages" (1761), noted that "the assignment of particular names, to denote particular objects, that is, the institution of nouns substantive, would probably, be one of the first steps towards the formation of language."[14]

For most theorists of the time, animals' inability to form abstract ideas and words represented a deficiency that marked the superiority of human language to animal communication. At the beginning of book 3 of *An Essay concerning Human Understanding,* in the chapter titled "Of General Terms," Locke argued that "all things that exist being particulars, it might perhaps be thought reasonable that words, which ought to be conformed to things, should be so too,—I mean their signification: but yet we find quite the contrary. The far greatest part of words that make all languages are general terms: which has not been the effect of neglect or chance, but of reason and necessity." Locke rejected the idealization of a language of particulars because he argued that "it is beyond the power of human capacity to frame and retain distinct ideas of all the particular things we meet with: every bird and beast men saw; every tree and plant that affected the sense, could not find a place in the most capacious understanding."[15]

A small but significant group of early modern thinkers, however, did argue that the animals' mode of communication, a language made up strictly of terms for particular ideas and therefore, to use Locke's terminology, "conforming to things" was in that respect potentially preferable to human languages. These individuals characterized animal communication in ways that resembled the idealized languages that some historians of linguistics have associated with what they call the seventeenth-century crisis of representation.[16] In contrast to Locke, Condillac, and Monboddo, these other thinkers idealized animal communication because they believed it was not subject to

---

14. Adam Smith, "Considerations concerning the First Formation of Languages," in *Lectures on Rhetoric and Belles Lettres,* ed. J. G. Bryce (Oxford: Oxford University Press, 1983), 203.

15. Locke, *An Essay concerning Human Understanding,* 2:14.

16. See among others, Robert Markley, *Fallen Languages: Crises of Representation in Newtonian England, 1660–1740* (Ithaca: Cornell University Press, 1993); Eco, *The Search for the Perfect Language;* Robert E. Stillman, *The New Philosophy and Universal Languages in Seventeenth-Century England: Bacon, Hobbes, and Wilkins* (Lewisburg, PA: Bucknell University Press, 1995).

the ambiguity implicit in abstract words. Because animal languages were free from such ambiguities, they reduced the potential for redefining moral terms in ways that could lead to vacuous speech or violent disputes.

Cureau de la Chambre on Animal Minds and Languages

In 1645, a French court physician and member of the Académie française, Marin Cureau de la Chambre (1596–1669), included a bold philosophical defense of animal intelligence and language in his *Caractères des Passions*. A section titled "De la connaissance des bestes" argued that animals use the faculty of the imagination to reason and communicate. Within a year, Pierre Chanet (fl. 1644–1649) responded vehemently in his *De l'instinct et de la connoissance des animaux avec l'examen de ce que M. de La Chambre a escrit sur cette matière* (1646). Chanet's criticism prompted Cureau de la Chambre to restate and explain his claims in his *Traité de la connoissance des animaux* (1648). Cureau de la Chambre adapted Aristotelian arguments about animal imagination and intention to insist that animals could reason and communicate linguistically.

Although Aristotle had famously stated that "man is the only animal whom [Nature] has endowed with the gift of speech,"[17] Cureau de la Chambre adopted Aristotle's own characterization of the faculty of *phantasia*, or imagination, as a faculty that generated ideas in the form of mental images to argue that animals did have ideas. Many early modern thinkers agreed with Aristotle's claim that since the imagination was a faculty of the sensitive soul and therefore possessed by at least the higher animals, these animals could form mental images or ideas. "The word *Imagination*," Cureau de la Chambre wrote, "should not be taken here as a faculty distinct from the common sense, from phantasy...but for a general faculty that includes all the powers of the sensitive Soul that aid Knowledge; in the same way that the word *Understanding* includes all the faculties of the intellective soul that lead to knowledge of things, such as the apprehensive, the cogitative, the discursive, the active and passive Intellect, etc."[18] He summed

---

17. Aristotle, *Politics,* ed. Richard McKeon (New York: Random House, 1941), 1129.
18. Marin Cureau de la Chambre, *Traité de la connaissance des animaux* (Paris: Fayard, 1989), 26.

up his argument concerning the uses of the imagination in the following three statements: "1) The Imagination, to know things, must make Images of them. 2) The Imagination can unite the Images that it has formed and consequently make Propositions. 3) The Imagination can unite several Propositions and tie them together by common terms, in which Reasoning consists."[19] He concluded from these three statements that "there is no difference between the union that [the Imagination] makes and that made by the Understanding when it assembles an Idea with another to make an Affirmative proposition."[20]

Aristotle had, however, drawn a significant difference between the kinds of images formed by the imagination and those formed in the faculty of understanding, which was possessed only by beings, like humans, who had intellective souls. Aristotle had maintained that while the sensitive soul passively formed mental images of particular objects, the intellective soul had the ability to transform those images, specifically by actively forming abstract ideas out of them. For Aristotle, then, the possession of an intellective soul marked the ability to form abstract ideas and a language of abstract terms.

Cureau de la Chambre followed Aristotle in insisting that the types of images that could be formed by animals had to be of particulars and should not to be construed as universal or abstract ideas. He argued that by stringing together such particular ideas, animals could form propositions and ultimately use the imagination to form sorites, or cumulative syllogisms.[21] He called such syllogisms "particular judgments." Thus Cureau de la Chambre argued that even without an intellective soul it was still possible to use the imagination to form particular images that could be united into propositions and that these propositions could then be strung together to form judgments.

Cureau de la Chambre also argued that animals emitted sounds intentionally, something that almost every earlier discussion of animal sounds had denied in order to insist that they were not truly linguistic.[22] Cureau de

---

19. Ibid., 24.
20. Ibid., 84.
21. A sorites is a syllogism formed by a series of propositions, in which the predicate of each is the subject of the next, the conclusion being formed of the first subject and the last predicate.
22. See Serjeantson, "The Passions and Animal Language," 432–433.

la Chambre admitted that the intention to communicate among animals was not of the same character as that in humans, who had intellective souls and "understanding."[23] He distinguished, however, between two types of willing—will *proper* and will *as impulse*—to argue that animals used language intentionally. By characterizing impulses as a form of willing, he could argue that the absence of the faculty of understanding "does not exclude...other Resolutions and other Designs besides those of the understanding." In this way, he concluded that with animals "the appetite never stirs itself without the judgment of the Imagination that proposes and commands to it what is to be done."[24] For Cureau de la Chambre, then, imagination, which he claimed could form certain kinds of propositions, was also responsible for the intentions that animals had when they communicated. "The Imagination," he wrote, "does not only command [the animal] to make its limbs move,...but even proposes the action, which is the end and the goal to which the Animal tends.... It is necessary that the judgment of the Imagination precede the movement of the muscles that form the voice, and that it know that the voice must form itself by its means, and that it commands the Animal to cry out. Now, if it knows and if it commands, it has Design and Intention to form the voice."[25] Cureau de la Chambre even went so far as to distinguish such intentional animal actions and sounds from "others that occur...without the Soul's intention to produce them."[26]

Animal Communication as Clear Language: Webster's Illuminations

If the system used by animals to communicate with one another consisted only of terms for particular ideas, then it could be characterized as free from the dangers of the ambiguities that crept into the definitions of words for abstract ideas. Although Locke explicitly denied that a language made up strictly of particular terms would be preferable to one that had terms

---

23. Cureau de la Chambre, *Traité de la connaissance des animaux*, 292.
24. Ibid., 293.
25. Ibid.
26. Ibid., 295.

for abstract ideas, he nonetheless did recognize its appeal. He wrote, "[A]ll things that exist being particulars, it may perhaps be thought reasonable that words, which ought to be conformed to things, should be so too."[27] Some of Locke's near contemporaries who worked on schemes to invent a real character were motivated by their fantasies of finding a transparent language, one that would be free from semantic and logical ambiguity. James R. Knowlson notes that in the late seventeenth century, an idealized language was usually "praised as being simpler, briefer, and more regular, hence easier to learn, remember, and use.... [I]t was also described as more directly representative of the natural world.... In this way, language would not only be a means of acquiring knowledge; it would itself *be* knowledge, since each 'word' would provide an accurate description of the thing signified."[28] One of the ways that some early modern thinkers tried to correct the supposed defects of ambiguous European languages was to find a system of communication in which each term stood for one particular thing in a stable and unambiguous relation to it. They sought to find what one early modern thinker called a language "adapted to the exact and perfect representation of things."[29] Indeed, Thomas Sprat's (1635–1713) linguistic comments in his *History of the Royal Society* (1667) recommended "return[ing] back to the primitive purity, and shortness, when men deliver'd so many *things,* almost in an equal number of *words.*"[30] Thus, for such thinkers an ideal language would be a language with such an extensive lexicon that every particular thing would have its own distinct word. Unlike Locke, then, some language schemers did hope to find a language in which ambiguity, error, and misunderstanding, as well as the violence to which these often lead, would be impossible.

If animals communicated with one another using only terms for particulars, then animal languages shared a property with the kind of ideal language for which some of the early modern language schemers were looking. Indeed, Cureau de la Chambre's strongest critic, Pierre Chanet, recognized the potential that his characterizations of animal communication had for

---

27. Locke, *An Essay concerning Human Understanding,* 2:14.
28. Knowlson, *Universal Language Schemes,* 8.
29. Jan Comenius, *Via Lucis* (1668), 187, quoted in Knowlson, *Universal Language Schemes,* 88.
30. Thomas Sprat, *History of the Royal Society of London* (London: Printed by T. R., 1667), 113.

making animals appear to be superior to humans.[31] While Cureau de la Chambre denied this implication, there were nonetheless some who did argue that animal communication, as a language of particulars conforming to things, was preferable to human languages.

A couple of decades before Cureau de la Chambre's claims for animal language appeared, the mystic Jacob Böhme (1575–1624), in his *Mysterium Magnum* (1623), had already put forward a theory of the language of nature in which he suggested that animals communicated more effectively than people. Böhme argued not only that God had instituted this language of nature at the moment of creation and that it was common to all earthly creatures but also that "when all People spoke in one Language, then they *understood* one another." "But," he added, "when they would not use the *natural* genuine Tongue, then the true and right Understanding was put *out* in them; for they brought the Spirits of the genuine Tongue of Sense into an *external gross* Form... and learned to speak out of the *Form only*." Böhme contrasted "the *bare* contrived Form of the gross compounded Words" of languages that fallen human societies had instituted with the more perfect language of nature that "no people do any more understand" but which "the Birds in the Air and the Beasts in the Fields [continue to] understand." Böhme advised that "*Man* may well think and consider what he is deprived of" and blamed this human inability to communicate using the language of nature for "the Contention and Strife wherewith Men contend and jangle about God and his Will."[32]

The English educational reformer John Webster (1611–1682) similarly claimed that animals possessed not only a genuine linguistic capacity but also one that was preferable to human languages. After losing his position as an Anglican minister, Webster became a nonconforming chaplain and surgeon in the parliamentary army, and in that role he saw firsthand the bloody violence of the English civil wars.[33] Like many of his contemporaries who had lived through the unprecedented period of religious and civil violence, he searched for a way to guard against disputes that might lead to physical violence. In his own time, Webster was known especially for criticizing, in

---

31. Pierre Chanet, *De l'instinct et de la connoissance des animaux avec l'examen de ce que M. de la Chambre a escrit sur cette matière* (La Rochelle: Par Toussaincts de Govy, 1646), 93.

32. Jacob Böhme, *The Works of Jacob Behmen, the Teutonic Theosopher* (London: Printed for G. Robinson, 1772), 3:195 and 196.

33. See Peter Elmer, *The Library of Dr John Webster: The Making of a Seventeenth-Century Radical* (London: Wellcome Institute for the History of Medicine, 1986), 1.

his *Academiarum Examen, or thee Examination of Academies* (1654), what he took to be corruptions in the universities. The book caused a stir among conforming clergy and members of what eventually became the Royal Society of London. They included the language schemers Seth Ward (1617–1689), bishop of Salisbury, who answered him in his *Vindiciae Academiarum* (1654), and Wilkins, who wrote a prefatory letter to Ward's reply. Wilkins was generally dismissive of Webster as "a kind of credulous fanatick reformer," but he singled out for special derision the influence that Böhme's notion of the language of nature had had on Webster's views.[34]

In his *Academiarum Examen*, Webster had taken up and paraphrased some of Böhme's linguistic claims. He wrote, for instance, that "the voices of birds, and beasts (though we account them inarticulate) are significative one to another." Webster added that "by the altering, and varying of those sounds, they express their passions, affections and notions, as well as men, and are thereby understood by one another." Following Böhme in calling it the "language of nature," Webster also made similar claims concerning the superior virtues of animal communication. Webster, however, devoted a large section of the *Academiarum* to the topic "Of Tongues or Languages." In this section he developed Böhme's more mystical discussion of the language of nature by linking it to the language schemers' desires for communicative transparency:

> What a vast advancement had it been to the Republick of learning, and hugely profitable to all mankind, if the discovery of the universal Character...had been wisely and laboriously pursued and brought to perfection? That thereby Nations of divers Languages might have been able to have read it and understood it, and so have more easily had commerce and traffick one with another, and thereby the sciences and skill of one Nation, might with more facility have been communicated to others.... This would have been a potent means to repair the ruins of Babell.

Webster proposed that the requirements for a universal language might be met by a wide variety of language schemes. He listed, for example, (1) "the most pregnant and notable waies by signes and gestures" with which

---

34. Seth Ward and J. Wilkins, *Vindiciae academiarum, Containing Some Briefe Animadversions upon Mr. Wesbter's Book, Stiled, The Examination of Academies* (Oxford: Printed by Leonard Lichfield, 1654), 5.

the "deaf and dumb" "express their minds," (2) "*Dactylogy*," and 3) the "characters" that "in *China,* and some other Oriental Regions...are real, not nominal, expressing neither letter nor words, but things, and notions." Webster's reference to the "reality" of Asian characters, their capacity to express things and notions—i.e., *res* rather than *verba*—suggests that his ideal language would be one consisting of particular rather than abstract words. Finally, Webster came to the language of animals. "I cannot...passe over with silence," he wrote, "that signal and wonderful secret...of the language of nature: but out of profound consideration, must adumbrate some of those reasons, which perswasively draw my judgment to credit the possibility thereof." Like the mystic Böhme, Webster suggested that "every creature understands and speaks the language of nature, but sinful man who hath now lost, defac't and forgotten it." For both Böhme and Webster, then, animals spoke the same language that Adam had spoken in Eden. They both believed that it was only as a consequence of a sinful act that people had lost their ability to speak and understand this language of nature, and they both believed that if people could recover this universal language, it would be the key to the regeneration of humanity.[35]

If the language of animals was merely one of many candidates for a universal language, it had many rivals, like sign language, universal writing systems, and even Latin. His reason for preferring animal language over these others was that he took it to be a *real* language. His insistence that the universal language would not be, as he put it, "nominal" puts Webster in contrast to many of his contemporary language schemers, like Ward and Wilkins, and even Descartes, who thought that a conventional language that simply managed to rigidly designate every particular object would make communication transparent and make the disputes and errors arising from ambiguity virtually impossible. While Wilkins and Descartes, for example, believed that a universal language might be created, their universal language was to be built out of arbitrary signs that represented

---

35. John Webster, *Academiarum Examen, or thee Examination of Academies* (London: Printed for Giles Calvert, 1654), 31, 24–25, 25, 26, and 27. Although he was Webster's sharpest critic, Wilkins shared his belief that the prelapsarian language was better than existing human languages. See John Wilkins, *Essay towards a Real Character and a Philosophical Language* (London: Printed for Sa. Gellibrand, and for John Martyn, 1668), 19. What marks the main point of contention between them is that Wilkins believed that the prelapsarian language could not be recovered, while Webster argued it was still spoken by beasts.

simple or particular ideas. Knowlson has noted that "the language of real characters that both Wilkins and Ward had in mind is...expressly dissociated from the mystical notions of Webster and continental writers, and Ward proceeds to explain that his conception of the proposed character will be based instead upon a description of things by their qualities and their relations."[36]

Historians have variously treated Webster as a Baconian modern, a superstitious mystic, and an "ignorant critic" who had "fantastic hopes to turn judicial astronomy, magic, and the arcane of hieroglyphics and emblems to the betterment of mankind."[37] All these historians, despite their varying characterizations of Webster, follow his seventeenth-century critics in emphasizing his anti-Aristotelianism, making him a linguistic Platonist. While there is no question that he was explicitly critical of elements of Aristotelian and Galenic medicine and of other elements of Aristotelian thought,[38] as Peter Elmer has shown through an analysis of Webster's catalog of his library, Webster was also remarkably eclectic in his reading and had a "solid grounding in the learning of the 'ancients,' and in particular Aristotle."[39] Elmer stresses "that Webster, despite his public dismissal of Galenism, was neither ignorant of, nor unconversant with, the more traditional forms of medical theory and practice. Like Aristotle, Galen was not held entirely to blame by Webster for the excessive trust which the physicians and natural philosophers of his day placed in his writings."[40] It should not be surprising, then, to find that he accepted the idea that the mind receives particular images of sensory objects to which particular terms can attach and that error can thus be linguistically transcended.

Like those whom Locke represented as thinking that a language made up strictly of terms for particular ideas and "conforming to things" might be preferable to conventional human languages, Webster complained that

---

36. Knowlson, *Universal Language Schemes*, 14.
37. For Webster as a "modern," see Richard Foster Jones, *Ancients and Moderns: A Study of the Rise of the Scientific Movement in Seventeenth-Century England* (Berkeley: University of California Press, 1961), 101–115. For Webster as a superstitious mystic, see Phyllis Allen, "Scientific Studies in the English Universities of the Seventeenth Century," *Journal of the History of Ideas* 10, no. 2 (1949): 219–253, esp. 237. For Webster as an ignorant critic, see Mark H. Curtis, *Oxford and Cambridge in Transition 1558–1642* (Oxford: Clarendon Press, 1959), 232.
38. See, for instance, Webster, *Academiarum Examen*, 106–107.
39. Elmer, *The Library of Dr John Webster*, 20.
40. Ibid., 25.

in human languages "there is not absolute congruency betwixt the notion and the thing, the intellect and the thing understood, and so it is no longer verity, but a ly, and a falsity." Webster's objection to human languages was therefore that their words did not rigidly conform to things, and his claim for the superiority of animal language therefore rested on his belief that animal languages were free from this defect. Likening the universe to a "great fabrick or machine," he argued that "every individual creature is as a several cord or string inbued with a distinct and various tone, all concurring to make up a catholick melody." Although he was somewhat influenced by Böhme's mysticism, Webster presented the language of animals as a kind of speech in which each word corresponds exactly and particularly to the "individual creatures" of the universe. In the language of nature everything has "an adequate name" that "manifests" its "nature." Webster explained that such an adequate name is "exactly conformable, and configurate to the *Idea* in [the speaker's] mind; the very prolation, and sounds of the word, contain[s] in it the vive expression of the thing."[41]

Webster concluded his discussion of the language of animals with a restatement of the significant merits of his "natural" language. "*The mind*" he wrote, "*receiveth but one single and simple image of every thing.*" Each of these particular mental images, he argued, "is expressed in all by the same motions of the spirits,... but men not understanding these immediate sounds of the soul,... have instituted, and imposed others, that do not altogether concord, and agree to the innate notions." Webster, therefore, called "for the recovery of the Catholique language in which lies hid all the rich treasury of natures admirable and excellent secrets."[42] As mystically Platonic as his writings were, this and other passages in his writing come very close to Cureau de la Chambre's characterization of animal communication as involving a language of particular terms that rigidly designate particular ideas.[43] In this characterization of animal language Webster believed he had found an argument for recovering a form of communication, i.e., animal language, that would put an end to bitter civil and religious

---

41. John Webster, *Academiarum Examen*, 30 and 28.
42. Ibid., 32 (emphasis added).
43. Webster's library included a copy of Cureau de la Chambre's *Discourse of the Knowledge of Beasts*. See Elmer, *The Library of Dr John Webster*.

conflicts caused by the fallen and therefore semantically ambiguous human languages.

Hobbes and the Suppression of Moral Redescription

The fact that Webster was a Puritan preacher in Cromwell's New Model Army and a political radical might be taken to suggest that the belief that the language of animals was a model of communicative clarity and a means to regenerate society was predominantly a Radical Protestant phenomenon. Certainly, the biblical account of a prelapsarian communicative and therefore social harmony was a powerful image wherein a common language united not just humanity but all terrestrial creatures. As Knowlson points out, "[F]or this reason it offered an ideal of religious harmony that was fundamental to many of those Christians who, in the middle decades of the century, were striving to bring about the reunification of the churches. Many of these reformers, belonging to Protestant groups located in various countries throughout Europe, regarded the invention and adoption of a universal language as likely to remove one of the greatest obstacles to the religious harmony that they had so much at heart."[44] While it is true that much of the impulse for recovering a prelapsarian language came from Radical Protestants, who insisted on the role of human languages in corrupting communication and veiling truths, they hardly had an exclusive claim to the ideal of a language that conformed to things.

Thomas Hobbes (1588–1679) developed his argument that animals communicate more clearly than humans while he was in France, where he had fled out of fear he would be persecuted as a royalist during the English civil war. Hobbes, like Webster, believed that from the moment that people invented languages, they became subject to disputes that always threatened to disrupt the kind of peaceful social existence manifest among sociable animals.

Hobbes first articulated his argument in Latin in the second section of his *De Cive* (1642). There he noted that Aristotle counted as political animals "not man only, but divers others, as the ant, the bee, &c.; which...so

---

44. Knowlson, *Universal Language Schemes*, 10.

direct their actions to a common end, that their meetings are not obnoxious unto any seditions."⁴⁵ Hobbes set out to explain why it was that many animals managed to live agreeably with one another while human societies were plagued with violent disputes. One of the six reasons he developed was that while animals managed to communicate with one another, they did so without what he called "that art of words which is necessarily required to those motions in the mind, whereby good is represented to it as being better, and evil as worse than in truth it is." By contrast, Hobbes claimed, "the tongue of man is a trumpet of war and sedition: and it is reported of Pericles, that he sometimes by his elegant speeches thundered and lightened and confounded whole Greece itself."⁴⁶ Thus, unlike animals, humans tried and often succeeded in deceiving others with words, and verbal disputes spilled over into physical violence.

The moral and political import of the difference between animal and human forms of communication reappeared nine years later in a key passage of Hobbes's *Leviathan* (1651). "Certain living creatures, as Bees, and Ants," Hobbes noted, "live sociably one with another,...and yet have no other direction, than their *particular judgments* and appetites; nor speech, whereby one of them can signifie to another, what he thinks expedient for the common benefit: and therefore some may perhaps desire to know, why Mankind cannot do the same."⁴⁷ He answered "that these creatures, though they have some use of voice, in making knowne to one another their desires, and other affections; yet they want that art of words, by which some men can represent to others, that which is Good, in the likeness of Evill; and Evill, in the likeness of Good; and augment, or diminish the apparent greatness of Good and Evill; discontenting men, and troubling their Peace at their pleasure."⁴⁸ Hobbes thus reiterated with only slight changes his earlier answer to this fundamental question about why it was that certain animals managed to live together peaceably while human communities frequently erupted into civil violence.

Though he did not consider animal communication "linguistic," Hobbes's account in his *De Corpore* (1655) and *Leviathan* of how animals

---

45. Thomas Hobbes, *The English Works of Thomas Hobbes* (London: John Bohn, 1841), 2:66.
46. Ibid., 67.
47. Thomas Hobbes, *Leviathan* (New York: Penguin, 1968), 225 (emphasis added).
48. Ibid., 226.

desired, judged, and represented things and communicated these representations closely resembled Cureau de la Chambre's account. According to Hobbes, the fundamental difference between animal and human minds was that animals had only particular desires and therefore formed and communicated only particular judgments.[49] Human beings, by contrast and ultimately as a consequence of their distinct capacity for curiosity, formed and communicated abstract ideas. For Hobbes this crucial difference between animal and human minds depended ultimately on the fact that human languages had abstract terms, or what he called "common" or "universal" names. Philip Pettit has argued that this claim that animals represented and communicated only particular things while human beings had the capacity to represent and communicate things under general aspects is "the most startling and original claim that [Hobbes] makes in the whole of his philosophy."[50]

While the human invention of a language of terms to represent abstract ideas had made it possible for human beings to improve their faculties "to such a height, as to distinguish men from all other living creatures," Hobbes did not see this distinction as an unqualified good. Indeed, on this point he was explicit: "[B]y speech man is not made better but only given greater possibilities."[51] According to Hobbes, the creation of defective human languages was the principal source of misunderstanding and civil violence. Like Locke, Hobbes believed that there was "nothing in the world universal but names; for the things named, are every one of them individual and singular."[52] Hobbes blamed the process of abstracting properties from particular objects and of assigning abstract or general terms for them, particularly in the case of evaluative or moral terms like "good" and "evil," for the ambiguity that led to disagreement and violence.

In his study of the place of rhetoric in Hobbes's philosophy, Quentin Skinner shows that in the late 1630s Hobbes rejected his earlier humanism and the value it placed on rhetoric. Central to this rejection of humanism and rhetoric was Hobbes's belief that the rhetoricians' claims that virtues

---

49. See Thomas Hobbes, *Leviathan*, 103–104.
50. Philip Pettit, *Made with Words: Hobbes on Language, Mind, and Politics* (Princeton: Princeton University Press, 2008), 25.
51. Thomas Hobbes, *De Homine* 10.3, quoted ibid., 97.
52. Hobbes, *Leviathan*, 102.

could be redescribed as vices through various techniques, had prevented people from developing a true science of society.[53] Hobbes rejected the belief that vices were merely neighboring virtues and that they therefore could always be redescribed as virtues. It was precisely this technique that Hobbes linked with the human capacity for abstract language and that therefore distinguished human from animal societies: the art of words by which humans could make evil seem good and good seem evil. For Hobbes, just as for the mystic Böhme and the Puritan Webster, animal forms of communication remained grounded in the realm of particulars and so were not subject to the dangers of ambiguity, equivocation, and redescription.

Hobbes did argue, however, that human societies could transcend what he took to be the unfortunate implications of the human abuse of abstract words. Indeed, as Skinner notes, in the *Leviathan,* "Hobbes [was] seeking to replace the dialogical and anti-demonstrative approach to moral reasoning encouraged by the humanist assumption that there are two sides to any question, and thus that in the moral sciences it will always be possible to argue on either side of the case. He is chiefly reacting, in short, against...the 'rhetorication' of moral philosophy."[54] In Hobbes's view, this replacement of rhetorical language by a demonstrative "civil science" would be accomplished by an agreement giving a sovereign individual or assembly the authority to fix strict and clear definitions. Skinner explains that, for Hobbes, "since our use of evaluative language will inevitably be conditioned by our passions and interests, the only method of avoiding disputes and hostilities will be to appoint an arbitrator to decide how such language should be used."[55] Hobbes, for example, wrote that to prevent violent disputes "the parties must by their own accord, set up for right Reason, the Reason of some Arbitrator, or Judge, to whose sentence they will both stand, or their controversie must either come to blowes, or be undecided, for want of a right Reason constituted by Nature."[56] With this agreement to rigidly manage the definitions of abstract terms and so create a better, if not perfect, human society, people could hope to transcend conflict

---

53. Quentin Skinner, *Reason and Rhetoric in the Philosophy of Hobbes* (Cambridge: Cambridge University Press, 1996).
54. Ibid., 299.
55. Ibid., 341.
56. Hobbes, *Leviathan,* 111.

and reproduce the happy state of sociable animals. In this sense, Hobbes's absolutist conception of speech was a redemptive response to a perceived defect in fallen human languages. For Hobbes the fall away from a state of communication that relied on particulars and into languages made up of defective abstract terms was what made human lives in the state of nature nasty, brutish, and short. Hobbes's political and linguistic doctrines should be thought of as his attempt to redeem fallen languages and to restore at a more reflective and refined level the kind of clear communication apparent among the sociable animals.

Rousseau on the Abuse of Abstract Words

Another seventeenth-century thinker to comment on the superiority of animal communication was the Calvinist humanist Isaac Vossius (1618–1689). This son of the famous Dutch scholar Gerard John Vos (1577–1649) spent much of his time in England, where he often attended the court of Charles II. In his *De Poematum cantu et viribus rythmi* (1673), he claimed "that the state of animals, which are generally thought stupid, seems far better than ours in this respect, namely they express their feelings and thoughts without mediation, more manifestly, and perhaps more propitiously, than any humans do."[57] Although there is no evidence that he meant his comments to reflect the belief that the animal imagination consisted of particular images of particular things to which particular words corresponded, this passage would be used in exactly this way by later thinkers in arguing for the communicative superiority of beasts.

Vossius's comments on animal communication reappeared spectacularly in a note to Jean-Jacques Rousseau's (1712–1778) *Discours sur l'origine et les fondements de l'inégalité parmi les hommes* (1755). Rousseau quoted Vossius's comments with the following gloss: "I well would guard myself from embarking upon philosophical reflections that are to be made on the advantages and inconveniences of the institution of languages: I am not permitted to attack vulgar errors.... Let us therefore allow those to speak who are not accused of committing a crime whenever they dare sometimes

---

57. Isaac Vossius, *De Poematum cantu et viribus rythmi* (Oxford: Sheldonian Theater, 1673), 66.

to take the side of reason against the opinion of the multitude."[58] It was at this point in his essay that Rousseau discussed the transition from natural to artificial language in human communication. He argued that "the first language of man, the most universal language,... is the cry of nature."[59] He wrote that humans

> first gave to each word the sense of a whole proposition. When they began to distinguish the subject from the attribute and the verb from the noun,... substantives were then no more than proper names,... and regarding adjectives, this notion must have developed only with great difficulty because every adjective is an abstract word, and abstractions are painfully difficult operations and hardly natural.
>
> Each object thus received a particular name,... and all the individual things presented themselves in isolation to their [the people who invented languages] minds as they are in the scene of nature.[60]

Rousseau thus repeated the argument that the language of nature was a language of the imagination in which particular objects produced particular images in the mind and had particular terms to designate them. For Rousseau's theory of language, at least the one he developed in his second *Discourse,* the imagination was a representational faculty that did not err in producing mental images of sensory things to which individual signs could be tied. It was the intellect that introduced error by leaving the realm of particular and concrete objects to create abstract ideas and abstract terms that might not correspond to sensory things. He wrote that "every general idea is purely intellectual; as soon as the imagination gets involved, the idea instantly becomes particular.... Purely abstract beings see themselves in the same manner, or they only conceive by way of discourse.... As soon as the imagination stops, the mind marches on only with the aid of discourse."[61] In his *Essay on the Origin of Languages,* Rousseau argued, "I do not doubt that animals that work and live together, such as Beavers, ants, bees, have some natural language as a means of communicating with one

---

58. Jean-Jacques Rousseau, «Discours sur l'origine et les fondements de l'inégalité parmi les hommes,» in *J.-J. Rousseau, oeuvres politiques,* ed. Jean Roussel (Paris: Bordas, 1989), 39.
59. Ibid., 39.
60. Ibid., 38–39.
61. Ibid., 39–40.

another. There is even reason to believe that the language of Beavers and that of ants are gestural and speak only to the eyes."[62] Rousseau thus characterized animal communication as a transparent gestural sign language.

According to Rousseau, "Conventional language belongs to man alone. That is why man makes progress in good as well as in evil, and why animals do not. This single distinction seems to be far-reaching."[63] As Sophia Rosenfeld has noted, "the idea that many negative consequences stemmed from the insincere, inaccurate, and ambiguous use of words—or the *abus des mots,* as it was commonly called in eighteenth-century France—had a long prior history."[64] The early modern concern with the dangers of abstract words goes back at least to Francis Bacon, who included "Names...rashly and irregularly abstracted from Things" among "the *Idols* [of the Market Place] which Words impose upon the Understanding."[65] He argued that the dangerous errors "raised by a wrong and unskillful Abstraction, [are] intricate and deep rooted."[66] Hobbes, Locke, Rousseau, and many other late-seventeenth- and eighteenth-century thinkers frequently blamed abstract words for interminable and sometimes violent disputes.

While the context in which Rousseau made his remarks was very different from that of Hobbes or Webster, there are nonetheless significant similarities. Each shared a vision of a language of particular terms applied to the particular images in the faculty of the imagination. Each thus also shared the same vision of animal communication as a language free from the dangers of abstraction and that, in Locke's terms, conformed to things. These thinkers presented animals as communicating in a language in which ideas of particular things were conveyed clearly and therefore without ambiguity. Taken on these terms, the particularist systems of animal communication fulfilled the language schemers' quest for clarity. Each of these thinkers idealized animal communication to criticize the sophistical

---

62. Jean-Jacques Rousseau, "Essay on the Origin of Languages," in *Jean-Jacques Rousseau: The First and Second Discourses together with the Replies to Critics and Essay on the Origin of Languages,* ed. Victor Gourevitch (New York: Harper Torchbooks, 1990), 244.

63. Ibid.

64. Sophia Rosenfeld, *A Revolution in Language: The Problem of Signs in Late Eighteenth-Century France* (Stanford: Stanford University Press, 2001), 16.

65. Francis Bacon, *The Philosophical Works of Francis Bacon,* ed. Peter Shaw (London: Printed for J. J. and P. Knapton, 1733), 2:358.

66. Ibid., 358.

potential of any language with a lexicon that had terms for poorly abstracted ideas, which they perceived as the main cause of disagreement, dissimulation, and moral degeneration.

Among the thinkers discussed in this chapter, only Webster believed that it might be possible for people to adopt the language used by animals. He believed that the easy communication of knowledge among the learned, not to mention the uncovering of "the rich treasury of nature's admirable and excellent secrets," would result from a recovery of animal language. For Webster, without the language of nature, speech could lead only to moral confusion and civil discord. In a sermon he delivered at All Hallows, on June 23, 1653, Webster complained that people had turned values upside down and that man's wisdom was now accounted folly, "his Righteousness, Sin;...his Heaven, Hell."[67]

Rousseau asked his readers "which life, the civil or the natural, is most subject to becoming insupportable to those who enjoy it?"[68] He avoided an explicit answer to the seemingly rhetorical question. He nonetheless made the following remark: "[W]e see virtually no one around us except people who complain about their existence, many even who deprive themselves of it as much as they can."[69] For Rousseau, the stage of social evolution in which abstract terms were introduced into human communication was the one that led to the "excess of corruption"[70] that he associated with modern "polite" and commercial sociability. It was because of faulty abstractions that humanity was led into a state in which "sociable man, always outside himself, does not know how to live any other way than in the opinion of others,...everything reducing itself to appearances, everything becomes factitious and staged....[I]n the middle of so much philosophy, humanity, politeness, and sublime maxims, we have nothing but a deceiving and frivolous exterior, honor without virtue, reason without wisdom, and pleasure without happiness."[71] The structure of this last sentence, in which Rousseau contrasted honor, reason, and pleasure with the implicitly preferable moral qualities of virtue, wisdom, and happiness, suggests the

---

67. John Webster, *The Vail of the Covering, Spread over All Nations* (London: Printed for J. Sowle, 1713), 27.
68. Rousseau, «Discours sur l'origine,» 41.
69. Ibid.
70. Ibid., 77.
71. Ibid., 78.

kind of sophistical moral redescription that was so much at issue in the early modern worries about the socially corrosive role played by human speech and the corresponding idealizations of animal language as models of clear communication. Although Rousseau thought it neither desirable nor possible to return to a prelapsarian linguistic state by simply adopting the languages of animals, he did share with Webster, Hobbes, and many of his contemporaries a desire to regenerate human society by reforming languages.[72] For Rousseau, this linguistic regeneration would be a Herculean task because a sophistic and sophisticated language of abstract terms was both the instrument to be fixed and the instrument required to do this fixing. Rousseau wrote, for instance, that "all the kinds of knowledge that demand reflection, all those acquired only by the concatenation of ideas and perfected only successively, appear to be utterly beyond the grasp of savage man, owing to the lack of communication with his fellow-men, that is to say, owing to the lack of the instrument which is used for that communication, and to the lack of the needs that make it necessary."[73]

For some early modern thinkers, then, the example of an unambiguous animal language was intended to be redemptive. The redemptive linguistic impulse of discussions of animal communication therefore echoed that of the early modern language schemers. Humans, Webster and Böhme argued, had fallen away from the purity of a language that conformed to things, that had been divinely instituted at the moment of creation, and that animals continued to use in order to communicate. Theirs was a story of decline over time, a decline that had led to the ambiguity that permitted people to mischaracterize vices as virtues and also ultimately led to civil violence. For others, like Hobbes and Rousseau, the model of animal communication was also meant to be redemptive but in the sense that it was intended to spur contemporaries to reflect on the defective abstract

---

72. Rousseau made this clear in a long note to the text, in which he asked, "What then! Must we destroy societies...and return to live in the forests with bears?" He concluded, "As for men like me, whose passions have forever destroyed their original simplicity, who can no longer feed on grass and acorn[s], nor get by without laws and chiefs;...those, in a word, who are convinced that the divine voice called the entire human race to the enlightenment and the happiness of the celestial intelligences; all those latter ones will attempt, through the exercise of virtues they oblige themselves to practice while learning to know them, to merit the eternal reward that they ought to expect for them." See Rousseau, *Discourse on the Origin of Inequality* (Indianapolis: Hackett, 1992), 80 n. 9.

73. See ibid., 74 n. 6.

terms in their lexicon so that a progressive clarification of lexical meaning could proceed with a new reflective intensity that would serve ultimately as a panacea to civil violence. In the cases of both retrospective restoration and prospective reformation, appeals to an idealized animal language may have played only a small role, but it is a revealing one that historians have up to this point never examined.

Early modern idealizations of animal language could also serve competing ideological ends. Despite being English contemporaries placed on opposite sides of religious and political controversies, Webster and Hobbes shared the belief that animals lived in more cooperative and peaceful communities because they were not subject to the kinds of ambiguity and equivocation that distinguished human forms of communication. Although both Webster and Hobbes were criticized by opponents in the Royal Society, they all shared a worry about the role of abuses of ambiguous language in the social and political crisis of mid-seventeenth-century England. Webster would have agreed with the Anglican latitudinarian Samuel Parker (1640–1688), who claimed that "the different Subdivisions among the [dissenting] Sects themselves are not so much distinguish'd by any real diversity of Opinions, as by variety of Phrases and Forms of Speech, that are the peculiar *Shibboleths of each Tribe*."[74] Thus the Puritan revolutionary, the skeptical royalist, and latitudinarian Restorationists could put forward a vision of an ideally clear and static language to replace an ambiguous and unstable language that they took to be the source of civil conflict, social disorder, and religious factionalism.

In late-eighteenth-century France, uses of an ideal of clear animal communication similarly crossed the ideological spectrum. For example, the same comment from Vossius in favor of animal communication that Rousseau appealed to in his *Discourse on Inequality* resurfaced during the later years of the French Revolution in Urbain-René-Thomas LeBouvyer-Desmortiers' *Mémoire, ou considérations sur les sourds-muets de naissance* (1800). In this little-known work, the author, a medical doctor and member of the Société des Observateurs de l'Homme, like Rousseau, appealed to Vossius's preference for animal over human language: "[He] thinks that the human species would not be less happy if, renouncing usage of those

---

74. Samuel Parker, *A Discourse of Ecclesiastical Politie* (London: Printed for John Martyn, 1670), 75.

languages that often produce such fatal confusions and abuses, men agreed to no longer explain themselves by any means but signs."[75] LeBouvyer-Desmortiers appealed to Vossius during the waning years of the Directorate to reiterate the regenerative themes of the Revolution. As he put it in the *Mémoire,* he believed that the deaf "would not have created these destructive systems which, for the last ten years, have ravaged and bloodied the four corners of the world. Happy nation! How sweet it would be to lose the ability to hear or to speak if one would be admitted into your bosom!"[76]

For LeBouvyer-Desmortiers, the deaf, who had never known conventional human languages and instead had relied on a natural language of gestural signs, were in linguistic circumstances resembling Vossius's animals and therefore in a state preferable to that of the French during the logomachic days of the Revolution, when the Jacobins and sansculottes could use and abuse abstract terms to violently impose the Terror. As Rosenfeld and Paul Friedland have shown, both Jacobins and their counterrevolutionary enemies blamed each other for having abused abstract terms to build their destructive ideological castles in the sky.[77] The fact that some early modern thinkers turned to beasts as models for ideal forms of communication is a testament to the undeniable importance of clarity as a linguistic ideal and of worries about ambiguity and abstract words in early modern Europe.

---

75. Urbain-René-Thomas LeBouvyer-Desmortiers, *Mémoire, ou considérations sur les sourds-muets de naissance* (Paris: F. Buisson, 1800), 46.

76. Ibid., xxiv.

77. Rosenfeld, *A Revolution in Language,* 123–226; Paul Friedland, *Political Actors: Representative Bodies and Theatricality in the Age of the French Revolution* (Ithaca: Cornell University Press, 2002), 228–250.

2

HOMO RISUS

Making Light of Animal Language

> Man is the merriest species of the creation, all above and below him are serious. He sees things in a different light from other beings.
>
> JOSEPH ADDISON, *The Spectator* (1711)

While a number of early modern language theorists accepted that in order to guard against abuses of ambiguous and equivocal words, abstract terms had to be clarified by scrupulously regulating their definitions, others embraced the notion that certain kinds of verbal ambiguity were precisely what made human languages superior to those of sociable animals. These thinkers argued that a fundamental virtue of human languages was the polysemous and equivocal quality of words that generated a potential for the kind of ambiguity that Hobbes and Rousseau sought to correct. This chapter will argue that some early modern thinkers celebrated human forms of language for the way they allowed speakers to represent and communicate the many contrasting perspectives from which to view a thing or idea. By permitting and even encouraging the communication of contrasting perspectives, the distinctively human form of polysemous language gave rise to the uniquely human capacities to produce wit and laughter, which they presented as central not only to conversation and humor but also to the acquisition of new ideas. In arguing that the capacity to be witty and to laugh represented humanity's special claim to superiority over beasts, these thinkers valorized semantic contingency and deliberation over transparency and certainty in communication.[1] Indeed, many saw these distinctively human forms of communicative engagement as the best means with which to combat enthusiasts who falsely claimed for themselves a privileged and transparent access to truth.

Mandeville and the Virtues of Moral Redescription

In 1656, the French Jesuit and mathematician François du Verdus (c. 1620–1675) sent his friend Hobbes a letter that raised an objection to his characterization of the difference between human and animal communication and sociability. "Who can be sure," Du Verdus asked Hobbes, "that ants and bees do not have a language? That having a King they revere, their obedience is not, as it is with men, *ex institutio*? That they have neither honors nor dignities?... Even if they agree to make their honey in the same hive, can we say for all that that they never have any disagreements?... And who can say that... they are not ruled, like men, out of fear?"[2] Du Verdus thus suggested the possibility that bees had the same "art of words" that, according to Hobbes, was the source of human discord and that, like humans, bees might also have to regulate their private interests by agreeing to live under the rule of a terrifying sovereign.

Fewer than fifty years later, Bernard Mandeville created something of a scandal when he published his verse fable *The Grumbling Hive: Or, Knaves Turn'd Honest* (1705). This fable was a story about a thriving colony of lying and cheating bees that collapses as a result of the bees' agreement to become, as the title suggests, honest. In other words, the knavish colony of bees declines because of their virtuous decision to replace their equivocal and deceptive speech with clear communication. In this respect, the fable was an ironic reversal of Hobbes's suggestion that human societies

---

1. For a treatment of early modern claims that the capacity to truly laugh is uniquely human, see Erica Fudge, *Brutal Reasoning: Animals, Rationality, and Humanity in Early Modern England* (Ithaca: Cornell University Press, 2006), 15–21.

2. François Du Verdus, "Endroits que je n'entens pas de vostre Leviathan," in *The Correspondence of Thomas Hobbes*, ed. Noel Malcom (Oxford: Clarendon Press, 1994), 1:349.

could establish civil harmony by emulating the more direct and rigid form of animal communication. In 1714, Mandeville's poem reappeared as part of *The Fable of the Bees: Or, Private Vices, Publick Benefits*. The choices of a society of communicating bees as the subject of the earlier edition of the fable and of the subtitled *Private Vices, Publick Benefits* for the 1714 edition suggest the themes of animal communication and moral redescription that were central to Hobbes's characterization of the difference between animal and human communication. Though he gave no direct indication of taking his subtitle from Hobbes, Mandeville was familiar with Hobbes's doctrines.[3] Mandeville, in fact, was acquainted thoroughly with many of the contemporary debates over the nature of animal faculties and behavior. As a medical student in Leyden, he wrote an essay in 1689 that was essentially a mechanistic account of animal behavior.

By the time he wrote his fable, Mandeville essentially agreed with Hobbes that in the earliest stage of human social development, before the invention of speech, human beings "differ'd from Brutes in nothing but the outward Figure."[4] Like Hobbes, Mandeville was especially sensitive to the role of language in transforming human nature. His earliest claims about the role of language in distinguishing human and animal sociability appeared in his tale of the merchant and the lion. This particular fable was about a Roman merchant who got shipwrecked on the coast of Africa and encountered a lion. The lion spoke to the merchant, "assuring him withal, that he should not be touch'd, if he could give him any tolerable Reasons why he should not be devoured." The merchant "pleaded his Cause with abundance of good Rhetorick." Suggesting that rhetoric played no role in animal communication, Mandeville wrote that the merchant's "Flattery and fine Words made very little impression." The merchant then turned to "reasoning from the Excellency of Man's Nature and Abilities, [and] remonstrated how improbable it was that the Gods should not have designed him for a better use than to be eat by Savage Beasts." After listening to the merchant's argument, the lion finally replied, "[Y]our violent Fondness to change, and greater Eagerness after Novelties...perverted your Nature and warp'd your Appetites."[5]

---

3. See F. B. Kaye, introduction to *The Fable of the Bees: Or Private Vices, Publick Benefits*, by Bernard Mandeville (Oxford: Clarendon Press, 1924), 1:cix.
4. Mandeville, *The Fable of the Bees*, 1:43–44.
5. Ibid., 176. Edward Hundert discusses this fable in his *The Enlightenment's Fable* (Cambridge: Cambridge University Press, 1994), 87–90.

Thus, like Hobbes, Mandeville argued that a key step in the transformation of human nature occurred when humans invented languages with abstract terms that facilitated their use of rhetoric.

Whereas Hobbes had blamed this art of words for the appearance of civil violence among humans, Mandeville tended to celebrate it as the source of civil prosperity and harmony that he associated with the rise of commercial society. Mandeville argued that "those that have undertaken to civilize Mankind...being unable to give so many real Rewards as would satisfy all Persons for every individual Action, they were forc'd to contrive an imaginary one." In this way, moral values and particularly the idea of "honor" were invented and inculcated into human societies. As Mandeville put it, humans "agreed...to call everything, which, without Regard to the Publick, Man should commit to gratify any of his Appetites, VICE;...And to give the Name of VIRTUE to every Performance by which Man, contrary to the impulse of Nature, should endeavour the Benefit of others, or the conquest of his own Passions out of a Rational Ambition of being good." Much as Hobbes had argued, Mandeville claimed that "the Notions of Good and Evil, & the Distinction between *Virtue and Vice,* were...the Contrivance of Politicians." The shift from the bestial to the civilized state therefore represented for Mandeville the shift from a transparent mode of communication, in which words conformed to things, to more abstract, contingent, imaginative, and rhetorical uses of language. For Mandeville, however, it was precisely this move from a language of particulars and clear communication to a language of abstraction and ambiguous communication that contributed to making human civil communities peaceably and prosperously sociable.[6]

In 1729, Mandeville published a series of six dialogues in which one of the characters, Cleomenes, tries to defend Mandeville's fable to the other character, named Horatio. In the "Sixth Dialogue," which is essentially devoted to the issue of the human inventions of language and writing, Cleomenes explains to Horatio that although human beings have a natural "Capacity beyond other Animals" and although "Nature has made all Animals of the same kind...intelligible to one another, as far as is requisite for the Preservation of themselves," the superior human capacity remains merely potential until the invention of human "speech."[7] One of the things

---

6. Mandeville, *The Fable of the Bees,* 1:42, 48–49, and 50.
7. Ibid., 2:269.

that Cleomenes suggests distinguishes the language of nature from the languages developed by humans is that, with the former, beings can "say more without guile" than with the latter. In other words, the natural language can communicate information in a way that does not allow for deception. For Cleomenes, however, this is not necessarily a good thing.

According to Cleomenes, the problem with the language of nature is that it is "too significant" for human civil societies to be peaceful and prosperous.[8] When Cleomenes rejects Horatio's assertion that "the Design of Speech is to make our Thoughts known to others" and Horatio responds with surprise, asking "What! Don't Men speak to be understood?" Cleomenes explains that "the first Design of Speech was to persuade others."[9] According to Mandeville, the great virtue of the equivocal human languages that supplant a more direct and transparent natural language is that human languages allow people to hide or mask their inward thoughts and feelings. By doing this, an all-important distance is established among people. This distance is a form of "politeness" that contributes to the attenuation of civil violence. Thus, for Mandeville, the difference between sociable humans and animals lies in the former's ability to substitute imaginary for real objects of desire as well as to establish a buffer of politeness between potentially antagonistic people.[10] It is precisely this "encrease in...Cunning," as Mandeville called it,[11] that is made possible by the invention of human languages and that permits humans to redescribe virtues and vices. In doing so, it helps human societies manage their definitions in ways that will symbolically contain their dangerous potential for physical civil violence.

Jonathan Swift: *Deus Est Anima Brutorum*

Where Hobbes had called for the rigid regulation of potentially equivocal words and Rousseau lamented that such words encouraged the loss of a brutal authenticity and liberty, Mandeville celebrated them as the source of a modern commercial and polite sociability that was fundamentally

---

8. Ibid., 287.
9. Ibid., 289.
10. See Hundert, *The Enlightenment's Fable*, 90.
11. Mandeville, *The Fable of the Bees*, 2:267.

both peaceful and prosperous. Jonathan Swift (1667–1745) similarly celebrated the equivocal and redescriptive nature of human communication as a virtue that made it superior to the more limited, if clearer, form of animal communication. Like Mandeville, Swift presented his suggestion that humans do on the whole communicate more effectively than beasts as a parody of a putatively perfect community of animals. Although there is a long-standing tradition of interpreting the fourth part of *Gulliver's Travels* (1726) as presenting the sociable and communicative Houynhnms as more virtuous than humans, there are good reasons to believe that Swift was in fact, like Mandeville, specifically parodying those who claimed that animals communicated more effectively than people.

Swift's "The Logicians Refuted" is one of the many early modern poems in the "satire-on-man" genre, in which authors seem to denigrate humanity by characterizing their claims to rationality and virtue as vain delusions.[12]

> Logicians have but ill defined
> As rational, the human kind;
> Reason, they say, belongs to man,
> But let them prove it if they can.
> Wise Aristotle and Smiglesius,
> ...
> Have strove to prove, with great precision,
> With definition and division,
> *Homo est ratione præditum;*
> But for my soul I cannot credit 'em,
> And must, in spite of them, maintain,
> That man and all his ways are vain;...
> And that brute beasts are far before 'em.
> *Deus est anima brutorum.*[13]

---

12. Robert Gould's *Satire on Man* (1708) set the terms for describing this kind of poem. See Arthur O. Lovejoy, *Reflections on Human Nature* (Baltimore: Johns Hopkins University Press, 1961), 16. See also George Boas, *The Happy Beast in French Thought of the Seventeenth Century* (Baltimore: Johns Hopkins University Press, 1933).

13. Jonathan Swift, "The Logicians Refuted," in *The Works of Jonathan Swift*, ed. Sir Walter Scott (Boston: Houghton, Mifflin, 1883), 14:215–217. The two Latin lines quoted above mean "Man is endowed with reason" and "God is the soul of beasts."

This poem along with another, titled "The Beasts' Confession to the Priest, on Observing How Most Men Mistake Their Own Talents,"[14] that Swift first published in 1732 might seem to suggest that Swift shared Hobbes's and Rousseau's belief that animals are in some significant way superior to people. Indeed, *Gulliver's Travels* has often been interpreted as just such a satire of human nature that culminates in a final voyage to the land of the Houyhnhnms, where Gulliver meets animals that look like horses but speak and live in perfect harmony. A parenthetical comment in Swift's poem "The Beasts' Confession to the Priest" that "When beasts could speak, (the learned say / They still can do so every day)"[15] suggests his familiarity with the argument that animals have not only a genuine language but even an ideal one.

Swift did, in fact, devote a large part of the third chapter of the fourth voyage to the Houyhnhnm language and, throughout the fourth voyage, some of the linguistic features that Gulliver stresses resemble those emphasized by Webster, Hobbes, and Rousseau in their own idealizations of animal language. The Houyhnhnms, for example, communicate with the "most significant Words."[16] The Houyhnhnms lack terms for various abstract ideas, particularly those relating to political speech. Gulliver notes that "Power, government, war, law, punishment, and a thousand other things, had no terms, wherein that language could express them."[17] Gulliver also relates that, in the Houyhnhnm language, there are no terms for falsehoods or lies:

> I remember in frequent Discourses with my Master...having Occasion to talk of *Lying,* and *false Representation,* it was with much Difficulty that he comprehended what I meant.... For he argued thus: That the Use of speech was to make us understand one another, and to receive information of Facts; now if any one *said the Thing that was not,* these Ends were defeated; because I can not properly be said to Understand him; and I am so far from receiving information, that he leaves me worse than in Ignorance; for I am led to

---

14. Ibid., 282–290.
15. Jonathan Swift, "The Beasts' Confession to the Priest, on Observing How Most Men Mistake Their Own Talents" (1732), in Scott, *The Works of Jonathan Swift,* 14:284.
16. Ibid., 325.
17. Jonathan Swift, *Gulliver's Travels* (London: Penguin, 1967), 291.

believe a thing *black*, when it is *white;* and *short*, when it is *long*. And these were all the Notions he had concerning the Faculty of *Lying*.[18]

Gulliver's narration therefore draws a sharp contrast between human beings, who can play on the ambiguities in their languages to give new and sometimes contrary meanings to abstract moral and political terms, and the Houyhnhnms, who never use words ambiguously or equivocally. Given the similarity between the arguments of those who idealized animal communication and the manner in which Swift characterizes the Houyhnhnm language—especially Gulliver's comment that, unlike humans, the Houyhnhnms are not able to redescribe moral terms—Swift appears to have shared their indictment of the ambiguity implicit in human languages and to have intended his description of the Houyhnhnms to be a representation of the model speech community of beasts.

Although there is a long tradition of reading *Gulliver's Travels* as a satire of human nature and of seeing the Houyhnhnms as Swift's ideal of a rational, virtuous, conversable society, Kathleen Williams has shown that there are several difficulties with such a reading. Most significantly, this interpretation assumes "that [Swift's] satiric method is much more simple and direct than elsewhere, and that the attitude of mind is quite different from that which his other work has led us to expect. In recent years, there has been increasing support for the view that Swift did not intend his Houyhnhnms as a simple positive standard...."[19] Swift clearly intended certain parts of *Gulliver's Travels* to be satires of other prominent late-seventeenth-century schemes to guarantee linguistic clarity. When Gulliver visits the School of Languages at the Academy of Lagado, for example, he uncovers two ridiculous language projects. "The first Project was to shorten discourse by cutting polysyllables into one, and leaving out verbs and participles; because in reality all things imaginable are but nouns." The second project Gulliver encounters involves abolishing words altogether: "Since words are only names for *things,* it would be more convenient for all men to carry about them, such *things* as were

---

18. Ibid., 286.
19. Kathleen Williams, *Jonathan Swift and the Age of Compromise* (Lawrence: University of Kansas Press, 1958), 177.

necessary to express the particular business they are to discourse on."[20] Swift presented both projects to parody the language schemers' fantasies of establishing a language with perfect lexical clarity and making words conform to things. Anne Kline Kelly points out that, as they are described by Gulliver, both of these language schemes "oppress rather than liberate."[21] If Swift meant to ridicule those who dreamed of inventing a perfectly clear system of communication, then it seems difficult to believe that he could have intended the similarly perfect language of the Houyhnhnms to be any less ludicrous. While the Houyhnhnms might seem on the surface to be the kind of model speech community that Hobbes and Webster had associated with sociable animals, the fact that their language precludes any use of genuinely deliberative conversation and wit, both of which often depend on verbal ambiguities, suggests that Swift intended this ideal community to be a derisive parody of that model and those who subscribed to it.

The witty management of semantic ambiguities to communicate perspectives that might not otherwise have been apparent was in fact central to Swift's own practices as a satirist. In his *Epistle to a Lady* (1727), Swift presented himself as someone who used laughter and ridicule as alternatives to violent dispute. He wrote,

> I, who love to have a fling
> Both at senatehouse, and king;
> That they might some better way tread,
> To avoid the publick hatred;
> Thought no method more commodious,
> Than to show their vices odious;
> Which I chose to make appear,
> Not by anger, but a sneer.
> As my method of reforming,
> Is by laughing, not by storming.[22]

---

20. Swift, *Gulliver's Travels*, 230.
21. Anne Cline Kelly, *Swift and the English Language* (Philadelphia: University of Pennsylvania Press, 1988), 77–78; see also Deborah Baker Wyrick's *Jonathan Swift and the Vested Word* (Chapel Hill: University of North Carolina Press, 1988), 4 and 44–46.
22. Jonathan Swift, *The Works of the Rev. Jonathan Swift* (New York: William Durell and Co., 1812), 11:43–44.

Swift associated vice with a false pretense to moral gravity, which wit can expose and laughter can correct.

In one of his *Lectures on Rhetoric and Belles Lettres,* Adam Smith extensively discussed Swift's uses of ridicule. Smith wrote, "[I]t is [Swift's] talent for ridicule that is most commonly and I believe most justly admired." The definition of ridicule that Smith used in this discussion corresponds closely to a fairly commonplace early modern definition of wit or humor as the practice of reversing the moral valence of things to render them fresh and new. "Whatever we see that is great or noble," Smith wrote,

> excites our admiration and amazement, and whatever is little or mean on the other hand excites our contempt. A great object never excites our laughter, neither does a mean one, simply as being such. It is the blending and joining of those two ideas which alone causes that Emotion. The foundation of Ridicule is either when what is in most respects Grand or pretends to be so or is expected to be so, has something mean or little in it or when we find something that is really mean with some pretensions and marks of grandeur. Now this may happen either when an object which is in most respects a grand one, is represented to us and described as mean, or e contra when a grand object is found in company as it were with others that are mean; or e contra when our expectation is disappointed and what we imagined was either grand or mean turns out to be the reverse. These different combinations of ideas afford each a different form or manner of ridicule.

Smith noted that the type of ridicule that Swift employed was chiefly that which results "when mean objects are exposed by considering them as Grand." He also pointed out that "when [Swift] has a mind to throw a great degree of ridicule on any subject he puts it into the mouth of some other person as in Gulliver's travels.... The most common manner in which he throws ridicule on any subjects when he speaks in another character is to make them express their admiration and esteem for those things he would expose."[23] In other words, Gulliver's admiration of the Houyhnhnm language should be read as an instance of ironic and witty moral redescription, in which Swift tended to revel.

---

23. Adam Smith, *Lectures on Rhetoric and Belles Lettres* (Indianapolis: Liberty Classics, 1981), 43, 43–44, 48, and 49.

In a short essay on John Gay's *Beggar's Opera* (1728) that appeared in *The Intelligencer,* Swift explicitly took up the subject of humor. He wrote, "I agree with Sir *William Temple,* that the Word [humour] is peculiar to our *English Tongue,* but I differ from him in the Opinion, that the thing it self is peculiar to the *English Nation*... and particularly, whoever hath a *Taste* for *True Humour,* will find a Hundred Instances of it in those Volumes Printed in *France,* under the name of *Le Theatre Italien,* to say nothing of *Rabelais, Cervantes,* and many others."[24] In fact, Swift's early patron, Sir William Temple (1628–1699), also had argued, in his essay "Of Popular Discontents,"[25] that of all the proposed "distinctions" between mankind and beasts only "laughter" is "proper and peculiar to man, without any traces or similitude of it in any other creature."[26] In his *Intelligencer* essay Swift added that "a Taste for *Humour* is in some manner fixed to the very Nature of Man.... And as this *Taste* of *Humour* is purely Natural, so is *Humour* it self."[27] Swift characterized "what we call *humour*" as "the most useful and agreeable species of [*wit*]" and added, "[I]t is certainly the best Ingredient towards that kind of Satyr, which is most useful, and gives the least Offence; which instead of lashing, Laughs Men out of their Follies and Vices."[28]

Béat-Louis de Muralt (1665–1749), who had spent a good deal of time with Temple and Swift during his visit from Switzerland to England, commented that the English "have what they call *Houmour.*" "This *Houmour,*" he explained to his readers, "is approximately, that which constitutes the *diseurs de bons mots* among the French.... But,... they understand by it, a certain fecundity of Imagination, which in general tends to reverse the ideas of things to render them fresh and new."[29] Unlike those who

---

24. Jonathan Swift and Thomas Sheridan, *The Intelligencer,* ed. James Woolley (Oxford: Clarendon Press, 1992), 61.

25. Temple wrote "Of Popular Discontents" in 1681, but Swift was the first to publish it in his 1701 edition of Temple's *Works*. It appears in the same volume with the essay "Of Poetry," in which Temple made the claim about humor that Swift cited in *The Intelligencer.*

26. Sir William Temple, "Of Popular Discontents," in *The Works of Sir William Temple* (New York: Greenwood Press, 1968), 3:31.

27. Swift, *The Intelligencer,* 61–62.

28. Ibid., 62.

29. Béat-Louis de Muralt, *Lettres sur les Anglois et les François,* ed. Charles Gould (Paris: H. Champion, 1933), 122. Muralt's comments echoed those made by Temple himself in his essay "Of Poetry," published in the same volume of his *Works* as the essay "Of Popular Discontents." See Temple, *The Works of Sir William Temple,* 3:437.

blamed the verbal abuses of redescribing moral terms for outbreaks of civil violence, Muralt argued that the moral inversions generated by the imagination not only are sometimes amusing but can also render ideas "fresh and new."

Elena Russo's study of stylistic issues in the French Enlightenment points to the importance of early modern debates about the value of wit. Russo shows that Locke "separated wit (the English equivalent of *ingenium*) from judgment and...denied wit any significant role in the process of reason. To him, only judgment offered clear and distinct ideas, whereas wit yielded nothing more than confused representations."[30] Indeed, Locke wrote,

> [M]en who have a great deal of wit and prompt memories, have not always the clearest judgment of deepest reason. For *wit,* lying most in the assemblage of Ideas, and putting those together with quickness and variety, wherein can be found any resemblance or congruity, thereby to make up pleasant pictures and agreeable visions in the fancy; *judgment,* on the contrary, lies quite on the other side, in separating carefully, one from another, ideas, wherein can be found the least difference, thereby to avoid being misled by similitude, and by affinity to take one thing for another. This is a way of proceeding quite contrary to...that entertainment and pleasantry of wit, which strikes so lively on the fancy.[31]

For Locke, wit clouded and confused while judgment clarified. As Russo points out, however, a number of early-eighteenth-century thinkers agreed that by drawing together notions that were conventionally kept distinct, wit could generate surprise and wonder, which in turn helped to focus the mind and move it to discover something new and significant.[32] Lord Kames, in his *Elements of Criticism* (1762), argued, for example, that "nature hath providently superadded curiosity, a vigorous propensity, which never is at rest. This propensity attaches us to every new object; and incites

---

30. Elena Russo, *Styles of Enlightenment: Taste, Politics, and Authorship in Eighteenth-Century France* (Baltimore: Johns Hopkins University Press, 2007), 147.

31. John Locke, *An Essay concerning Human Understanding,* ed. Alexander Fraser Campbell (New York: Dover, 1959), 1:203.

32. Russo analyzes the complicated early-eighteenth-century network of related concepts such as *je ne sais quoi,* grace, wit, *inquiétude,* and *esprit* in her *Styles of Enlightenment,* 141–166.

us to compare objects, in order to discover their differences and resemblances." Kames added that

> resemblance among objects of the same kind, and dissimilitude among objects of different kinds, are too obvious...to gratify our curiosity in any degree: its gratification lies in discovering differences among things where resemblance prevails, and resemblances where difference prevails. Thus a difference in individuals of the same kind of plants or animals, is deemed a discovery; while the many particulars in which they agree, are neglected: and in different kinds, any resemblance is greedily remarked, without attending to the many particulars in which they differ.[33]

This idea that the mind can be pushed to make new discoveries by bringing together in curious and surprising ways objects that would at first sight seem to be unrelated comes very close to the way Swift and some of his contemporaries defined wit or humor as a "fecundity of Imagination, which reverses the ideas of things to render them fresh and new."

Wit, some argued, also played an important role in making people sociable because by introducing surprising resemblances between otherwise dissimilar ideas, it kept conversation from becoming too tedious and dull. Kames wrote, for instance, that wit often "depends, for the most part, upon chusing a word that hath different significations: by that artifice hocus-pocus tricks are play'd in language, and thoughts plain and simple take on a very different appearance." He added, "Play is necessary for man, in order to refresh him after labour; and accordingly man loves play, even so much as to relish a play of words: and it is happy for us, that words can be employ'd, not only for useful purposes, but also for our amusement. This amusement, tho' humble and low, unbends the mind; and is relished by some at all times, and by all at some times." Kames explained that this kind of amusement arises only once "a language is formed into a system, and the meaning of words is ascertained with tolerable accuracy." At a certain point in the progress of linguistic development, some words take on multiple meanings and "by the double meaning of some words, [opportunity is afforded for expressions that] give a familiar thought the appearance of

---

33. Henry Home, Lord Kames, *Elements of Criticism,* ed. Peter Jones (Indianapolis: Liberty Fund, 2005), 1:197.

being new; and the penetration of the reader or hearer is gratified in detecting the true sense disguised under the double meaning."[34]

A number of Swift's near contemporaries also argued that the capacity for polite conversation, like wit, distinguishes humans from beasts. In his essay "Of Study and Conversation," Charles de Saint-Évremond (1613–1703), for example, had argued that even though animals do communicate linguistically, "Conversation is an Advantage peculiar to Man.... It is the bond of Society, and by it the Commerce of a Civil Life is kept up."[35] "The State of a Solitary man," he added, "is a State of violence.... To live then as Man, it is necessary to converse with Men; it is fit that Conversation should be the most agreeable Pleasure of Life."[36] Swift agreed that conversation is one of the distinguishing marks of humanity. In his "Hints Toward an Essay on Conversation," he wrote that conversation, like humor, "requires few talents to which most men are not born, or at least may not acquire, without any great genius or study. For nature has left every man a capacity of being agreeable."[37] Swift's ideal of conversation left plenty of room for repartees, replies, rejoinders, and circumlocutions. For Swift, conversation also frequently required the deft management of verbal ambiguities or, as he wrote, "double *entendres*" and "innuendoes."[38] Neither any of these characteristics of conversation, nor the laughter with which they would be "attended," could exist in the perfect language of the Houyhnhnms. Swift, like many other early modern writers on the art of conversation, believed that conversation should be an exchange of contrasting points of view. Anne Cline Kelly has noted that "Swift continually stresse[d] that an accurate picture of the world can be assembled only through collective effort, with each person's perspective providing

---

34. Ibid., 273. Kames linked this phenomenon with "words held to be synonymous." See chapter 5 for a discussion of the ways that early modern French thinkers attributed the *légèreté* of the French national character to the "apparent synonymy" of an exceptional number of French words.

35. Charles de Saint-Évremond, *Oeuvres de Monsieur de Saint-Évremond* (Londres: Chez Jacob Tonson, 1711), 6:118.

36. Ibid., 120.

37. Jonathan Swift, "Hints Toward an Essay on Conversation," in *A Tale of a Tub, The Battle of the Books, and Other Satires* (London: Everyman's Library, 1909), 227.

38. Jonathan Swift, "A Complete Collection of Genteel and Ingenious Conversation," in *A Tale of a Tub*, 244–245.

a small piece of the whole. Swift believed that to ensure the efficacy of conversation, one needs to expose oneself to a wide range of views."[39]

The suggestion that Swift intended his representation of Houyhnhnm communicative practice to be an ideal model therefore cannot be right. Gulliver relates, for example, that "Reason among [the Houyhnhnms] is not a point as problematical as with us, where men can argue with plausibility on both sides of a question; but strikes you with immediate conviction." Gulliver's characterization of the Houyhnhnm language is strikingly similar to the idealizations of a language in which the meanings of words are never ambiguous. The Houyhnhnms, as Gulliver relates, do not even have the idea of opinion. Swift wrote, "[I]t was with extreme difficulty that [Gulliver] could bring his master to understanding the meaning of the word *opinion*, or how a point could be disputable." Without an idea of opinion, they also can never have genuine deliberations. Though they have what Gulliver calls "Grand Assemblies," these always involve only "unanimous consent."[40] The one and only debate that ever occurred among the Houyhnhnms, according to Gulliver, had to do with the question "whether the Yahoos should be exterminated from the face of the earth."[41] In fact, the debate occurred only because Gulliver himself had introduced his novel opinion.[42]

In the end, the Houyhnhnm are strikingly similar to violent fanatics and savage enthusiasts. In fact, by the end of the century, William Godwin (1756–1863) pointed out the fundamentally uncivil nature of Swift's Houyhnhnm in his essay "Of Politeness" (1797). The "Houyhnhnm is a savage," Godwin noted, "who cries repeatedly to the unfortunate wanderer to go faster, and never discovers his incapacity or his pain, till it is in the most express manner represented to him."[43] Neither the Houyhnhnm nor the enthusiast is willing to tolerate difference civilly or with anything like a sense of humor. They refuse to really consider the opinions of those who disagree with them because they believe that with their unambiguous words they can not fail to always reason correctly and so come to the only

---

39. Kelly, *Swift and the English Language*, 40.
40. Swift, *Gulliver's Travels*, 202.
41. Ibid., 205.
42. He had suggested that the Yahoos could be castrated to render them tame. *Gulliver's Travels*, 205–206.
43. William Godwin, *The Enquirer: Reflections on Education, Manners, and Literature* (London: Printed for G. G. and J. Robinson, 1797), 331.

right conclusion. In the face of difference and contrasting opinions, the Houyhnhnms, like the religious and political fanatics of the sixteenth and seventeenth centuries, resort to violent extermination.

In fact, as a parody of the idea that animal languages are semantically unambiguous, Swift's representation of the Houyhnhnms suggested, not unlike Mandeville's characterization of his colony of bees, that humans are superior to beasts precisely because only humans have the capacity to ironically redescribe moral terms. This distinctly human capacity makes it possible to recognize and communicate novel opinions and to begin to engage in genuine ethics and politics. Indeed, as Swift explained in *Contests and Dissentions,* anything resembling an ideal state must be one in which competing interests and opinions remain in harmonious balance. As Anne Cline Kelly argues, Swift believed that "the civil equilibrium is an analogue to good conversation; all parties benefit and none suffers."[44] Although there is no direct evidence tying Swift's *Gulliver's Travels* to Mandeville's fable, it is nonetheless safe to assume that Swift, like any literate person, would have known about the fable, especially after the grand jury of Middlesex recommended in 1723 that its publisher be prosecuted for having printed a book that had "a direct Tendency to the Subversion of all Religion and Civil Government."[45]

The "Fourth Voyage" in *Gulliver's Travels,* then, should not be read so much as a critique of the human inability to reach a final consensus on theological, ethical, or political issues as a critique of those who are so enraged by dissenters and by their inability to achieve consensus that they are led ultimately to a ridiculous hatred of humanity itself. This fact comes out most visibly in Swift's correspondence with Viscount Bolingbroke, who was one of the great believers in the virtues of an illuminating rationality that must lead finally to consensus in any question. In September of 1724, Bolingbroke commented to Swift just months before reading the "Voyage to the Houyhnhmland" that "the faculty of distinguishing between right and wrong, true and false, which we call reason or common sense, which is given to every man... is the light of the mind, and ought to guide all

---

44. Kelly, *Swift and the English Language,* 78.
45. See W. A. Speck, "Bernard Mandeville and the Middlesex Grand Jury," *Eighteenth-Century Studies,* 11, no. 3 (Spring, 1978): 363. This publishing scandal surrounding Mandeville's fable occurred precisely during the period from 1720 to 1726 when Swift was working on *Gulliver's Travels.*

the operations of it." Bolingbroke therefore defined humanity as *animal rationale*. About one year later Swift wrote to Pope, "I have got materials toward a treatise, proving the falsity of that definition *animal rationale*, and to show it would be only *rationis capax*. Upon this great foundation...the whole building of my Travels is erected." Bolingbroke, after Pope presumably showed him the letter, replied to Swift, "Your definition of *animal capax rationis*, instead of the common one *animal rationale*, will not bear examination." But Swift's final answer was that despite the fact that humanity was not absolutely rational, it was nonetheless not to be despised. "I tell you after all," he wrote to Pope late in 1725, "that I do not hate mankind: it is *vous autres* who hate them, because you would have them reasonable animals, and are angry for being disappointed. I have always rejected that definition, and made another of my own." When one reads Gulliver's "Fourth Voyage" against the grain of Swift's writings on wit and conversation, it becomes apparent that his ideals of linguistic communication implied that those like Webster, Hobbes, and Rousseau who held up animal communication as a model of clarity were themselves ultimately ridiculous promoters of incivility. By contrast, for Swift, the polysemous nature of human languages made them significantly superior to the unambiguous but rigidly static, mentally constraining, and socially uncompromising forms of animal communication.[46]

Bougeant's Beastly Amusements

Fewer than fifteen years after the appearance of *Gulliver's Travels*, the French Jesuit Guillaume-Hyacinthe Bougeant (1690–1743) published his *Amusement philosophique sur le langage des Bêtes* (1739), a work that purported to show not only that animals communicated linguistically but also that animal languages were significantly better than human languages.[47] Bougeant followed Swift in presenting his idealizations of animal communication as

---

46. *The Correspondence of Jonathan Swift 1718–1727*, ed. F. Erlington Ball (London: G. Bell and Sons, 1912), 3:209, 277, 297, and 293.

47. On the popularity of the work, its editions, and commentaries see Hester Hastings, *Man and Beast in French Thought of the Eighteenth Century* (Baltimore: Johns Hopkins University Press, 1936).

parody of those who believed that animals communicated more effectively than humans. Bougeant's *Amusement* made a sufficient public impact to lead the Abbé Yvon (1720–1790) to make note of its currency in his *Encyclopédie* article on "animal souls."[48]

In the *Amusement,* Bougeant singled out beavers as exemplars of sociable and cooperative existence to prove that animals communicate linguistically. The beaver dam, he noted, "is perfectly constructed; it is the admiration even of Men; and the little [beaver] society...never dreams of anything more than to live tranquilly.... Is it not evident that an enterprise, which is executed so well, necessarily supposes that these animals talk to one another and have among them a language, by which they communicate their thoughts?" Bougeant followed Cureau de la Chambre, Hobbes, and Rousseau in insisting that animals have "no abstract ideas and consequently, no Metaphysical reasonings." As a consequence, he suggested, they appear to have distinct communicative advantages over human beings. Animals, he wrote, have "no other science than that...of self-preservation,...and of procuring for themselves that which is good. Also we have never seen any of them haranguing in public, or disputing over causes & their effects." Since many of the vicious ideas that trouble human societies are abstract ones, their absence means that they cannot trouble sociable animals. "Glory, grandeur, riches, reputation, ostentation & luxury," he argued, "are words unknown among the Beasts & which you will not find in the dictionary of their language." Bougeant concluded that animal languages must be "very restricted" since they are free from abstract words. He seemed to follow Hobbes in suggesting further that animal societies might therefore also be free from the disturbances generated by abuses of abstract words. He wrote,

> [T]he language of Beasts does not seem to us to be so narrowly confined except in relation to our own which is maybe too diffuse.... Would it not be

---

48. Abbé Claude Yvon, "Ame des Bêtes," in *Encyclopédie, ou Dictionnaire Raisonné des Sciences, des Arts et des Métiers,* ed. Denis Diderot and Jean le Rond d'Alembert (Stuttgart-Bad Cannstatt: Frommann, 1966), 1:351. Besides his writings on animal communication, Bougeant wrote many other works, and at least some of his contemporaries considered him to be "one of the best writers of the eighteenth century." See Guillaume-Hyacinthe Bougeant, *Amusement philosophique sur le langage des bêtes; avec le supplément, ou plutôt la critique de cet ouvrage...* (Peking: Chez Gogué et Née de la Rochelle, 1783), 5.

something to be wished for, at least from certain perspectives, that our language were less abundant and less prolix? Men are naturally great talkers, & if I dare say, chatterers. They never have enough words to express everything that they wish to say. Little contented with simple ideas, they like to dissect them, so to speak, into subdivisions: they seem sometimes to want to dissect an idea or sentiment, like a Surgeon dissects the head. So many new words that have to be created as a consequence; & what words! Words so empty of sense, obscure, equivocal, and more suited to give rise to disputes, than to enlightenment.

At first glance, Bougeant seems to have argued, like Hobbes and Webster, that there were significant ethical and cultural advantages to animal forms of communication. He wrote that humans abused "their facility for speaking which nature has given them." "What errors and lies," he complained, "are the ordinary subjects of our conversations!...If the Beasts were to hear us converse, chatter, lie, slander, exaggerate, would they have any reason to envy us the uses we can make of speech?...They speak little, but they never speak but to the point and with a knowledge of the issue. They always speak the truth and never mislead." Following Swift, Bougeant seemed to be presenting animal communication and the societies they entailed as models for humans to emulate. "There is commonly but one single expression for each object," he wrote. "Compare the pretences of our amplifications, of our metaphors, of our hyperboles, of our contorted sentences, and always you will find among the Birds simplicity and truth, and in human language a whole lot of verbiage and out-and-out lying." For Bougeant, animal communication was a language where distortions of rhetoric could have no place.[49]

A superficially literal reading of Bougeant's *Amusement* seems to place it directly in line with those who claimed that animal language might be the perfect language conforming to things that was the stuff of language schemers' fantasies: "Is it not to be wished," Bougeant wrote, "as some have at times proposed, that humans establish on this model a universal

---

49. Guillaume-Hyacinthe Bougeant, *Amusement philosophique sur le langage des bêtes*, ed. Hester Hastings (Genève: Librairie Droz, 1954), 75, 85–86, 87–88, and 95. On the idea that beavers are exemplary sociable, reasonable, and communicating animals, see Gordon M. Sayre, *Les Sauvages Américains: Representations of Native Americans in French and English Colonial Literature* (Chapel Hill: University of North Carolina Press, 1997), 218–247.

language that would be understood throughout the Universe?"⁵⁰ Bougeant seemed to have gone to great lengths to demonstrate that animals are better off in many ways than humans as a result of their languages. Without words for abstract ideas, he pointed out, animals do not engage in seemingly frivolous inquiries. Unlike humans who converse too much about apparently meaningless things, animals are ideals of taciturnity. Animals do not create ambiguous and equivocal neologisms. They never lie, exaggerate, harangue, or dispute. Much like Gulliver's idealized world of the Houyhnhnm, Bougeant seemed to present the speech community of the beasts as a model of logical coherence and semantic transparency and consistency; unlike humans, they never resort to such potentially equivocal and ambiguous rhetorical figures as metaphor, irony, and hyperbole.

The fact that Bougeant presented these thoughts on animal communication in the form of an amusement suggests that, like Swift, he ultimately intended his treatise to be received as an amusing parody of those who held up animal communication as a model for human emulation. Hester Hastings, the editor of a modern edition of the *Amusement*, described him as having a "playful humor" and a "bantering temperament."[51] Many of Bougeant's contemporaries similarly appreciated his witty sense of humor. The editor of one of the many eighteenth-century editions of the *Amusement* described it as "the fruit of a bantering & laughing imagination."[52] The 1744 obituary notice for Bougeant that appeared in the *Journal de Trévoux* indicated his tendency to avoid overly serious subjects. He did not follow up on his most serious work, the *Histoire du Traité de Westphalie* (1727), because of his "exquisite and fine taste, which does not content itself easily with subjects of a certain importance."[53] Jean Sgard and Geraldine Sheridan, the editors of a work in which Bougeant parodied the emerging genre of the novel, have described Bougeant as a worldly wit who was at home in the conversable and amusing sociability of the French salon.[54]

---

50. Bougeant, *Amusement philosophique*, ed. Hastings, 96.
51. Hester Hastings, introduction to Bougeant, *Amusement*, ed. Hastings, 11.
52. See Bougeant, *Amusement philosophique*, ed. Hastings, 22.
53. "Éloge historique du P. Bougeant" (1744), in *Journal de Trévoux, ou Mémoires pour servir à l'histoire des sciences et des arts* (Geneva: Slatkine Reprints, 1968), 44:246.
54. Jean Sgard and Geraldine Sheridan, preface to *Voyage merveilleux du Prince Fan-Férédin*, by Guillaume-Hyacinthe Bougeant, ed. Jean Sgard and Geraldine Sheridan (Saint-Étienne: Publications de l'Université de Saint-Étienne, 1992), 10.

They describe Bougeant's sense of humor as his characteristic operational style and method: "[H]umor is his mark, his style, his method of analysis. He excelled in making this romantic, used-up, worn-out machine function according to his own agendas; he turned it into a machine to process texts, into a writing workshop specifically for endlessly rewriting absurdities."[55] Bougeant's near contemporary the abbé de Voisenon referred to his love of "canards": "When he needed money to buy coffee, or chocolate, or tobacco, he would say naively: *I will make a monster that will bring me a louis;* it would be a little sheet that announced the encounter of a very extraordinary monster that had been seen in a far-off country, & that never existed."[56]

By the time he had published the first edition of his *Amusements,* moreover, he had, like Swift, already earned a reputation as a satirist for a series of politically and religiously potent satirical comedies: *La Femme docteur, ou la théologie tombé en quenouille* (1731), *Les Quacres français, ou les nouveaux trembleurs* (1732), *Arlequin janséniste* (1732), and *Le Saint déniché, ou la banqueroute des marchands de miracles* (1732). In these plays, Bougeant satirized the Jansenists, the Jesuits' eighteenth-century confessional rivals. In his *Arlequin janséniste,* for example, one of the characters asserts: "[W]e comedians are like Doctors of humankind,... all the vices, and all the foibles, and all the passions, all the ridicules of the world reside in our domain; they are the game we hunt."[57] Bougeant prefaced another of his anti-Jansenist comedies with a letter in which he pretended to beg his editor not to publish the play. Bougeant asked, "To what are you exposing me?" He claimed, "I imagine myself already hearing the clamors of a thousand people.... What! They will say, to place partisans of grace and charity on the stage like ridiculous characters!"[58] He noted that people might be offended by the representation of ostensibly grave religious figures as ridiculous. He also described how some enemies of the Jesuits might react with a pretense to be offended: "To treat the most holy matters of Theology and Religion in a Comedy! What an abuse! What profanation!... what

---

55. Ibid., 14.
56. L'Abbé de Voisenon, "Anecdotes litteraires," in *Œuvres complettes de M. l'Abbé de Voisenon* (Paris: Moutard, 1781), 4:126.
57. Guillaume-Hyacinthe Bougeant, *Arlequin janséniste* (Cracovie: Jean Le Sincere, 1732), act 2, scene 2.
58. Guillaume-Hyacinthe Bougeant, *La Femme docteur, ou la théologie janséniste tombée en guenouille, comédie* (Amsterdam: E. Ledet, 1731), 3–4.

sacrilege!" Bougeant suggested that the Jesuits' enemies would try to deflect his satire by pretending to be offended at his treating a religious subject in a comedy, "for that is their style."[59] Bougeant, however, defended himself from such charges by reminding his readers that the Jansenist "Pascal treated the same matters before" in his *Provincial Letters,* "which are nothing but Comedy." "But," Bougeant complained, "I would try to make them see reason in vain. They inundate the public with insipid and tasteless jibes; they are permitted all this.... But we, poor Molinists, let us not venture to want to laugh in our turn. The proverb that half the world laughs at the other is not made for us. We must suffer others to laugh at our expense without daring to laugh in our turn."[60] Bougeant thus argued that the Jesuits had to meet their enemies on the field of wit and appeal to the imaginations of the reading and theatergoing public.

Bougeant had so successfully mastered the art of redescriptive wit that, for the first and only time, under his literary influence the Jesuits regained the upper hand in their quarrel with the Jansenists over the legitimacy and limits of Christian uses of raillery.[61] Indeed, his comedies were such theatrical successes that the Jansenists, normally the enemies of theater, felt compelled to publish their own comedy attacking the Jesuits in the manner of Bougeant.[62] One eighteenth-century commentator emphasized the regenerative effects that Bougeant's uses of redescriptive humor had on French society:

> Father Bougeant is not the first to have found in theological disputes a subject for Comedy; but he has the distinction of having put, more than anyone else, wit into these sorts of Works. He turns the Jansenists to ridicule; & that

---

59. Ibid., 4. The reference is to the *Nouvelles Ecclesiastiques,* the Jansenists' periodical publication. This issue of whether or not certain subjects, particularly religious ones, because they were by their nature too grave or important, should be shielded in principle from ridicule was the central question famously addressed by the eleventh of Pascal's *Provincial Letters* (1656) and by Shaftesbury's *Sensus Communis* (1711). The issue was taken up over and over throughout the eighteenth century in such works as John Brown's *An Essay on Satire: Occasion'd by the Death of Mr. Pope* (London: Printed for R. Dodsley, 1745). See Alfred Owen Aldridge, "Shaftesbury and the Test of Truth," *Publications of the Modern Language Association of America* 60, no. 1 (1945): 129–156.

60. Bougeant, *Femme docteur,* 4.

61. On this quarrel see Marc Fumaroli, *L'Âge de l'éloquence* (Paris: Albin Michel, 1994), 327.

62. An example was the *Arlequin, esprit folet* (1732). According to André Dabezies, it was considered bad and was unsuccessful. See André Dabezies, "Érudition et humour: Le Père Bougeant (1690–1743)," *Dix-Huitième Siècle,* no. 9 (1977): 267.

is what gave such a vogue to his Comedy, in a time when minds were very heated by all that concerned the P. Quesnel, the Bull of Unigenitus, the Appellants to the Council, &c. Up to that point no one had disputed so lightheartedly upon these matters, which, on the contrary, had often caused a thousand chagrins to those who got involved with them.[63]

This commentator characterized confessional conflicts as usually the stuff of heated minds, or what others would have characterized as enthusiasm or fanaticism. The commentator argued, however, that Bougeant had found a better way to deal with these heated disputes: he directed them away from the domain of physical violence associated with civil and religious war and toward the domain of symbolic or verbal violence associated with humor and ridicule.[64]

Reading Bougeant's claims about the superiority of animal communication against the background of his literary personality and productions, it becomes evident that he shared Swift's belief that the human capacity for communicating wit was the distinguishing mark of human superiority over the beasts. In his *Amusement,* Bougeant noted that, as commendably taciturn as animals might be, they nonetheless lacked one particular but especially important human capacity. Bougeant begged his readers, "Permit me to make a little digression about joy. Do you know that our ancient Philosophers have alleged that Beasts do not laugh at all, and that laughter is an essential property of Man alone to the exclusion of Beasts?" Bougeant toyed with the idea that animals might laugh since they can feel joy. "Is this not an old error," he asked, "and is it not evident that Beasts laugh very well in their own way, and just as well as Man? ... Is it essential to laughter that it occurs as in Man by a movement of the lips and the mouth with a convulsive sound of the voice?" He entertained the possibility that "laughter is nothing but an expression of joy.... Man laughs in his

---

63. See Bougeant, *Amusement philosophique,* 18–19.

64. The contest between the Jesuits and the Jansenists, though largely a theological conflict, spilled onto the political stage at certain points through the course of the eighteenth century. Dale Van Kley has argued that developments in this dispute were one of the fundamental causes of the French Revolution. See Dale Van Kley, *The Religious Origins of the French Revolution: From Calvin to the Civil Constitution, 1560–1791* (New Haven: Yale University Press, 1996). See also James E. Bradley and Dale K. Van Kley, eds., *Religion and Politics in Enlightenment Europe* (Notre Dame: University of Notre Dame Press, 2001).

way, & the Dog laughs in his. What matter that it be by a burst of voice, or by a simple movement of the ears and tail...? It is still laughter."[65]

The construction to this point suggests that Bougeant expected his audience to agree that animals must laugh, albeit in their own way. Bougeant, however, continued, "I beg you, suspend your decision a moment."[66] In the end, Bougeant concluded that animals must lack the capacity for laughter because laughter is an expression of a very distinct and special type of joy. "I agree with the ancient Philosophers," he wrote, that "while Laughter is an expression of pleasure & of joy, not all pleasure & joy produce laughter."[67] According to Bougeant, only humans could laugh because only humans could experience the specific joy that comes from perceiving the tensions apparent in a combination of otherwise incompatible ideas that produce a novel, unexpected, and therefore amusingly surprising composite:

> The only joy that produces laughter is that which is accompanied by surprise, & that is borne in us at the sight of some bizarre combination of two ideas, or of two incompatible things, such as a Magistrate dressed as a Harlequin, or of a blunderer who wishes to seem capable.... It is necessary as a consequence, in order to be able to laugh, to be able to compare together two ideas, & to perceive their incompatibility. Yet, that is what the Beasts do not know how to do, because they only have direct knowledge. They have sentiments of satisfaction, of pleasure & of joy, & most of them express them very distinctly, but they can in no way have that joy that is born of reflection or comparison. Thus the Beasts never laugh, and the ancients were right.[68]

Bougeant, like Swift and others, saw the true mark of human superiority in the distinct capacity for wit and laughter generated by redescriptions that depended ultimately on a particular kind of ambiguity and that can lead to novel discoveries. It is because they lacked this linguistic tool required for wit that, as he noted, animals make "no curious researches into all the objects that surround them."[69]

---

65. Bougeant, *Amusement philosophique*, ed. Hastings, 91.
66. Ibid.
67. Ibid.
68. Ibid., 91–92.
69. Ibid., 85–86.

Bougeant's *Amusement* and Swift's *Gulliver's Travels,* both of which parodically turned beasts into exemplars of virtue and reason, were thus both examples of this witty and redescriptive rhetoric.[70] This was precisely the spirit in which the Abbé Claude Yvon presented Bougeant's *Amusement.* In fact, Bougeant's own experiences after publishing his *Amusement* resembled Gulliver's fate. Like Gulliver, who was exiled from the land of the Houyhnhnms because they were unable to recognize him as anything other than a Yahoo, Bougeant's enemies used a witty but potentially heretical comment in his *Amusement* to have him exiled. His suggestion was that animal rationality might be explained by presuming that God punished rebellious angels by trapping their immortal souls in the bodies of beasts. As Yvon interpreted his case, Bougeant had been the victim of his witless and pretentiously grave enemies who could not bear to have religion treated with humor, especially by someone like Bougeant, who was a member of a religious order. "Gallantry is never forgivable in a philosophical work," Yvon noted, "except when the author is a man of the world; and even then many think it is out place. In reasoning with a light touch and raising interest by way of banter, one often falls into ridicule; and one always causes scandal, if one's status does not permit the imagination to give itself over to witticisms." Yvon concluded, however, that "they have too harshly censored our Jesuit for what he said.... It is easy to see that he never regarded his system as anything but a bizarre and almost crazy fantasy. The title of *Amusement,* which he gave to his book, and the pleasantries which made it sparkle, are enough to see that he never believed it to be built on

---

70. Also, the redescriptive element in Bougeant's discussion of the differences between animals and humans was echoed in chapter 7 of his *Voyage du Prince Fan-Férédin,* where Bougeant explicitly referred to *Gulliver's Travels.* After discussing the fact that Gulliver was both big to the Lilliputians and small to the Brobdignagians, Bougeant wrote that "it was not worth the trouble of making such a grand voyage, to learn what we already knew, that in the world there is no absolute grandeur, and that great or small stature is a thing indifferent to human nature." See Guillaume-Hyacinthe Bougeant, *Voyage merveilleux du Prince Fan-Férédin* (Saint-Etienne: Université de Saint-Etienne, 1992), 75. Bougeant followed this comment on the relativity of certain human characteristics with a discussion of talking animals in novels (75–76). The author of the critical "Lettre à Madame la Comtesse de ***, pour servir de Supplément à l'Amusement Philosophique sur le langage des Bêtes" (see the 1783 edition of Bougeant's *Amusement*) explicitly connected Bougeant's *Amusement* to the fourth part of *Gulliver's Travels.* He wrote that, in Bougeant's *Amusement,* "you will find some strange Philosophers.... It... could serve as a sequel to the ridiculous voyage made by Gulliver in the country of the *Houyhnhnms"* (202).

a foundation to generate any real persuasion."⁷¹ Another commentator, a few years later, described Bougeant's *Amusement* as a "jeu d'esprit that he perhaps should not have permitted himself and which his ardent enemies treated with too much rigor."⁷² In other words, Bougeant was one of the worldly wits of his day who fought with limited success against what he took to be pretentiously and ridiculously grave fanaticism. He participated in the light sociability of early modern French salon culture, and he put his ideas about what it was that made human sociability better than that of animals to the service of defending the Jesuit order against Jansenist attacks. He did this by trying to direct the potential physical violence of religious enthusiasm into the symbolic domain of wit and ridicule.

Conclusion

In his *Essai philosophique sur l'âme des bêtes* (1728) David-Renaud Boullier (1699–1759) emphasized the "vicissitudes of opinion" that surrounded the question of animal communication. "Nothing," he wrote, "appears more humiliating for the human mind than that flux and reflux of opinions, which we see among Philosophers throughout the centuries. What is certainly remarkable is that the same man cannot long apply himself to the study of Truth without experiencing in himself these same vicissitudes."⁷³ For Boullier, then, the fact that so many thinkers had deliberated questions like whether animals had souls for such a long time and without ever reaching any final resolution must be evidence of the weakness of the human mind. A number of early modern French and British thinkers would have agreed with Boullier that humanity's incapacity to finally reach an absolute consensus on answers to moral questions was a human failing. Unlike animals, whose unambiguous communication provided them with a clear relationship to their social and material surroundings,

---

71. Yvon, "Ame des Bêtes," 1:353.

72. Louis-Mayeul Chaudon, *Bibliothèque d'un home de goût*...(Avignon: J. Blery, 1772), 2:339.

73. David-Renaud Boullier, *Essai philosophique sur l'âme des bêtes précédé du Traité des Vrais Principes qui Servent de Fondement à la Certitude Morale* (Amsterdam: Chez François Changuinon, 1737), 177. Boullier was a Protestant theologian originally from France who not only was anti-Cartesian but also published a *Défense des pensées de Pascal* against Voltaire.

humans tended to take advantage of the ambiguities in certain defective abstract terms to redescribe moral categories. Hobbes, Webster, and Rousseau saw this as a singular defect of human communication and one that generated and perpetuated civil violence.

A second group of thinkers, however, not only accepted the ambiguities in human languages but believed that such ambiguities served crucial purposes in helping to focus the human mind's attention on novel phenomena and in making humans peaceably and amusingly sociable. While some insisted that the distinctively human capacity for moral redescription was the most fundamental source of physically violent human conflict, Swift, Bougeant, and Mandeville suggested that it was precisely the ambiguity in human language that allowed people to converse, laugh, and deliberate. Swift characterized the Houyhnhnms as ridiculous in their incapacity not only to recognize that Gulliver was neither a Houyhnhnm nor a Yahoo but also to properly deliberate the question of what to do with him. By the end of the story, although Gulliver returns to his former human society, he spectacularly fails to reintegrate and becomes the central ridiculous character of the novel through his pretensions to being essentially different and superior to other people whom he can now only recognize as Yahoos. Separated from the Houyhnhnms, whose language he now speaks, he gallops around, shuns any human contact—especially that of his family, for whom he has only contempt—and spends all his time in the barn pretending to talk to his horses. The satiric target of the fourth voyage is therefore not humanity's incapacity to recognize and communicate the dictates of a chimerical transparent reason but rather the people who criticize and hate humanity for not being able to do so. Bougeant offered the most explicit argument that laughter and wit marked humans' superiority over brutes. He, like Temple and others, characterized wit as the ability to perceive and represent incongruities through rhetorical redescriptions of virtue and vice. For Bougeant, as for others, this distinctly human ability allowed people to guard against the impostures of truth. Mandeville presented a similar but ultimately far more radical argument for the positive influence of humanity's tendencies to rhetorical redescription. He insisted that without this tendency to manage verbal ambiguities, humans, unable to find either real or imaginary values, would be unable to live together peaceably.

Part II

SAVAGE ELOQUENCE

3

WARMING SAVAGE HEARTS AND HEATING ELOQUENT TONGUES

> Men of exalted minds, and... Noble in characters and manners, are very little disposed to laugh; for, though they perceive the Ridiculous, they are not delighted with it. This we observe among the Indians of North America, whom we call Savages; for not only in their public assemblies..., there is the greatest gravity and dignity of behaviour observed, but in their private conversation there are none of those violent bursts of laughter which we see among us.
>
> JAMES BURNET, *Origin and Progress of Language* (1792)

> The words which issued all on fire from the lips of this Christian were received in hearts colder than marble: but it is a seed which the Holy Ghost will cause to sprout when he pleases.
>
> JÉRÔME LALEMENT, *Jesuit Relations* (1640)

John Quincy Adams (1767–1848) reported in his *Memoirs* that in July of 1794 he attended a smoking ceremony between American dignitaries, including then American president George Washington (1732–1799), and members of the Chickasaw Nation.[1] "Whether this ceremony be really of

---

1. Adams was describing the audience that Chief Piomingo had in Philadelphia with President Washington on July 11, 1794.

Indian origin," Adams commented, "I have some doubt.... These Indians appeared to be quite unused to it, and...it looked as if they were submitting to a process in compliance with *our* custom. Some of them smiled with such an expression of countenance as denoted a sense of *novelty,* and of *frivolity* too; as if the ceremony struck them, not only as new, but also as ridiculous."[2] Adams drew attention to the conventionality of Chickasaw dress, noting that "there was nothing remarkable in their appearance.... They were none of them either painted or scarified.... And I do not recollect observing any other ornaments upon them."[3] If Adams was suggesting that the belief that American Indians were somehow essentially different from whites was a silly mistake, he nonetheless repeated one early modern commonplace about the American Indians as "noble savages." He described the scene in which Washington read a speech that was then translated for the Chickasaw by an interpreter. As soon as the translator had finished each sentence, Adams noted, "the five Chiefs all together would utter a sound, importing their approbation. The sound was strong or faint, in proportion to the degree of satisfaction they had in what was said.... It resembled a horse's neighing as much as anything, and more than once reminded me of the Houynhms [*sic*]."[4] One might easily wonder whether by associating the speech of the Chickasaw with the language of the Houyhnhnms Adams was suggesting that American Indians were ideal speakers who, like the Houyhnhnms, never said "the thing that was not."

While Adams gave no other indication that he thought Native Americans spoke an ideal language, by the end of the eighteenth century the characterization of Indian speech as supremely eloquent had become firmly established. In his *Notes on the State of Virginia* (1782), Thomas Jefferson, for example, celebrated a speech by Captain John Logan (c. 1725–1780), a Mingo chief, citing it to illustrate his belief that Indians had an "eminence in oratory."[5] Jefferson insisted, "I may challenge the whole orations of Demosthenes and Cicero, and of any more eminent orator, if Europe

---

2. John Quincy Adams, *Memoirs of John Quincy Adams,* ed. Charles Francis Adams (Philadelphia: J. B. Lippincott & Co., 1874), 1:34–35.

3. Ibid., 35–36.

4. Ibid., 35.

5. Thomas Jefferson, *Notes on the State of Virginia,* ed. William Peden (New York: Norton, 1972), 62.

has furnished more eminent, to produce a single passage superior to the speech of Logan."[6]

As this chapter will show, however, not all early modern accounts of Indian languages and speakers insisted on their virtues. Early modern Europeans tended initially to cast Indian speakers and their languages as defective. This chapter will explore the emergence of the idea of the supremely eloquent Indian orator within the context of Christian missionizing and the following chapter will show how this idea migrated into linguistic discourses that attributed Indian eloquence to characteristics of so-called savage languages. Early modern discourses about the relative merits of languages thus not only made competing claims for transparency and levity; some also idealized the warmth and energy that they associated with savage speech. Chapters 3 and 4 will therefore examine the uses of a thermal metaphor of communication in which savage speech was characterized as transmitting an emotional energy and moving warmth to generate a sublime eloquence and guarantee sincerity.[7]

If some early modern thinkers sought to overcome a perceived problem of communication by correcting the ambiguities implied in moral redescriptions, scripture itself provided many instances not only of irony but also of God's own turning of vice into virtue in what could be called a divine form of redescription. The New England Puritans who collaborated in publicizing their missionary work among the so-called Praying Indians were particularly attuned to this notion of God as a moral redescriber inasmuch as they saw the conversion of the Indians as a process in which God was taking what one Puritan called "the veriest ruines of mankind" and turning them into exemplars of grace to humble white Christian audiences. Language was central to the missionary account of this ironic transmutation. Christian missionaries, both Puritan and Jesuit, who often described un-Christianized Indians as linguistically deficient, unbearably noisy, and rhetorically inept, also frequently noted that God's grace, in melting Indian hearts and warming their affections, transformed

---

6. Ibid.
7. For a contrasting use of the thermal metaphor of speech in colonial America, see Robert Blair St. George, "*Heated* Speech and Literacy in Seventeenth-Century New England," in *Seventeenth-Century New England,* ed. David D. Hall and David Grayson Allen (Boston: Colonial Society of Massachusetts, 1984), 275–322.

these noisy savages into silver-tongued Christian orators who moved their audiences to tears.

Early modern accounts of Indians often characterized them as barbarians. Anthony Pagden has shown that "the barbarian was a specific cultural type who could be characterized in terms of a number of antitheses to the supposed features of the civil community."[8] New England Puritans like Cotton Mather (1612–1727), for instance, referred to Indians as "doleful creatures,... the veriest ruins of mankind" and listed several "conveniencies of human life" that they lacked.[9] Language was a key characteristic that classical thinkers believed barbarians lacked. The invention of language was central to their account of the historical emergence of the boundary between civilization and barbarism. As Pagden puts it, "the barbarian... was thought to live in a world where this all-important *communicatio* was ineffective, where men failed to recognize the force of the bonds which held them to the community, where the language of social exchange itself was devoid of meaning. In most respects the barbarian was another animal altogether."[10] Seventeenth-century discussions of Indians commonly insisted on the deficiencies of their languages. Paul Lejeune (1591–1664), a Jesuit missionary and the editor of *Jesuit Relations*, remarked, for example, that "the poverty [of their language] appears in a million articles.... All the utterances, all the terms, all the words and all the names that have to do with the world of goods and grandeur, must be absent from their dictionary; this is a great dearth."[11]

Richard Rath has shown that English-language descriptions of Indians frequently commented on their wild noises. John Smith (1580–1631), for example, described the Potomacs as "showting, yelling, and crying, as we rather supposed them to be so many divels."[12] George Percy (1580–1632) described Powhatan's people as making "a noise like so many Wolves or

---

8. Anthony Pagden, *The Fall of Natural Man: The American Indian and the Origins of Comparative Ethnology* (Cambridge: Cambridge University Press, 1982), 20.

9. Cotton Mather, *Magnalia Christi Americana or, The Ecclesiastical History of New England...* (Hartford, CT: Silas Andrus and Son, 1853), 1:558.

10. Pagden, *The Fall of Natural Man*, 21.

11. Reuben Gold Thwaites, ed., *The Jesuit Relations and Allied Documents* (New York: Pageant, 1959), 7:20.

12. Richard Cullen Rath, *How Early America Sounded* (Ithaca: Cornell University Press, 2003), 151.

Devils." Percy also described a scene in which "an old savage made a long Oration." According to Percy, this oration, however, was nothing more than the "making [of] a foule noise" and "vehement action."[13] In discussing the funeral for one of the Praying Indian children, Thomas Mayhew contrasted the behavior of the Praying Indians to that of other Indians, stating, "[T]ruly they gave an excellent example in this also, as they have in other things; here were no...hellish howlings over the dead, but a patient resigning of it to him that gave it."[14] Cotton Mather, who referred to Indian languages as a "Barbarous Linguo," recommended that "the best thing we can do for our Indians is to Anglicise them," because "their Indian Tongue is a very penurious one."[15]

Rhetorical Primitivism and the Christian Grand Style

Recent discussions of missionary accounts of Native Americans have tended to take at face value the New England Puritan caricatures of both Indian speech and Jesuit communicative approaches as being fundamentally oral and rhetorical, as focusing on *verba* more than *res,* and of Puritan approaches as being fundamentally textual and logical, as focusing on *res* more than *verba*. In doing so, these historians have missed an important feature shared by Jesuit and Puritan representations of Indians: the supreme eloquence of the converted savage. In fact, Puritans frequently pointed to the eloquence of the Indians' Christian oratory: their conversion narratives and preaching.

Historians also have tended to view Puritan discussions of savage eloquence as "reveal[ing] their anxiety about the uses of eloquence in their own communities."[16] Sandrah Gustafson, for instance, insists that "Puritan writers...excoriated the figure of the eloquently manipulative Indian

---

13. George Percy, *Observations by Master George Percy, 1607* (New York: Scribner's, 1907), 13, online facsimile edition at http://www.americanjourneys.org/aj-073/ (accessed May 22, 2009).
14. Michael P. Clark ed., *The Eliot Tracts: With Letters from John Eliot to Thomas Thorowgood and Richard Baxter* (Westport, CT: Praeger, 2003), 183.
15. Quoted in *The Letter-Book of Samuel Sewall,* Collections of the Massachusetts Historical Society, 6th ser., 1:401–402 (Boston, 1886).
16. Sandra M. Gustafson, *Eloquence Is Power: Oratory and Performance in Early America* (Chapel Hill: University of North Carolina Press, 2000), 33.

orator."[17] Behind this view is the belief that "Europeans...identified textuality, particularly the use of Scripture, as the crucial difference between Puritan preaching and Indian sacred oratory."[18] Edward Gray similarly places a heavy emphasis on Puritan textual practices, arguing that, for Puritans, "an expression [of faith] could be neither received nor conveyed in the ambiguous form of signs, symbols, or gestures—media that, by their figural form, were assumed to inadequately convey God's word. Indeed to present God's word in media other than print was merely to continue the alienation of the believer from God. It was to insert an obstacle between believers and Scripture in its least fluid—and truest—form: the printed form."[19] While such arguments appeal to the well-documented distinctions between Reformed and Catholic, especially Jesuitical, stylistic commitments[20] and to the obvious differences resulting from the fact that Indians did not have alphabetic writing systems, they nonetheless give the misleading impression that Puritans were antagonistic either to rhetoric or to oral and performative communication.

This historiographical implication of drawing the distinction between the Puritans' commitments to script or text and the Indians' oral culture is overdrawn to the extent that it obscures Puritan missionary interests in the oral performances of converted Indians. In fact, the missionaries' concern was generally not that Indians communicated orally; it was that, not being Christians, their speech was not divinely inspired and, as such, could be neither eloquent nor trustworthy. It was not so much that Puritan missionaries mistrusted Indians because they inhabited an oral culture as that they sought to ensure the *sincerity* of Indian conversions. In fact, Puritans not only did not ignore Indian speech, but they closely scanned rhetorical performances of the Indians for evidence of genuine inspiration and sincere conversion. Their reports of Indian conversion therefore represent an important stage in the development of the commonplaces of savage eloquence.

---

17. Ibid.
18. Ibid., 35.
19. Edward G. Gray, *New World Babel: Languages and Nations in Early America* (Princeton: Princeton University Press, 1999), 50.
20. Walter Ong, *Orality and Literacy: The Technologizing of the Word* (London: Methuen, 1982), and James Axtell, *The Invasion Within: The Contest of Cultures in Colonial North America* (Oxford: Oxford University Press, 1985).

Jefferson's well-known comment that Logan was at least as eloquent as the classical exemplars of eloquence, whether Jefferson knew it or not, was made possible by early modern missionary adaptations of Saint Augustine's theory of rhetorical primitivism that made it possible to conceive of a speaker as being both unfamiliar with the sophisticated theories of rhetoric and nonetheless supremely eloquent. It was largely within this Christianized theory of rhetorical primitivism that European missionaries began to recognize and comment on Indian oratory. The early modern reconfiguration of the *genera dicendi,* the hierarchy of rhetorical styles, to combine the high and low styles and create the "Christian grand style" was decisively influenced by Augustine's *De doctrina Christiana* (AD 427). According to Augustine, when one "is making ready to speak before the people...God may place a good speech in his mouth,"[21] but such a speaker is eloquent "more through the piety of his prayers than through the skill of his oratory."[22] For Augustine, the grand style thus retained the "forceful...emotions of the spirit"[23] but lost the full and formal artifice of the Ciceronian grand style to become a passionate but plain style. This Augustinian grand style, therefore, represented a fusion of the expressive and forceful sublimity of the Asiatic style and the simple, extemporal, and unrefined character of the Attic style.

The Augustinian insistence on the centrality of pathos in the grand style distinguished it from Platonic and Stoic conceptions of eloquence that tended to bifurcate reason and passion. While Plato and the Stoics tended to associate passionate persuasion with deception,[24] Augustine held that "grand eloquence...[moves] the minds of listeners...that they may do what they already know should be done."[25] Since he maintained that affect and volition were inseparable, Augustine held that the passions were allied with reason in the search for the divine and truth. Just as Christian holiness was, for Augustine, a gift of grace and not of good works, so Christian eloquence was a gift of grace and not of artful manipulation. Augustine

---

21. Saint Augustine, *On Christian Doctrine,* trans. D. W. Robertson, Jr. (New York: Macmillan, 1958), 168.
22. Ibid., 140.
23. Ibid., 150.
24. See Deborah Shuger, *Sacred Rhetoric: The Christian Grand Style in the English Renaissance* (Princeton: Princeton University Press, 1988), 44–46.
25. Saint Augustine *On Christian Doctrine,* 137.

wrote that while the grand style often "uses almost all of the ornaments, it does not seek them if it does not need them.... It is enough for the matter being discussed that the appropriateness of the words be determined by the ardor of the heart rather than by careful choice."[26]

The fate of this Christian grand style in the sixteenth and seventeenth centuries in England and France is a relatively complicated story intertwined as it is with the Protestant Reformation, Renaissance humanism, and the emergence of the New Philosophy. Recent scholarship in the history of rhetoric, however, suggests that these three movements each contributed to and drew on a reinvigorated Augustinian conception of the grand style in the seventeenth century.[27] In both France and England, the advocates of the Christian grand style tended to be from those groups with affinities for Reformed doctrines: the Jansenists in France and the Puritans in England.

Augustine thus laid the foundation for a Puritan acceptance of the importance of verbal eloquence, and even a superficial survey of New England Puritan culture and ideas will show that rhetoric and techniques of verbal eloquence were fundamentally important to Puritans.[28] Cotton Mather, for example, singled out the Puritan missionary John Eliot's (1604–1690) *"way of preaching"* as "very powerful;...when he was to use reproofs and warnings against any sin, his voice would rise into a warmth which had in it very much of energy...; he would sound the trumpets of God against all vice, with a most penetrating liveliness, and make his pulpit another Mount Sinai for the flashes of lightning."[29] One important but largely overlooked discourse about the verbal eloquence of the untrained but inspired savage therefore lies at the intersection of Puritan prophecy, scriptural commentary, and English encounters with Algonquian-speaking Indians.

---

26. Ibid., 150.

27. Marc Fumaroli, in *L'Âge de l'éloquence* (Paris: Albin Michel, 1994) for example, has traced the contests between the *parlementaires'* austere atticist styles and the Jesuits' florid asianist styles in the emergence of French classicism. The magistrates in the *parlements* had stylistic affinities with the Jansenists, the Jesuits' doctrinal and stylistic enemies.

28. See E. Brooks Holifield, *Era of Persuasion: American Thought and Culture, 1521–1680* (Boston: Twayne, 1989), 93.

29. Mather, *Magnalia Christi Americana*, 1:548.

Conversion Narratives and Suspicion in the Eliot Tracts

The suggestion that Indians were supremely eloquent, although well established by the eighteenth century, sat rather awkwardly next to frequent seventeenth-century claims that their languages were deficient and that Indians made little more than "hellish howlings." The locus for Puritan representations of savage eloquence, however, was the converted Indian. In representing American Indian eloquence, Puritans frequently followed Augustine's insistence that it was God who made speakers eloquent by affecting their hearts and thereby placing eloquent speech in their mouths.

Roger Williams, in his *Key into the Language of America* (1643), noted that he was impressed with the verbal eloquence of newly Christianized Indians. In his preface, addressed "To the Reader," he commented on "that great Point of their *Conversion*" and noted, "I know there is no small *preparation* in the hearts of Multitudes of them. I know their many solemne *Confessions* to my self, and one to another of their lost *wandering conditions*."[30] Williams reported that during his visit to the dying Pequot or Niantic sachem Wequash, who had aided the English at the siege of the Pequot fort at Mystic, Wequash told him that their earlier discussions concerning Christian conversion "were never out of my heart."[31] According to Williams, the dying Wequash regretted his failure to convert. Williams reported that the last words he heard from Wequash were "Me so big naughty Heart, me heart all one stone!" Williams called these last words from Wequash "savory expressions."[32] Williams's comment here is noteworthy for the way in which it attributed a rhetorical salt to the speech of this Pequot sachem, who had at the moment of his death taken the important first step toward Christian regeneration. Indeed, Williams represented Wequash's lament about his having failed to convert and his having a heart of stone by characterizing it as spoken with a *humilitas* that was one of the hallmarks of the Christian grand style. Puritans frequently remarked on similarly savory expressions of the converted Indians, who, with the help

---

30. Roger Williams, "To the Reader," in *A Key into the Language of America*... (London: Gregory Dexter, 1643), no page no.
31. Ibid.
32. Ibid.

of divine grace, had turned from speaking with beastly howling voices to speaking with the energetic eloquence of a divine voice.

As Kristina Bross has recently pointed out, "the story of Puritan evangelism in America and of the invention of the Praying Indians begins in 1643, with the publication of *New Englands First Fruits*, [which...] describes the Christian conversion of several Indians."[33] In this and other tracts that followed it, the divine light of grace warmed and enlivened speech as much as it clarified it. The thermal metaphor of energizing enlightenment was connected to the heart in the same way that the visual metaphor of clarifying enlightenment was connected to the intellect. The Eliot Tracts, a series of short works published in London that Eliot and his supporters wrote between 1647 and 1670 and which purport to describe the conversion narratives of certain so-called Praying Indians, demonstrate how Puritans used this Christian language of divine enlightenment to characterize the energetic eloquence of converted Indians.

Historians have long been aware that Puritans established what Edmund Morgan has called a *"morphology of conversion,* in which each stage could be distinguished from the next ... by a set of ... recognizable signs."[34] Morgan summarizes this morphology in the following terms:

> First comes a feeble and false awakening to God's commands and a pride in keeping them pretty well, but also much backsliding. Disappointments and disasters lead to other fitful hearkenings to the word. Sooner or later true legal fear or conviction enables the individual to see his hopeless and helpless condition and to know that his own righteousness cannot save him, that Christ is his only hope. Thereafter comes the infusion of saving grace, sometimes but not always so precisely felt that the believer can state exactly when and where it came to him. A struggle between faith and doubt ensues, with the candidate careful to indicate that his assurance has never been complete and that his sanctification has been much hampered by his own sinful heart.[35]

The Eliot Tracts are accounts of the signs that some Indians genuinely were converting to Christianity, and they conform to Morgan's descriptions of

---

33. Kristina Bross, *Dry Bones and Indian Sermons: Praying Indians in Colonial America* (Ithaca: Cornell University Press, 2004), 3–4.
34. Edmund S. Morgan, *Visible Saints: The History of a Puritan Idea* (New York: New York University Press, 1963), 66.
35. Ibid., 91.

the morphology of conversion. Cotton Mather remarked, for example, that "the Churches of New-England... required very signal demonstrations of a *repenting* and a *believing* soul, before they thought men fit subjects to be entrusted with 'the rights of the kingdom of Heaven.'"[36] He explained that "the Indians were... called in considerable assemblies convened to that purpose, to make open *confessions* of their faith in God and Christ, and of the efficacy which his word had upon them for their conversion to him."[37] These confessions "were scanned by the people of God."[38]

The belief that certain changes became evident with the infusion of grace was central to the morphology of conversion. Puritans maintained that a transformation in speech involved some of the most important signs of a genuine conversion. The English Puritan Joseph Alleine (1634–1668), in his *A Sure Guide To Heaven* (1672), noted that when people who "before were the instruments of sin, are now become the holy utensils of Christ's living temple," their "heart, that was a sty of filthy lusts,... becomes an altar of incense, where the fire of divine love is ever kept burning, and from which the daily sacrifice of prayer and praise, and the sweet incense of holy desires, ejaculations and prayers, are continually ascending."[39] On this theory, divine grace warmed the converted heart, and the Christianized speaker suddenly became an eloquent orator. Alleine focused particularly on the sonic transformations that took place at the moment of regeneration. "The mouth" of the converted, he wrote, became "a well of life; his tongue as choice silver, and his lips feed many." He continued his explanation of the eloquence of the converted speaker in the following terms: "Now the salt of grace has seasoned his speech..., and cleansed the man from his filthy conversation, flattery, boasting, railing, lying, swearing, backbiting, that once came like flashes proceeding from the hell that was in the heart (Jas iii 6). The throat, that once was an open sepulcher, now sends forth the sweet breath of prayer and holy discourse, and the man speaks in another tongue." Alleine concluded that the tongue of the divinely inspired convert became a "silver trumpet... and the best member that he has."[40] Puritans thus believed that the individual's divine regeneration was

---

36. Mather, *Magnalia Christi Americana*, 1:565.
37. Ibid.
38. Ibid.
39. Joseph Alleine, *A Sure Guide to Heaven* (Edinburgh: The Banner of Truth Trust, 1959), 35.
40. Ibid., 36.

made most apparent in the radical transformations of both the sound and the substance of a person's speech.

This Puritan insistence that divine grace regenerated the filthy noise issuing from a person's mouth to turn it into eloquent speech was central to the development of the theory of savage eloquence; by frequently characterizing Indian speakers as making wild noises, seventeenth-century writers were, sonically speaking, portraying them as especially well suited to regeneration. That there was a communicative criterion to evaluating the efficacy of Indian conversions is indicated by Cotton's grandfather, Richard Mather (1596–1669), who wrote:

> To see and hear Indians opening their mouths, and lifting up their hands and eyes in prayer to the living God...; to see and hear them exhorting one another from the word of God; to see and hear them confessing the name of Christ Jesus, and their own sinfulness; sure this is more than usual! And though they spoke in a language of which many of us understood but little, yet... we saw and heard them perform the duties mentioned with such grace and sober countenances, with such comely reverence in their gesture, and their whole carriage, and with such plenty of tears trickling down the cheeks of some of them, as did argue to us that they spake with the holy fear of God, and it much affected our hearts.[41]

In this passage, where Mather remarks on the "more than usual" scene of savage eloquence, a number of the commonplaces of the Christian grand style make an appearance: the pathos and the sublimity of the *actio,* each presented with "grace," "sobriety," and "comely reverence." Mather's remarks on the manner of speaking of the converted Indians, therefore, cast them in precisely the terms of the Christian grand style in which a divine grace warmed the heart and generated a moving eloquence.

Patricia Caldwell argues that New England Puritans tended to play down the linguistic advantages of a gracious condition in conversion narratives. The Puritan leaders' prudence in the face of the language and rhetoric of conversion narratives was tied to their awareness of what Caldwell calls "the sinful distortion of language during the Antinomian

---

41. Mather, *Magnalia Christi Americana,* 1:565.

troubles."⁴² Thus, while out of fear of Antinomian enthusiasm, Puritan leaders encouraged the speakers of their own non-Indian communities to temper their uses of the Christian grand style, these same leaders encouraged the opposite from Indians.

If Puritan missionaries were suspicious of the workings of grace on Indians, they remained convinced that in time they would genuinely convert the Indians. In fact, Eliot insisted that "it is a day of small things with us: and that is Gods season to make the single beauty of his humbling Grace, to shine in them, that are the veriest ruines of mankind that are known on earth."⁴³ Thomas Shepard's (1605–1649) *The Clear Sun-shine of the Gospel Breaking Forth upon the Indians New-England* (1648) similarly worried about the possibility that Indian conversions were false but ultimately reassured readers of their authenticity. He opened his tract by confessing, "I dare not speake...what I thinke about their conversion, I have seen so much falsenesse in that point among many English, that I am slow to believe herein too hastily concerning these poor naked men." Despite this awareness, he nonetheless concluded, "[C]ertainly 'tis not so in all, but that the power of the Word hath taken place in some, and that inwardly and effectually."⁴⁴

Shepard recorded the following comment from Eliot: "that it was true indeed, that some of the English did so far suspect them for sundry reasons."⁴⁵ Shepard wrote that "this their own testimony of themselves being propounded with much sweetnesse and seriousness of affection, may be the...confirmation of some inward worke among them; which I looked upon as a speciall providence that such a speech should be spoken and come to my eare...; the Lord himself I believe and no man living, putting these words into their own hearts."⁴⁶ Shepard thus concluded that it was the Praying Indians' eloquence that provided the final assurance that

---

42. Patricia Caldwell, *The Puritan Conversion Narrative: The Beginnings of American Expression* (Cambridge: Cambridge University Press, 1983), 145.

43. John Eliot, *Tears of Repentance or a Further Narrative of the Progress of the Gospel amongst the Indians in New England* (London: Printed by Peter Cole in Leaden-Hall, 1653), no page no.

44. Thomas Shepard, *The Clear Sunshine of the Gospel Breaking Forth upon the Indians in New-England...* (London: Printed by R. Cotes for J. Bellamy, 1648), 2. Shepard helped develop and police the requirements of a genuine confession of religious experience and faith for admission to membership in the congregation. See his *The Sincere Convert* (1641) and *The Sound Believer* (1645).

45. Ibid.

46. Ibid.

God's grace was really at work.[47] In fact, the Puritan missionaries took the Praying Indians' confessions to be signs that, in good Augustinian fashion, God was regenerating them and placing eloquent speeches in their mouths. Eliot frequently noted that the Praying Indians' confessions consisted of what "the Lord assist[ed] them to utter."[48] Elsewhere, he wrote, "I see evident demonstrations that Gods Spirit by his word hath taught them, because their expressions, both in Prayer, and in the confessions which I have now published, are far more, and more full, and spiritual, and various, then ever I was able to express unto them." He continued: "There is a great Spirit of Prayer powred out upon them, to my wonderment; and you may easily apprehend, That they who are assisted to express such Confessions before men, are not without a good measure of inlargement of Spirit before the Lord."[49] The way Eliot framed his reports of the Indians' confessions shows that he took their utterances to be inspired by, if not direct manifestations of, God's own divine eloquence. Thus it is clear that Puritan missionaries did not distrust the eloquence of the Praying Indians, as has been suggested by some, but rather their eloquence became for these missionaries the guarantee of the authenticity of their regeneration. After commenting on the Indians' confessions, Eliot on one occasion added that "they have not any writing, or like helps, only their memory, and the help of Gods Spirit, to read in their own hearts, what they utter."[50] The Praying Indians' very lack of writing, therefore, was what guaranteed that their eloquence was unstudied and thus more likely to be an authentic manifestation of the workings of grace in their hearts.

Heating Hard Hearts

The Puritan missionaries' confidence in the authenticity of Indian conversions rested on the belief that the inspiration of divine grace affected

---

47. In the next century, Joseph Priestley published a tract on the Pentecostal miracle of the "gift of tongues." The apostles' plain but passionate style was for Priestley the evidence of their sincerity. See Joseph Priestley, *An Essay on the Gift of Tongues, Proving That It Was Not the Gift of Languages in a Letter to a Friend* (Bath, 1786), 133–139.
48. John Eliot, *A Further Account of the Progress of the Gospel amongst the Indians in New England*... (London: Printed by John Macock, 1660), 36.
49. Eliot, "To the Reader," in *Tears of Repentance,* no page no.
50. Eliot, *A Further Account of the progress of the Gospel,* 46.

the Indians by warming their hearts. As Charles Cohen points out, Puritans criticized those who cultivated what the New England Puritan Thomas Hooker (1586–1647) called "a cold luke warme temper."[51] "Puritans," Cohen notes, "were a 'hotter sort' of Protestant, and what kept them bubbling was a religious sensibility intimately bound up with conversion, an emotional confrontation with grace borne by the Holy Spirit in the Word."[52] That those who missionized among the Indians understood divine enlightenment not only in visual but also—and even more fundamentally—in thermal terms is evident where Eliot wrote that "there is grace in [the Praying Indians'] hearts, a spark kindled by the Word and Spirit of God that shall never be quenched."[53] The following admonishment appears in Shepard's *Clear Sunshine of the Gospel upon the Indians in New England* (1648): "We have the *light* of former times, but we want the *heat...; we* have a *form* of Godliness, but want the *power....* Let these poor *Indians* stand up *incentives* to us...: who knows but God...hath *warmed* them, that they might *heat* us."[54] Discussing one Praying Indian's "variety of gracious expressions, and abundance of teares," Shepard favorably contrasted such emotional expressions of a divine enlightenment with its intellectual manifestations.[55] Shepard wrote that he "and some others, [who] have had so great light, and yet want such affections as they have, who have as yet so little knowledge," were "much ashamed."[56] Eliot not only noted that the heat of divine light had warmed the Indians but also prophesied that they would conduct this heat to English-speaking Christians. He wrote, "It were a very desireable mercy, that the practise and example of our native Brethren, yea of the native *Indians* in *New England* might kindle in us the fire of a blessed emulation in this matter."[57]

In the Puritan reports of their conversion performances, the 'Praying Indians' frequently referred to their hearts as initially stone cold but then noted that the heat of divine grace melted them. Several passages in the

---

51. Thomas Hooker, *The Soules Vocation or Effectual Calling to Christ* (London: 1638), 273.
52. Charles Lloyd Cohen, *God's Caress: The Psychology of Puritan Religious Experience* (Oxford: Oxford University Press, 1986), 4.
53. Clark, *The Eliot Tracts*, 205.
54. Shepard, *Clear Sunshine of the Gospel*, no page no. In the same letter, Shepard wrote that "where the *power* is lost, God will not *long* continue the *form,* where the *heat* is gone, he will not *long* continue the light" (31).
55. Ibid., 36–37.
56. Ibid., 37. See also Clark, *The Eliot Tracts*, 85.
57. Eliot, *Further Account,* no page no.

Eliot Tracts describe the divine light of grace not only as breaking but also as melting the Indians' cold, hard hearts. One example is the confession of one Totherswamp, who stated: "[B]efore I prayed...not one good word did I speak...and full was my heart of evil thoughts."[58] His confession finished, Eliot reported, "Mr. Allin further demanded of him this Question, How he found his heart, now in the matter of Repentance. His answer was; I am ashamed of all my sins, my heart is broken for them and melteth in me."[59] In another reported confession, an Indian named Ponampam twice associated "the workings of the Word" not only with the breaking but also the melting of his heart.[60] In *The Glorious Progress of the Gospel amongst the Indians in New-England,* one contributor pointed to what he described as the Praying Indians' "sweet and affectionate melting under the word of grace" as evidence that their conversions were sincere.[61]

The Savage Eloquence of Praying Indians

Puritan missionaries argued that Indian eloquence was a sure sign that God was genuinely inspiring the Indians and warming their hearts. Shepard noted, for example, that "the *Spirit* also going forth in *power* and efficacy with it, in *awakening* and *humbling* of them, drawing forth those *affections* of sorrow, and expressions of *tears* in abundance, which no tortures or *extremities* were ever observed to *force* from them."[62] When they discuss Indian speakers, the authors of the Eliot Tracts frequently identified the characteristics of the Christian grand style, such the extemporaneousness, the pathos, and the plainness of their speeches.

According to Augustine, "the grand style frequently prevents applauding voices with its own weight, but it may bring forth tears."[63] In describing an oration of his own to the people of Caesarea, Augustine reflected on the effects of his use of the grand style. "I did not think that I had done anything when I heard them applauding," he wrote, "but when I saw them

---

58. Eliot, *Tears of Repentance,* 5.
59. Ibid., 7.
60. Ibid.
61. Ibid., 25.
62. Shepard, *The Clear Sunshine of the Gospel,* no page no.
63. Saint Augustine, *On Christian Doctrine,* 160.

weeping.... Tears indicated that they were persuaded.... There are many other experiences through which we have learned what effect the grand style of a wise speaker may have on men. They do not show it through applause but rather through their groans, sometimes even through tears."[64] It should not be surprising, then, to find that one of the most common signs that divine grace was melting Indian hearts was a flood of tears. Eliot described a scene in which, when one Indian confessed his sins, this Indian's "father burst forth into great weeping: hee did the same also to his mother, who wept also, and so did divers others; and many English being present, they fell a weeping, so that the house was filled with weeping on every side; and then we went to prayer, in all which time *Cutshamaquin* wept, in so much that when wee had done the board he stood upon was all dropped with his teares."[65] Eliot described one Indian who "manifested many teares in publike." He added "that there were so many, as that the dry place of the *Wigwam* where he stood was bedirtied with them, powring them out so abundantly. *Indians* are well known not to bee much subject to teares... and if the word workes these teares surely there is some conquering power of Christ Jesus stirring among them."[66] The Praying Indians did not simply shed plenty of tears; those tearful performances were so moving that they conducted the divine heat to audiences who in their turn similarly melted into puddles.[67]

While the Puritans took such tears to be reliable signs of divine inspiration, they also related other ways that the reality of inspiration manifested itself in the Indians' speech. They commented, for example, on the extemporal and plain character of the Indian confessions. Thomas Mayhew noted that on one occasion, "some of the Indians spake something for their benefit; and about ten, or twelve of them prayed, not with any set Form..., with much affection, and many Spiritual Petitions, savoring of a Heavenly

---

64. Ibid., 160–161.
65. Shepard, *The Clear Sunshine of the Gospel,* 23.
66. Ibid., 29–30.
67. Eliot reported that when one Toteswamp spoke, he did so "in more words, and much affection, and not with dry eyes: Nor could I refraine from teares to hear him." See John Eliot, *Late and Further Manifestation of the Progress of the Gospel amongst the Indians in New England* (London: Printed by M.S., 1655), 7. See also Clark, *The Eliot Tracts,* 91–92.

mind."[68] Eliot insisted, "I see evident demonstrations that Gods Spirit by his word hath taught them, because their expressions, both in Prayer, and in the confessions...are more full, and spiritual, and various, then ever I was able to express unto them."[69] Shepard related that when Eliot offered to give some clothes to an "old [Indian] man [who] hath much affection stirred up by the Word," this Indian "affectionately brake out" into a speech. Shepard noted that this was "a blessed, because a plain hearted affectionate speech, and worthy *English* mens thoughts."[70] According to Shepard, "This same old man...after an *Indian* Lecture, when they usually come to propound questions; instead...began to speak to the rest of the *Indians,* and brake out into many expressions of wondering at Gods goodnesse unto them.... This speech expressed in many words in the *Indian* Language and with strong, actings of his eyes and hands, being interpreted afterward to the *English,* did much also affect all of them that were present [at] this Lecture also."[71] Shepard's description is a good example of how Puritans tended to cast the eloquence of the Praying Indians. Shepard noted that this Indian broke out into speech and ignored the formal conventions of "propounding questions." He described this speech as "affectionate" but also "plain hearted." He also noted other characteristics of the Augustinian passionate but plain style. There were, for example, clear marks of *humilitas* in the speaker's wonderment, and Shepard noted the strength of the *actio* in the "actings of eyes and hands," both of which contributed to passionately moving the audience.

Others similarly cast the Praying Indians as speaking with a passionate but plain eloquence. Among the letters that Whitfield printed in his *Strength out of Weaknesse,* one by John Endecott (1588–1665) cast the moving eloquence of the Praying Indians as a sign of "the inlarging of the Kingdome of [God's] deare Sonne...amongst the Heathen *Indians.*" Endecott told his readers, "[T]ruly Gentlemen, had you been eare and eye-witnesses of what I heard and saw..., you could not but be affected therewith as I was." "I could hardly refraine teares for very joy," he continued, "to see

---

68. Thomas Mayhew, "To the much Honored Corporation in London...," in Eliot, *Tears of Repentance,* no page no.
69. Eliot, "To the Reader," no page no.
70. Shepard, *The Clear Sunshine of the Gospel,* 12.
71. Ibid., 13.

their diligent attention to the word first taught by one of the *Indians,* who before his Exercise prayed.... The matter I did not so well understand, but it was with such reverence, zeale, good affection, and distinct utterance, that I could not but admire it;... [he] continued in his Exercise full halfe an houre or more..., his gravitie and utterance was indeed very commendable."[72] These reports of speeches by converted Indians emphasized their passionate but plain eloquence.

In a letter he sent to Johannes Leusden (1624–1699), professor of Hebrew at the University of Utrecht, Cotton Mather's father, Increase (1639–1723), drew attention to a number of churches in which the pastors were Indians. Increase noted that in these churches the "preacher always begins with prayer, and *without a form, because from the heart.*" Cotton Mather glossed this part of his father's letter by insisting on the extemporal, passionate, and sincere manner in which the converted Indians prayed. He argued that the Indians who "pray with much pertinence and enlargement" "would much wonder at it, if they should hear of an English clergy that should 'read their prayers out of a book,' when they should 'pour out their souls' before the God of Heaven."[73] Among the Eliot Tracts there are similar remarks on the special eloquence of Indian preachers. John Wilson, for example, commented as follows after he and a handful of other colonists listened to one Indian preacher: "[W]e understood him not... excepting now and then a word or two, he discoursed..., with great devotion, gravitie, decency, readiness and affection, and gestures very becoming, and sundry mentions he made of Jesus Christ,... and the rest of the *Indians;* diverse old men and women, and the younger did joyne and attend with much Reverence, as if much affected therewith; then he ended with prayer as he beganne."[74] In a "postscript" to his reproduction of exhortations made by six Praying Indians in 1658, Eliot commented, "These things argue a good savor of spirituall things in the speaker, and here is spirituall food for the hearer. I doe know assuredly that many Godly and savory matters and passages have slipped from me, and these expressions are but a little of a great deal. I know not that I... have let slip, much which they spake."[75]

---

72. Clark, *The Eliot Tracts,* 242.
73. Mather, *Magnalia Christi Americana,* 1:569–570.
74. Clark, *The Eliot Tracts,* 232.
75. Ibid., 339.

In closing his tract in this way, Eliot not only insisted that the converted Indian speakers expressed their melted hearts with surprisingly moving eloquence, but he even suggested that they were more eloquent than he was able to convey.[76]

Roger Williams's presentation of Wequash's "savory expressions" uttered on his deathbed was, in fact, an abbreviated form of a distinct genre that was used by Puritans to present the eloquence of the converted savages: "dying speeches." Puritans generally used dying speeches, which were frequently either wholly fictional or highly edited, to demonstrate the effectiveness of grace in regenerating even the most fallen of people or to provide models of excellent lives, lived in the face of adversity and sin. There are significant instances of such dying speeches in the Eliot Tracts. Whitfield, for example, described at length the dying words of one Wamporas, "one of [the Praying Indians'] first and principall men." After describing the scene in which Wamporas "dyed praying," Whitfield wrote,

> [H]e said he feared not death, he was willing to dye, and turning to the Company which were present hee spake unto them... with many such words exhorting them, which could not heare without weeping. A little before his death hee spake many gracious words unto them.... His gracious words were acceptable and affecting, that whereas they used to flie and avoyde with terrour such as lye dying, now on the contrary they flocked together to heare his dying words, whose death and burial they beheld with many teares; nor am I able to write his Storie without weeping.[77]

---

76. The New England Puritans rejected levity as a communicational ideal. Consistently, these Puritans contrasted the gravity of the Praying Indians' speeches with the raillery of the unconverted Indians. In a number of the passages from the Eliot Tracts, the Indian speakers were characterized as speaking with a grave tone or with *gravitie*. See, for example, Thomas Mayhew, "To the much Honored Corporation in London." Though it is not surprising that Puritans emphasized that the Praying Indians took their conversions seriously and so spoke gravely, this characterization contrasts sharply with depictions of the unconverted Indians. Eliot, for example, noted that other Indians "mock and scoffe at those *Indians* which pray." See John Eliot, "The Letter of Mr. Eliot to T.S. concerning the Late Work of God among the Indians," in Shepard, *Clear Sunshine of the Gospel*, 18. In the reports of their confessions, the Praying Indians frequently remarked both that before they joined the Praying Indians, they were foolish and laughed much and that after they joined them, other Indians laughed at them and mocked them. See, for example, Eliot, *A Further Account*, 21, 29, 33, 39, 65, 68. See also Eliot, *Tears of Repentance*, 46, 50, 57, 65, 66, 67, 73, 74, 78.

77. Clark, *The Eliot Tracts*, 222–223.

In 1685, Eliot published a collection of eight dying speeches, in which a number of converted Indians eloquently professed the sinfulness of their lives and with notable *humilitas* counseled their family and friends to turn to Christianity.[78] Not only were the speeches meant to convey to the Indians a perceived need to convert, but by publishing them, Eliot presumably intended to demonstrate the hand of providence at work among "such Indians as dyed in the Lord."

Much of the Puritans' evidence of the authenticity of the Indian conversions therefore lay in the passionate but plain eloquence of the converted Indians' rhetoric, and the missionaries' accounts of the Praying Indians' dying speeches conform to this Christian grand style. The extemporal nature of expression, the apparent inattention paid to diction and construction, the insistence on the pathos and *humilitas* exhibited in these Indian utterances and the emphasis placed on *actio* in the gestures and tears give these characterizations of the converted Indians' speeches a performative and therefore highly rhetoricized quality. Yet if, as some historians have argued, the Puritans differed from both Jesuits and Indians because they excoriated verbal eloquence and took their emphasis on texts as a mark of their identity, it seems that at least in their representations of Indian speech the Puritans were not all that Puritanical.

The *Jesuit Relations*

If the Puritan missionaries were not so Puritanical in their rhetorical orientations, the Jesuit missionaries were also not so Jesuitical in theirs. Historians have long argued that French Jesuit accounts of their missionary work among the Indians contributed significantly to the creation of the commonplace of the noble savage.[79] The Jesuit representations of the nobility of certain Indians rested particularly on the apparent eloquence of converted Indians. In fact, Jesuit representations of the savage eloquence of converted Indians differed surprisingly little from those of the Puritans. Like the Puritan descriptions of Indian eloquence, those by Jesuits

---

78. See John Eliot, *The Dying Speeches of Several Indians* (Cambridge, 1685).
79. George R. Healy, "The French Jesuits and the Idea of the Noble Savage," *William and Mary Quarterly* 15, no. 2 (1958): 145.

also emphasized the heating effects of divine inspiration on the hearts of converted Indians, who consequently communicated far more movingly than conventional touchstones of Jesuit rhetoric like Cicero. Like the Eliot Tracts, the *Jesuit Relations* described Indian speech in terms that emphasized their passionate but plain style, a style that they insisted demonstrated the warming effects of divine grace and also guaranteed the sincerity of Indian speakers. Such similarities between Puritan and Jesuit appraisals of Indian speech should appear strange since historians have generally argued that Jesuit stylistic priorities were opposed to the Augustinian grand style, associated as it was with Reformed Christianity. Yet, these very *Relations* have been the focus of historians' discussions of savage eloquence.[80]

The *Jesuit Relations*, which record the French Jesuit missionaries' activities in the New World during roughly the same, if slightly longer, period than that covered by the Eliot Tracts, provided European readers with descriptions of Algonquin and Iroquois eloquence. For the most part, the *Relations* are the reports made by Jesuit missionaries that were collected and then edited by one hand. The first and arguably most influential of these editors was Paul Lejeune (1591–1664).[81] Lejeune was trained at the two educational centers of French Jesuit rhetoric, La Flèche and Clermont, and for several years was a teacher of rhetoric at Nevers and Caen. As a student of both rhetoric and theology, he was certainly familiar with the contrasting ideals of classical, Augustinian, and Jesuit rhetorical theory.

Lejeune's first *Relation* (1632) depicted the Indians as decidedly unrefined and uneducated but also as receptive to instruction and conversion. After drawing attention to what he characterized as their "barbaric" dancing and signing, Lejeune noted that "in New France there are only sins to destroy, and those in a small number; for these poor people, so far removed from all luxury, are not given to many offenses.... In truth, any one who knew their language could manage them as he pleased." Lejeune's linking of linguistic competence and the capacity to "manage" the Indians

---

80. See, for example, André Vachon, *Éloquence Indienne* (Montreal: Fides, 1968); James Axtell, *The Invasion Within: The Contest of Cultures in Colonial North America* (New York: Oxford University Press, 1985); Normand Doiron, *L'art de voyager: Le déplacement à l'époque classique* (Sainte-Foy, Québec: Presses de l'Université Laval, 1995); Holifield, *Era of Persuasion*.

81. The first eleven *Relations* (1632–1642) were from his hand, and from 1649, as procurer of the mission, he was charged with their annual publication.

prefigured the many references to the importance of speech in the *Relations* that followed.[82]

Lejeune recorded one of his earliest and most explicit statements of the eloquence of the divinely inspired Indian speaker in his *Relation* for 1633. There he described the Montagnais as a "wandering and vagabond people" and wished that they were "stable and permanent tribes." Lejeune added to this description that "it is Cicero who says that all nations were once vagabond, and that eloquence has brought them together; that it has built villages and cities." Lejeune therefore explicitly pointed to the ethically and socially transformative power of eloquent speech. After noting that "there is no place in the world where Rhetoric is more powerful than in Canada," despite the fact that the natural eloquence of the Indians "has no other garb than what nature has given it" and "is entirely simple and without disguise," Lejeune added, "If the voice of men has so much power, will the voice of the Spirit of God be powerless?" Lejeune therefore recognized the place of oratory among the Algonquin tribes but in doing so suggested its inferiority to a divinely inspired eloquence. In fact, though Jesuit missionaries referred to native traditions of oratory, these were comparatively infrequent; they more frequently commented on the divinely inspired eloquence of converted Indians. By asking, in this early *Relation,* whether divine eloquence could be less effective than worldly eloquence, Lejeune anticipated the transfiguration of nature by grace that would become visible in later *Relations* of savage eloquence. As in the Eliot Tracts, in the *Relations* the supreme eloquence of Indian speakers was a guarantee of the sincerity of their claims to have been genuinely converted.[83]

In his early *Relations,* Lejeune thus oriented representations of savage eloquence toward the ideals of the Christian grand style. This style, which was typically the domain of Reformed traditions, did not sit easily

---

82. Reuben Gold Thwaites, ed., *The Jesuit Relations and Allied Documents,* 73 vols. (Cleveland, 1896–1901), 5:29 and 35.

83. Ibid., 191 and 193. Lejeune also reported the speech of a Montagnais speaker who said, in referring to the French promise to build a settlement, that "we shall no longer go to seek our living in the woods; *we shall no longer be wanderers and vagabonds*" (207). It was a commonplace in classical descriptions of the rise of civilization to insist, as Cicero did, that when "men with stammering voices uttering unformed and confused sounds," discovered language they were "thus united by the delightful bond of speech." See *De re publica* 3.2.3, quoted in Arthur O. Lovejoy and George Boas, eds., *Primitivism and Related Ideas in Antiquity* (Baltimore: Johns Hopkins Press, 1935), 245.

with the typical Jesuit preference for the florid ornateness of Ciceronianism. One explanation of this stylistic peculiarity may be that Lejeune was born into a Calvinist family and did not convert to Catholicism until he was sixteen, a mere five years before entering the novitiate of the Jesuits of Paris. Whether or not Lejeune's Calvinist background had a bearing on his representation of savage eloquence, he nonetheless set a stylistic agenda for the subsequent *Relations*.

Like the Eliot Tracts, the *Relations* exhibit the missionaries' desire to show that, while most Indians were particularly given to dissimulation and thus could not be trusted, those who spoke in a particular rhetorical register could be trusted as genuine converts. François du Peron (1610–1665), for example, described "the nature of the savage" as "thievish, lying, [and] deceitful." Lejeune similarly suggested that among the Indians "vice, only appears secretly and by stealth." The Jesuit missionary Louis André (1631–1715) reported that "the savages are too great liars to be Believed." Besides insisting that all unconverted Indians were inclined to lie, Jesuit missionaries also worried more particularly that catechized or baptized Indians merely *seemed* to accept the Christian doctrine without genuinely embracing it. Jean de Brébeuf noted in the 1636 *Relation,* for example, that the Hurons, "knowing the beauty of truth,... are content to approve it without embracing it. Their usual reply is, *oniondechouten,* 'Such is the custom of our country.' We have fought this excuse and have taken it from their mouths, but not yet from their hearts; our Lord will do that when it shall please him." Seventy years later the Jesuit Joseph Jouvency (1643–1719) worried that "from the...desire for harmony comes their ready assent to whatever one teaches them; nevertheless they hold tenaciously to their native belief or superstition.... What can one do with those who in word give agreement and assent to everything, but in reality give none?" The Jesuits were thus deeply suspicious that Indians who appeared to have converted might not have done so genuinely. Concerns with Indian duplicity led the Jesuits, as it did the Puritans, to scan their spoken words for reassuring signs of genuine conversion. And, as with the Puritans, the Jesuits found such assurances of the genuine workings of the Holy Ghost in the passionate but plain eloquence of certain converted Indian speakers.[84]

---

84. Thwaites, *The Jesuit Relations,* 15:155; 18:83; 57:295; 10:19; 1:275. Curiously, Brébeuf used an Indian metaphor for insincerity to cast Indians as insincere.

In the context of Augustinian rhetorical theory, instruction leads merely to knowledge, but divinely inspired eloquence has the moving force to radically transform a person's nature and make souls genuinely virtuous. Paul Ragueneau (1608–1680), for example, after reporting the speech of a recently baptized Attikamek Indian, wrote that "this Rhetoric is as holy as it is simple: it makes souls good, and that of Cicero and of Aristotle makes them wise." Ragueneau therefore took this Indian's holy yet simple eloquence as a sure sign of a sincerely converted soul and distinguished it from classical eloquence, which he characterized as instructing without persuading. Jesuit missionaries often commented on the converted Indians' eloquence in order to demonstrate the authenticity of their belief in Christian doctrine and the genuineness of their conversions. Barthélemy Vimont, (1594–1667), Lejeune's successor as the *Relations'* editor, for example, described how the Christianized Huron Charles Tsondatsaa returned to the mission after being away for months, and one of the other Christian Indians there told him he worried that Charles might have lost his faith while he was away. According to Vimont, Charles responded, "Since my Baptism, I have never wavered in the Faith. My feet have remained steadfast... It is he who holds the earth in his hand, as thou sayest, who has helped me.... Come, then, my brother... fear no longer. We are not half believers only; we believe entirely." Vimont concluded his account with a speech to the governor of New France by another Christianized Huron. After transcribing this speech, Vimont added, "Such eloquence is not derived from the Rhetoric of Aristotle or of Cicero, but from a school more loveable and candid." The school Vimont had in mind, of course, was the inspiration of divine grace. Vimont again noted the supreme eloquence of a Christianized Huron girl in his *Relation* for 1643 and 1644. He commented that he "would not have thought that the Savages could be so constant." Vimont reported that one of the missionaries, suspicious that her faith was insincere, asked her "what she said to God." "Without hesitation," Vimont noted, "she promptly replied: 'I speak to [God] in this way: 'My God, have pity on our Father; preserve him, and save him from being wrecked by too stormy winds, or too heavy waves. Take him to his own country, and bring him back to us. You can do all things.'" Vimont then glossed her reply by noting, "That is all her Rhetoric, which is better than that of Cicero."[85]

---

85. Ibid., 37:227; 22:87–89, 91, 25:237.

In the *Relation* for 1672, Claude Dablon continued to argue that suspicions that Indian conversions were not genuine could be laid to rest by paying attention to the eloquence of their oratory. Dablon noted that "the constancy of their Chief, Daniel Garakontié" "must give much joy to all who desire to see God glorified in these Peoples." Dablon wrote that when the baptized Garakontié had become ill, "his relatives and all the village... urged him with great importunity to permit, for the sake of being cured, the employment of the usual juggler's arts, which pass for remedies in that country." When he learned that the Indians had performed this ceremony, the Jesuit who was in that village "felt some suspicion that it had received the sick man's consent." Father Millet then went to visit Garakontié, who insisted to Father Millet, "I was much distressed on account of the ceremony which was performed, without my knowledge and out of my sight." Garakontié told him that in his distress he asked himself, "[W]hat will [Father Millet] think and say of me? He will believe me to be a hypocrite and dissembler." But he assured the Jesuit, "No, my Father, I have not changed my mind since my baptism." Dablon then related that Garakontié, while in Montreal, "displayed his Faith and zeal" before an "assembly of... more than five hundred Savages of various nations." According to Dablon, after the French and Indians gathered in the assembly had negotiated and ratified a peace treaty, Garakontié "raised his voice to tell them that he had formerly been as they were,—ignorant of the true God, given to the worship of his dreams, and observing all their superstitious practices; but that now he was a Christian.... He concluded his harangue by exhorting them, with his wonted eloquence, to imitate and follow him." For Dablon, as for others who contributed to the *Jesuit Relations,* the Christianized Indians' eloquence guaranteed that their conversions were authentic, that, as the Jesuits often put it, these wolves were genuinely transfigured into lambs.[86]

Dablon added to his description of Chief Garakontié's eloquent speech to the assembly that "such a speech, from the mouth of a Savage who thus frankly declares the feelings of his heart, often produces more effect upon these people's minds than the words of the most zealous Missionary." Dablon thus understood savage eloquence to be not only a mark of the

---

86. Ibid., 56: 41, 43, and 45.

genuine infusion of grace but also an effective vehicle for its communication to others. The conquering warmth of divine grace transformed noisy savages into silver-tongued orators who spoke with an eloquence that not only demonstrated a sincere faith but also was effective in moving audiences and generating further conversions.[87]

In his *Relation* of 1647 and 1648, Jérôme Lalement (1593–1673) described an episode in which "twelve of the most Considerable [Huron] Captains" from the Island of Saint Joseph pleaded with the Jesuit Fathers to "make that Island an Island of Christians." Lalement reported that these Hurons "spoke more than three whole hours,—with an eloquence as powerful to bend us as the art of Orators could furnish, in the midst of France, to most of those who call these countries barbarous." Lalement interpreted this eloquent speech in favor of Christianity by commenting that "their eloquence...conquered us. We could not doubt that God had chosen to speak to us by their lips; and although, at their coming, we all had entertained another design, we all found ourselves changed before their departure, and with a common consent we believed that it was necessary to follow God in the direction whither he chose to call us,—whatever peril there might be in it for our lives, and in whatever depth of darkness we may continue,—for the remaining future, which is not in our power." As with Terese's miraculous and conquering eloquence in favor of Christianity, the Jesuits presented the Huron captains as marshalling an energetic divine eloquence that miraculously conquered and transformed their audiences.[88]

The *Relations* often explicitly characterized Indian eloquence as miraculously inspired rather than studiously learned. Lalement wrote, "When God gives life to words, they have a thousand times more effect than the most forcible Rhetoric of an Aristotle or a Cicero." Lalement made this comment while discussing the baptism of Estienne Mangouch, a Nipissing Indian. Mangouch's baptism followed that of the Nipissing captain Eustache Alimoueskan. Lalement described Alimoueskan as displaying "an impetuous and arrogant character" before his baptism, but his conversion "made a lamb of him, and...changed him beyond recognition." Since

---

87. Like the Eliot Tracts and other seventeenth-century reports, the *Jesuit Relations* made frequent reference to the unconverted Indians as being especially noisy. For examples, see Thwaites, *The Jesuit Relations,* 10:19, 97; 12: 201–203; 15:41; 15:157; 50: 261; 19:221.

88. Ibid., 34: 209 and 211.

his baptism, he had "so exerted his courage in...scorning the banter of infidels...that whatever efforts [they] have made to induce him to commit sin, they have never been able to overcome him."[89]

The Jesuits frequently insisted that the eloquence of Christianized Indians had a divine foundation and derived from gracious inspiration rather than any other source. According to Father le Mercier's *Relation* of 1638, certain "Old Men" among the Huron reproached Father Brébeuf "for having too long deferred speaking to them about a matter of so much importance as is the life that awaits us after our death." Le Mercier added that they expressed this reproach "with an eloquence that showed nothing of the Savage." In his *Relation* for 1640 and 1641, after having written that "the Savages appear as cold as ice, but God is sure to warm and fire their hearts when it pleases him," Lejeune discussed an episode wherein certain Algonquins promised the Indians of the Saint-Joseph mission that if they would join them in a war party, on their return from war they would convert to Christianity. Lejeune reported that the Christianized Algonquin captain Jean Baptiste Etinechkawat replied with the following speech: "Your argument is not properly stated,—you have inverted your words: you say, 'Let us go to the war, and then we will be baptized;' reverse your language, and say: 'Let us be baptized, and then let us all go together to the war.' If you speak thus, your speech will be straightforward; you will not put yourselves in danger of being lost, and God our father, seeing his children together, will have favorable opinions of us." Lejeune added that "this speech...was not at all barbarous; and these sentiments are found only in a truly Christian heart." In his report on the state of the Jesuit missions for the year 1675, Charles Dablon (1619–1697) described a Christianized Indian named Paul as having spoken in favor of the Church with "a spirit, piety, and eloquence surprising in a savage."[90]

The Jesuits were fairly consistent in attributing this surprising savage eloquence to a divine source. In his *Relation* for 1640, for example, Lalement described a situation in which about a dozen Hurons began accusing the Jesuits of being "the ruin of their country." A Christianized Huron named Joseph Chihouatenhoua intervened and "began to speak to them so

---

89. Ibid., 27:57, 55, and 59. Note that in 1633, when Lejeune linked Capitanal's harangue with Aristotle and Cicero, he merely said it was *equal* to their art.

90. Ibid., 15:115, 20:159 and 167–169; 59:277.

appropriately, and with so much gentleness and effectiveness, that whereas they had come in as wolves, they returned thence as lambs." One of the accusers "so relished his words...that he desired to converse with him in private. In such talk he spent...three and four hours each day, without noticing how the time was passing; so much did the sayings of this good Christian,—or rather the holy Ghost, who spoke by his lips,—give him satisfaction." Lalement thus attributed the transfiguring eloquence of Chihouatenhoua's words to the Holy Ghost. In the same *Relation*, Lalement suggested the miracle of Pentecost when he compared Chihouatenhoua to the apostles after they had received the Holy Spirit. According to Lalement, Chihouatenhoua spoke to his brother and the other Hurons who were with him about the "wonders" of the Christian faith. Lalement commented that "he spoke to them with a superiority that the spirit of God gave him. All admired his eloquence (for he spoke whole hours with an air which they had never seen)...it is not by myself that I speak; the master whom I serve gives me thoughts, and renders me eloquent in maintaining his cause." According to Lalement, when his interlocutors then questioned the intentions of the French colonists and of the Jesuits, "he confounded them therein, and constrained them to avow that they were without sense. After all,...the words which issued all on fire from the lips of this Christian were received in hearts colder than marble: but it is a seed which the holy Ghost will cause to sprout when he pleases." For Lalement, as for the other Jesuit missionaries who contributed to the *Relations*, the supreme eloquence of the converted savages derived ultimately from a miraculous and gracious inspiration that warmed the heart and fired the tongue.[91]

Lejeune and the other Jesuits who prepared the *Relations*, like the Puritan missionaries, frequently represented God's grace as a divine flame that warmed Indian hearts and thereby generated divinely eloquent speech. In his second *Relation*, Lejeune expressed his hope "that, if a single village is converted, the fire will not be long in spreading to a great many others; and that the neighbouring tribes, which are very populous, will wish to warm themselves with the Hurons at this divine flame." By 1640, Lejeune's hopes seemed to have been realized. That year, Lalement reported that "one good Christian" Huron spoke to his elders "with a superiority

---

91. Ibid., 19:149, 151, 163, and 163–165.

that the spirit of God gave him." "All admired his eloquence (for he spoke whole hours with an air which they had never seen)." Lalement pointed out that this Huron recognized that in speaking this way he was merely transmitting a divine voice: "I am but a child and should be an arrogant fellow if I undertook by myself to convince you: it is not by myself that I speak; the master whom I serve gives me thoughts, and renders me eloquent in maintaining his cause." Lalement concluded that he had been assured that "words which issued all on fire from the lips of this Christian were received in hearts colder than marble: but it is a seed which the Holy Ghost will cause to sprout when he pleases." While Lalement reflected that the fiery eloquence of this converted Huron did not immediately move his auditors, it is notable that he used a thermal metaphor to represent the pathetic harangue as one that was divinely inspired.[92]

Lejeune remained confident that God's warming grace would not fail to be effective. He wrote in 1641 that "God has more power than nature," and that while "the Savages appear as cold as ice,...God is sure to warm and fire their hearts." In describing one Huron harangue that year, he wrote that it "was not at all barbarous; and [that] these sentiments are found only in a truly Christian heart." He also wrote in 1641 about another Huron speaker who prayed for his tormentors: "[H]uman nature does not go so far as this; these fruits are gathered only in the garden of grace." Lejeune then noted that he had "heard him...speak in so devout and tender a manner, that I have been greatly astonished; I am vexed with myself, that I have let escape from my memory the good sentiments that God gives him, and many others; but...we let slip away many of the holy affections of these good Neophytes."[93]

As with the Eliot Tracts, the *Jesuit Relations*' depictions of savage eloquence cited tears and humility as marks of sincere inward transfiguration. In the *Relation* of 1639 Lejeune related the speeches of the Algonquin whose converted name was Ignatius. As with Capitanal's speech reported by Lejeune, Ignatius's *humilitas* is made explicit. In one of the speeches

---

92. Ibid., 5:255; 19: 161, and 161–163. Lejeune reported, "Ah, how true it is...that God is a consuming fire; and that...there is no marble that it does not heat. Would I ever have believed that Barbarians born in cruelty, and fed upon human flesh, would become Preachers of Jesus Christ? I can assure you that I do not know any one who has given them these ideas of going to invite other nations to believe in God,—it is purely the work of the Holy Spirit" (18:111).

93. Ibid., 20:151, 159, 167, 201, and 201–203.

Lejeune attributed to Ignatius we read, "It seemed to me that I was only a poor little flea and I was surprised that so great a Captain consented to enter the heart of so insignificant a creature." Commenting on these speeches, Lejeune noted that he could not have "pulled such thoughts and sentiments from any other place than the living Book, which is Jesus Christ." Ragueneau, in his *Relation* for 1645 and 1646, told his readers that he would "finish this Chapter with the tears—but tears of zeal—of a good Christian of the Village of la Conception, named René Tsondihouonne." Ragueneau wrote, "[H]e could not contain his tears; and, wholly transported outside himself, and addressing Our Lord, he made to him complaints of himself, with as much faith and fervor as if he had seen him with his own eyes." According to Ragueneau, one of the Jesuit Fathers, overhearing him, "asked him who had taught him that prayer." "He answered, 'No one; but I felt in the depth of my heart that Our Lord was reproaching me at the little that I have done for him.'" Ragueneau added that Tsondihouonne expressed himself "nearly always with sentiments of devotion so tender and so powerful." Ragueneau's relation of this episode of savage eloquence included the tears, the humility, and the inspired voice of the same Christian grand style highlighted in the Eliot Tracts. Ragueneau concluded that "this good man, within the eight years since he has embraced the faith, makes us recognize in his exemplary life, even more filled with holiness than are his words, that God alone is his instructor." In Ragueneau's analysis, then, Tsondihouonne's eloquence moved those who listened to him and guaranteed that his conversion had been sincere.[94]

In the same *Relation* for 1645 and 1646, Ragueneau offered his readers a perfect example of how the divine flame transformed certain Indians into eloquent oracles. Ragueneau narrated how the Huron Estienne Totiri (fl. 1642–1646) saved "a poor miserable captive." Ragueneau told his audience that the "whole country was assembled...to burn...a poor miserable captive,—who,...was uttering frightful cries.... In the midst of these cries and these barbarous fires, [Totiri], animated with a more divine fire," began to speak. The Christian Totiri chided the other as-yet unconverted Hurons and warned them of the "flames that are forever inexorable to

---

94. Ibid., 16:123; 29:287–289, 289, and 291. Ragueneau added, "'Often,' he says, 'I speak, and I know not what I say. Some one speaks to me in the depth of my soul...; then I feel, as it were, a fire in my heart.'"

those who shall have refused in this world to experience the kindness of God...and acknowledge his power." Totiri's "harangue" was "so astonishing" to the other Hurons that they stopped tormenting their captive. Totiri, however, continued his energetic speech. He told his fellow Hurons that he had no intention of rescuing the captive from the earthly flames. "Death alone can put an end to his miseries....I fear for you, infidels,...flames more devouring,—for which your death will furnish a beginning, and which will never have an end." Ragueneau reported that "after having a long time spoken of the horrors of Hell...he said to them,...'Adore that great God...then Hell will have no more flames for you. But, if death surprise you in infidelity, those burning furnaces, and those subterranean fires, will be your portion.'" The audience's reaction to Totiri's harangue was mixed. "But," added Ragueneau, "I doubt not that...Heaven kindled it potently,—at least, it appeared efficacious for the salvation of this poor captive."

Totiri approached the poor captive and began speaking to him of salvation. "This poor man," Ragueneau wrote, "half roasted, begins to breathe afresh at these tidings....[Totiri] continues to instruct him, and finds a heart wholly disposed to our mysteries..., and which...asks for Baptism." At this the other Hurons "begin to offer resistance, and vigorously to oppose themselves to the salvation of their enemy,—shouting that his soul must be burned forever by the Demons of Hell....[Totiri]...seeking water for this Baptism, finds near him only fires and flames." Totiri fetches some water, all the while undergoing "a thousand insults and numerous blows,—each man pushing him, in order to make him spill his water." But, according to Ragueneau, "his zeal rendered him victorious over everything. So powerfully did it kindle the heart of that poor man of griefs that he seemed to forget his pain, having received holy Baptism, and to have no more voice, except to exclaim that he would be happy in Heaven." Ragueneau's account, rife with the rhetoric of redescription, moves from the earthly flames consuming the captive to a divine flame that inspires Totiri's heated speech, to Totiri's warnings of the hellfire that lies in store for the unconverted Huron, and then back to the divine flame that regenerates the speechless Indian in his dying moments.

After this incident, Totiri returned to the Christian Indians, and they tried to congratulate him for his zeal. Totiri, however, again adopted the passionate but plain register of the Christian grand style to remind them that his eloquence was only but the effect of a warming fire of divine grace. "'Alas! My brothers,' he said to them. 'I am an earthworm; it is not [Totiri] who has performed this Baptism, but our Lord who strengthened my weakness, and put in my heart the words which issued from my lips. I had received Communion this morning, and from that time I felt a fire which was burning in me, and which I could not have contained within myself." This last comment by Tortiri reflected the terms used by Ragueneau to frame his anecdote: "[W]hen the fire powerfully kindles a heart, it must needs at last have vent, and must drive its flames outward, in order to kindle the others with the same ardors which consume itself."[95] As with other descriptions in the *Jesuit Relations,* Ragueneau's story of how Totiri's eloquence saved the burning Iroquois Indian is an example, replete with a triangulation of the hellish, worldly, and divine fires, of a converted Indian's inspired, heated, authentic, and ultimately conquering oratory. For both Jesuits and Puritans, then, there was no need for the Indians to have studied a sophisticated rhetorical art; faith and grace alone sufficed to produce the plain but fiery eloquence of the savage orator. The heart melted, the emotions warmed, and the tongue fired off such a hot speech that all who heard it were left standing in a pool of tears; the Holy Spirit transfigured the Indian voices to create the image of a divine word that moves virtually everything in its path.

---

95. Ibid., 29:263, 263–265, 265, 267, and 269.

4

FROM SAVAGE ORATORS
TO SAVAGE LANGUAGES

> I answered him with all the frankness of a savage who knows not how
> to lie out of politeness.
>
> ALAIN-RENÉ LE SAGE, *Aventures du Chevalier Beauchêne* (1732)

> Cannot a simple Indian…
> With purest Flame acknowledge Love's sweet dart,
> And only speak the language of the heart?
>
> JOHN FENWICK, *The Indian* (1800)

As the previous chapter shows, missionaries, both Jesuit and Puritan, drew on Augustinian psychological and rhetorical theory to construct a representation of the converted savage as supremely eloquent in a passionate but plain key. In these cases, eloquence was taken to be a function of individual inspiration rather than the result of a study of the art of rhetoric. The tradition of the inspired Christian Indian orator continued into the eighteenth century. Dying speeches that represented Christianized American Indians as graciously inspired orators who moved their audiences to tears also continued to be published in the eighteenth century. One such dying speech by the Lenape Chief Ockanickon, which was first published in London in 1682, was reprinted in Philadelphia in 1740 by the Quaker Charles Woolverton (c. 1660–1746) along with a pamphlet titled

The Upright Lives of the Heathen. Even more than the New England Puritans, the Quakers tended to deploy a representation of God as an inward inspiration, and Woolverton's reprint of Ockanickon's dying speech touches on a number of the commonplaces of the converted Indian as an eloquent oracle. In the "Preface to the Reader," Woolverton introduced the dying speech by arguing that it shows how "the great Love of God to Mankind...led [Ockanickon]...to speak the Words of Truth and Soberness." Woolverton also reprinted the letter sent by one John Cripps to "a Friend in London," in which Cripps noted that, at Ockanickon's death, "many Tears were shed both by the Indians and English." In his dying speech, Ockanickon advised his nephew Jahkursoe how to "stand up in time of speeches" and to avoid "joining" any "evil speech" by either Indians or Christians. In his epilogue, Woolverton noted that in Ockanickon's dying speech "we may clearly see the divine Influence of the Spirit of Grace."[1]

Along with this Dying Speech, Woolverton reprinted another work titled *Epistles and Discourses betwixt Alexander the Conqueror and Dindimus King of the Brachmans*. Thomas Hahn has traced this edition back the Quaker Daniel Foote's *Alexanders Conference with Dindimus the Heathen...in the East-India* (c. 1650).[2] Hahn suggests that Foote's dialogue became the foundation for the "stirrings of seventeenth-century interest in the image of the virtuous Indians."[3] This series of texts suggest that certain Quakers drew parallels between the South Asian Dindimus, "King of the Gymnosophists" and Ockanickon, "an Indian King."[4]

What is particularly interesting from the perspective of early modern French and British interests in communication is that these dialogues, which contrasted the Christians' moral sluggishness with the untutored virtue of the non-European heathen, describe the Indian King as having

---

1. See Charles Woolverton, *The Upright Lives of the Heathen and the Dying-Words of Ockanickon, an Indian King* (Philadelphia: Printed by A. and W. Bradford, 1740), reprinted in Thomas Hahn ed., *Upright Lives: Documents Concerning the Natural Virtue and Wisdom of the Indians (1650–1740)*, Augustan Reprint Society, no. 209–210 (Los Angeles: William Andrews Clark Memorial Library, University of California, 1981), no page no.
2. Ibid., iii.
3. Ibid.
4. The suggestion of a parallel between these two "Indian" kings is made in Woolverton's edition by the juxtaposition of the two works in a single publication and in Sowle's 1683 edition by the fact that its Quaker publisher printed the dialogue in the same year he published William Penn's *Letter from Pennsylvania*.

a peculiar language in which lying may be impossible. Woolverton's edition reproduces the earlier passages in which Dindimus tells Alexander, "We be men of single speech, its common to us all not to lie. The God of all Grace is our God; for he hath liking in our Words and Deeds, by our manner of speaking."[5] This heathen Indian king contrasted his honest and authentic speech with that of Alexander, whom he accused of dishonesty and hypocrisy: "We be approv'd with few Words...and hold our Peace. Ye say what shall be done, and yet do it not: Your Wit and Wisdom is in your Lips."[6] Woolverton's interest in the figures of Dindimus and Ockanickon no doubt stemmed from his Quaker belief that God had placed an inner guiding light in every heart, that sophisticated theological and philosophical systems and scriptural authority were, if not an obstacle to apprehending divine truth, then at least unnecessary for it.[7] The Quakers' understanding of what they called the "inner light" had communicative dimensions similar to those of the Puritan and Jesuit missionaries, who emphasized the plainness and sincerity of inspired speech.[8]

In the second half of the seventeenth century, literary representations of New World Indians replaced the Old World Indian character of Dindimus as the mouthpiece for the belief that Europeans, as a consequence of their intellectual, cultural and linguistic refinement, hypocritically subscribed only to the *appearances* of truth and virtue. Whether Puritans like Eliot, Jesuits like Lejeune, Quakers like Woolverton, or Deists like Voltaire, many early modern Europeans agreed that Indians in the New World were closer to nature and therefore less liable to error and dissimulation. As Anthony Pagden has noted, "the 'Montezuma'... of Dryden's play the *Indian Emperor*... is lectured by a priest on the truthfulness of Christianity. Montezuma... consistently gets the better of his opponent. Finally the priest, driven into a logical corner, turns from argument to command. 'Renounce your carnal reason and obey,' he tells the Aztec. But Montezuma,... knows that: 'The light of nature should I thus betray, 'Twere to wink hard that

---

5. Woolverton, *The Upright Lives of the Heathen*, 6.
6. Ibid., 7.
7. See among others Roy Harvey Pearce, *Savagism and Civilization: A Study of the Indian and the American Mind* (Berkeley: University of California Press, 1988), 35–41.
8. Frederick B. Tolles, *"Of the Best Sort but Plain:* The Quaker Esthetic," *American Quarterly* 11, no. 4 (Winter 1959): 484–502.

I might see the light of day.' "[9] If Woolverton's juxtaposition of the Dindimus dialogue and the Ockanickon dying speech drew parallels between gymnosophists in India and the Indians in America, Dindimus's claim that his people had a peculiar *language* that prevented insincerity anticipated the development of an early modern representation of American Indian languages as sources of sublime eloquence and sincerity in large part because of their savage characteristics.[10]

Locke, Linguistic Clarity, and Savage Languages

Locke presented *An Essay concerning Human Understanding* to its readers as an attempt to solve the problems created by abuses of ambiguous words. In the preface he wrote that he had decided to write the book after he and his friends got into an insoluble dispute.[11] Locke intended his essay to be in large part a discourse on how people use words and argued that "amongst...men, who...confound [their ideas] with words, there must be endless dispute, wrangling, and jargon."[12] It is significant that Locke concluded his essay with an analysis of the sources of "enthusiasm," one of the early modern keywords for the sources of antisocial violence.

For Locke and his disciples, the problem with language was that it was often an opaque medium for the mental representation of perceptions

---

9. Anthony Pagden, *European Encounters with the New World: From Renaissance to Romanticism* (New Haven: Yale University Press, 1993), 122–123. Hahn argues that "it may well be that these [Quaker] writings drew Dryden's interest to the Indians." See Hahn, *Upright Lives*, iii.

10. Nicole Eustace has examined the continuing colonial concerns about Indian sincerity. Her focus, however, is mainly on the popularity of "the trope of the honest European and the insincere Indian," which contrasted with a European commonplace of the sincere savage speaker. See Nicole Eustace, *Passion Is the Gale: Emotion, Power, and the Coming of the American Revolution* (Chapel Hill: University of North Carolina Press, 2008), 82–95. Benjamin Franklin articulated an especially interesting colonial explanation for the rhetorical roots of Indian insincerity. He argued that the Indians' study of rhetoric led to a form of communicative "politeness" that they had "carried to excess." Franklin insisted that their excessive politeness did "not permit them to contradict, or deny the truth of what is asserted in their presence." "By this means," he added, "they avoid disputes; but then it becomes difficult to know their minds." Benjamin Franklin, *Two Tracts: Information to Those Who Would Remove to America. And, Remarks concerning the Savages of North America* (London: Printed for John Stockdale, 1784), 30.

11. John Locke, *An Essay concerning Human Understanding*, ed. Alexander Fraser Campbell (New York: Dover, 1959), 1:9.

12. Ibid., 1:236–237. See also 1:14–15 and 23.

and ideas. Many early modern thinkers therefore either searched for a transparent language or tried to reform their own ambiguous languages. As we saw in chapter 1, Locke and his followers argued that knowledge began with the mental representations of particular things, and individual thinkers associated representations of particulars in order to abstract their common properties by using abstract words.[13] One of the problems with languages was that over time people made errors when they introduced these general terms, that these general words continued to convey errors in representing the world long after they were introduced, and that they essentially did this without the speakers' being aware of it. What Locke called for, then, was a survey of the meaning of terms to make sure that they conformed to things. For many, this meant tracing back the introduction of abstract words to a supposed time when language consisted only of words for particulars.

Inasmuch as Locke believed that "in the beginning all the world was America," many of his eighteenth-century disciples, who adopted his "historical, plain method" of tracing the origins of ideas, believed that Indian languages existed in a developmental stage that predated the introduction of faulty abstract words.[14] For example, Rousseau, who held that "abstractions are painfully difficult operations," concluded that, in the earliest stages of human linguistic development, "each object... received a particular name."[15] When he speculated about the causes of civil inequality and discord, he therefore blamed the introduction of faulty abstract words into languages. By pursuing a similarly Lockean method, Pierre-Louis Moreau de Maupertuis (1698–1759) argued in 1748 that by studying "the *jargons* of the most savage peoples" one could not only "trace the first steps taken by the human mind" but also learn a great deal about "the influence that languages have on our understanding."[16] Maupertuis explicitly characterized this project "to understand the origin of the first propositions" as one that ultimately would make explicit the many mind-altering

---

13. Ibid., 2:14.

14. John Locke, *Second Treatise of Government* (London: Mentor, 1993), 285; Locke, *An Essay concerning Human Understanding*, 1:27.

15. Jean-Jacques Rousseau, *Discours sur l'origine et les fondements de l'inégalité parmi les hommes*, in *J.-J. Rousseau, oeuvres politiques*, ed. Jean Roussel (Paris: Bordas, 1989), 38–39.

16. Ronald Grimsley, ed., *Maupertuis, Turgot et Maine de Biran: Sur l'origine du langage* (Geneva: Librairie Droz, 1971), 32.

linguistic "errors" that crept imperceptibly into languages as they "became established."[17] Certain conjectural histories of language that were inspired by Locke's project therefore presumed that by tracing the presumed development of language from a savage to a civilized form, they would be able to clarify abstract words, thereby making error virtually impossible. This line of thinking represents one of the ways in which early modern language theorists became interested in Indian languages. As Maupertuis suggested, savage American and civilized European languages were radically and significantly different. In his examination of the Baron de Lahontan's *Dialogues with a Savage of Good Sense* (1703), Pagden argues that Lahontan deployed a representation of the difference between the Huron and European, which was built on this belief that there were "crucial lexical differences between civil and savage languages."[18] Pagden thus argues that one eighteenth-century commonplace about so-called savage languages presumed that they were "transparent" in representing "the nature of reality." "European languages," on the other hand "have the capacity to attribute…'an arbitrary character to things.' The savage's discourse, by contrast, is only about the true, the given, nature of the world."[19] The characterization of savage languages as especially clear thus turned on a visual metaphor of clarity and grounded a belief that these languages, like the idealized animal language, guarded against the potential dangers of moral redescriptions made possible by lexical ambiguity. Pagden rightly attributes to a Lockean linguistic theory this distinction between an idealized transparent savage language of particulars and an opaque and ambiguous civilized language of abused abstract words.

In his reading of early modern linguistic anthropology, Pagden simply follows those who have identified Locke as the most important theorist of language.[20] The tendency to make Locke the central, if not the only, figure in early modern linguistics has been unfortunate in two ways. First, Locke's

---

17. Ibid., 36.
18. Pagden, *European Encounters*, 129.
19. Ibid.
20. See, among others, Wilbur S. Howell, *Eighteenth-Century British Logic and Rhetoric* (Princeton: Princeton University Press, 1971), 7; Nancy Struever, ed., *Language and the History of Thought* (Rochester: University of Rochester Press, 1995), ix; and Edward G. Gray, *New World Babel: Languages and Nations in Early Modern America* (Princeton: Princeton University Press, 1999), 6.

An Essay concerning Human Understanding explicitly disparaged the use of persuasive rhetoric.[21] Second, the linguistic sections of the book deal almost exclusively with how individuals connect their words with their ideas to represent things. The more general questions about how societies use language to communicate were largely irrelevant to Locke. By making Locke the hero of early modern linguistics, historians have ignored a different but important early modern characterization of the virtues of savage speech.

This problem becomes apparent when one considers that many early modern commentators on savage speech, like the seventeenth-century missionaries, were more interested in its capacity to eloquently communicate energetic emotions than in its capacity to unambiguously represent clear ideas. In discussions of the virtues of Indian speech, early modern thinkers emphasized the linguistic virtues of energy as much as, if not more than, those of clarity. The Lockean linguistics of representational clarity does little to help explain the early modern fascination with savage eloquence. To understand this fascination one must turn to the different and equally important strand of early modern linguistic anthropology that emphasized emotional warmth rather than intellectual clarity in communication. Many thinkers worried about speakers' ability to coldly dissimulate and their inability to passionately move audiences.

Sheridan: The Paradox of the Orator

On November 30, 1762, the young James Boswell (1740–1795), visiting London from Edinburgh, recorded a meeting he had had with Thomas Sheridan (1719–1788), a transplanted Irishman, who had just the year before delivered a series of popular lectures in Edinburgh on the subject of English pronunciation.[22] Boswell reported that "Mr. Sheridan...was quite enthusiastic about oratory. He said Garrick had no real feeling; that his

---

21. Locke argued that "if we would speak of Things as they are, we must allow, that all the Art of Rhetorick, besides Order and Clearness, all the artificial and figurative application of Words Eloquence hath invented, are for nothing else but to insinuate wrong *Ideas,* move the Passions, and thereby mislead the Judgment; and so indeed are perfect cheats." See his *An Essay concerning Human Understanding,*. 2:146.

22. James Boswell, *London Journal 1762–1763,* ed. Frederick A. Pottle (New Haven: Yale University Press, 1950), 57.

talents for mimicry enabled him to put on the appearance of feeling, and that the nicety of his art might...make us cry, 'That's fine.' But as it was art, it could never touch the heart."[23] Just the day before, in fact, Boswell had seen the famous actor and director David Garrick (1717–1779), and a few days before that he had debated with some of his contemporaries about the relative happiness of savage and civilized societies.[24] Whether he realized it or not, Boswell's two conversations—the one about whether actors who, like Garrick, only pretend to be moved can really move their audiences and the other about the comparative merits of savage and civilized states—dealt with connected issues.

Sheridan's *A Course of Lectures on Elocution: Together with Two Dissertations on Language,* which appeared the year Boswell was in London, explicitly took up Locke's treatment of how "abuses of words," which led to "most errours in thinking" and "most controversies and disputes," "were owing to the want of clear and precise ideas being affixed to the terms used by the disputants." Sheridan then registered his disappointment that "the only remedy Mr. Locke suggests, is, that men should carefully examine the meaning of each word, and use it steadily in one sense. And that upon any difference of opinion, the parties should define such terms as are capable of ambiguity." Sheridan was therefore unsatisfied with the Lockean program for lexical clarity as a panacea to errors and disputes. Sheridan asked rhetorically, "[D]o men think, or reason more clearly, than they did before the publication of that book [Locke's *An Essay concerning Human Understanding*]? Have we a more precise use of language, or are the number of verbal disputes lessened?" "One would imagine," Sheridan complained, "that a philosopher, before he prescribed a cure, would have traced the disorder to its source." Sheridan explicitly presented his own work as an amendment to the failed project of Lockean linguistics.[25]

For Sheridan, the reason that disputes persisted despite the perennial popularity of Locke's essay was that Locke had dealt there only with one "part of the human mind." Sheridan pointed out that Locke had neglected the "two other parts of the human mind, with regard to which the world

---

23. Ibid.
24. Ibid., 55–56.
25. Thomas Sheridan, *A Course of Lectures on Elocution* (London: Printed by W. Strahan, For A. Millar et al, 1762), vii and ix.

is at this day, as much in the dark, as they were with respect to the whole, previous to the publication of Mr. Locke's essay." Sheridan described these other two parts as being "the seat of the passions,...the heart," and "the seat of the fancy; which is called the imagination." He argued that "all that is noble and praise worthy, all that is elegant and delightful, in man, considered as a social being, chiefly depends" on the very important part that the passions and imagination play in communication. Sheridan concluded that the frequency of European failures to resolve disputes derived from the Lockean "delusion that by the help of words alone, [speakers] can communicate all that passes in their minds." Sheridan insisted that Locke and his disciples "forget that the passions and the fancy have a language of their own, utterly independent of words, by which only their exertions can be...communicated." In other words, Sheridan's complaint was that a Lockean linguistics focused too much on introspective "private meditation" and neglected the more important sociable communication of "sentiments, when delivered in conversation."[26]

According to Sheridan, "in order to feel what another feels, the emotions which are in the mind of one man, must also be communicated to that of another." The social stakes of finding a surer means of communicating emotion were, according to Sheridan, incalculably high. He argued that a project like his, which aimed to better understand how to suppress "the passions...dangerous to society" and how to "invigorate" "those of the...social kind, calculated to promote the general good" "would tend more to the real benefit of this realm, than all the uninspired books that have been written from the creation of the world to this hour. Sheridan's project, as he understood it, was to understand how European languages had lost their capacity to effectively communicate emotions by diverging from what he called the "language of nature." The recovery of the characteristics of that emotive language of nature, he argued, would result in a society "approach[ing] as nearly to...a fellowship with angels, as the boundaries of the two worlds would permit."[27]

One of the principles that guided Sheridan's interest in reforming society by recovering the lost language of nature was his belief that the energetic communication of emotions is the surest means to sincerity and

---

26. Ibid., ix and viii.
27. Ibid., 99, xi–xii, xiii, and xiv.

persuasion. "To persuade others to the belief of any point," he wrote, "it must first appear, that the [speaker] is firmly persuaded of the truth of it himself; how can we suppose it possible that he should effect this, unless he delivers himself in the manner which is always used by persons who speak in earnest? How shall his words pass for words of truth, when they bear not its stamp?"[28] In diagnosing how it is that people who speak authentically are frequently not persuasive, while dissimulators are often believed, Sheridan focused on the particularly pernicious influence of writing on the language of nature, which operates mainly by means of sounds, tones, gestures, and expressions.[29] Sheridan's argument here resembles in many ways that of Rousseau's *Essay on the Origin of Languages* (1781) in supposing that the appearance of writing introduced the possibility and therefore the tendency to coldly dissimulate selfish desires among people who before had warmly and sincerely communicated with one another.[30] Sheridan held not only that the spelling of written language is often a poor indication of pronunciation but also that written language insufficiently indicates "the natural rests and pauses of discourse" and it does not at all indicate "the other articles of tones, accent, emphases, and gesture."[31] Sheridan added that such elements of communication "must be allowed to...contain in them, all the powers of strongly impressing the mind, captivating the fancy, rousing the passions, and delighting the ear."[32]

According to Sheridan, when people speak using a modern language, their speech passes through something like a textual filter that mutes or fails to adequately communicate their genuine emotions. The emotions of those who speak a primitive language, by contrast, "spontaneously start forth." Sheridan therefore concluded that "the best reading, must fall short of the power of speaking, in all articles which depend upon feeling." At this point in his argument, Sheridan considered the oral and visual performances of professional actors. Actors, he wrote, make it their profession "to speak...the sentiments of others; and yet to deliver them, as if

---

28. Ibid., 5.
29. Ibid., 7.
30. See Jean-Jacques Rousseau, "Essay on the Origin of Languages," in *Jean-Jacques Rousseau: The First and Second Discourses together with the Replies to Critics and Essay on the Origin of Languages*, ed. Victor Gourevitch (New York: Harper Torchbooks, 1990), 249–254.
31. Sheridan, *A Course of Lectures on Elocution*, 10.
32. Ibid., 11.

they were the result of their own immediate feeling." Sheridan argued that "it is not at the first, second, third, or even twentieth reading of their parts, that they are able to hit upon the exact manner, in which the words are to be delivered." Even when actors and orators have their lines perfectly memorized, Sheridan argued, "it is only by repeated trials, and constant practice in rehearsals, that they are able to associate to them, the just tones, looks, and gestures, that ought naturally to accompany them." According to Sheridan, actors' gargantuan difficulty is to adopt the right appearance of sincerity in feeling and believing something, but this is a difficulty that they are at great pains to overcome. That is, actors attempt coldly to apply techniques of verbal and performative dissimulation to communicate ideas and feelings that are insincere.[33] Sheridan commented to Boswell in November of 1762 to the effect that the speech of even the most talented and trained actor who pretends to be moved can never move an audience because such actors are ultimately working from a memorized script and speaking in a modern, rather than primitive, language.[34]

Sheridan believed that actors like Garrick and modern orators were simply the extreme cases of people who suffered from a much deeper and more diffuse problem caused by the inability of civilized languages to energetically communicate the warmth of genuine emotion. Indeed, Sheridan suggested that "public speakers" should "avoid all imitation of others." "Let him," he recommended to the would-be public speaker, "give up all pretensions to art, for it is certain that it is better to have none, than not enough.... Let him speak entirely from his feelings; and they will find much truer signs to manifest themselves by, than he could find for them." For Sheridan, "in order to know what another knows, and in the same manner that he knows it, an exact transcript of the ideas which pass in the mind of one man, must be made by sensible marks, in the mind of another; so in order to feel what another feels, the emotions which are in the mind of one man, must also be communicated to that of another, by sensible marks." Sheridan argued that "all our affections...and emotions, belonging to man in his animal state, are so distinctly characterized, by certain marks, that they can not be mistaken; and this language of the passions...excites also similar emotions, or corresponding effects in all minds alike." Sheridan

---

33. Ibid., 13.
34. Boswell, *London Journal 1762–1763*, 57.

claimed that "all the noble ends" that result from the communication of the genuine "internal operations, emotions, and exertions, of the intellectual, sensitive, and imaginative faculties of man," "are in a great measure lost to us," because "we have given up the vivifying, energetic language, stamped by God himself upon our natures, for that which is the cold, lifeless work of art, and invention of man." He added that civilized Europeans "have bartered that which can penetrate the inmost recesses of the heart, for one which dies in the ear, or fades on the sight." "In elocution," he noted, "nature can do much without art; art but little without nature. Nature, assaults the heart.... Force of speaking, will produce emotion and conviction; grace, only excites pleasure and admiration. As the one is the primary, and the other but a secondary end of speech, it is evident, that where one or the other, is wholly to take place, the former should have the preference." Sheridan therefore argued that unless one is genuinely and energetically moved and in possession of a language that is equal to communicating that emotional energy, little effect can be expected from any attempt to communicate and persuade. "Force of delivery," Sheridan argued, "is the necessary result of a...warm heart; provided...the speaker suffers his manner to be regulated wholly by his feelings and conceptions."[35]

Inasmuch as he believed that sincerity was required for effective and moving communication, Sheridan also held that some languages were better suited than others for such communication. In answering a question frequently posed in the eighteenth century—i.e. what is "the chief cause of [the] low state [of eloquence] amongst us"—Sheridan insisted "that an artificial manner, either from early institution, or subsequent imitation, has in general supplanted that which is natural in most public speakers and readers.... And this artificial manner, not being founded on true principles, and always differing from that which is natural, of course carries with it evident marks of art, and affectation. So that the restoring a natural manner of delivery, would be bringing about an entire revolution, in its most essential parts." Sheridan noted that there were "many instances in private life" of "persons who speak from their hearts, upon any topic, or incident which nearly concerns them." In "public discourses," however, "the speakers, have not their hearts affected by the subjects, upon which

---

35. Sheridan, *A Course of Lectures on Elocution: Together with Two Dissertations on Language*, 120, 99, 101, 110–111, 111, 121, and 121–122.

they harangue; or... an artificial manner, for the reasons before mentioned, has supplanted that of the natural kind." In a sense, Sheridan's rhetorical and linguistic theory was opposed to any diligent study of how to appear moved; instead, it called for communicating genuine emotion by attempting to recover the energetic primitive language of nature.[36]

Sheridan insisted that "there are two kinds of language... the one is the language of ideas; by which the thoughts which pass in a man's mind, are manifest to others.... The other is the language of emotions; by which... the passions, affections, and all manner of feelings, are not only made known, but communicated to others." Sheridan indicated his pre-eminent goal in promoting linguistic reform and the recovery of the language of nature: "To move therefore, should be the first great object of every public speaker; and for this purpose, he must use the language of emotions, not that of ideas alone, which of itself has no power of moving." "But he who is utterly without all language of emotions," he continued, "is not to be classed at all amongst public speakers." Ultimately, Sheridan directed his attempt to recover the energetic language of the emotions, to which he and many others attributed the eloquence of the so-called savages in America, at reforming British discursive practices with the ultimate aim of pushing back the rising tide of enthusiastic religious dissent.[37]

Sheridan's notion of the virtues of the natural language of the passions lent itself to a revision of earlier missionary representations of Indian eloquence. Instead of seeing such eloquence as resulting from divine inspiration, Sheridan's view of language suggested that the eloquence of savage oratory derived in some way from the primitive structure of their languages. Sheridan wrote, "We are told that amongst the Savages of North America, the spokesmen who come down with what is called by them *a Talk* to our governours, deliver themselves with great energy, untutored by any school-mistress but nature." "But were these savages," he continued, "to be taught our written language by our masters, we should soon find them delivering themselves as ill as we do."[38] Sheridan thus suggested that the energetic languages spoken by these savages facilitated their sincere and moving eloquence.

---

36. Ibid., 123 and 128.
37. Ibid., 132–133 and 133–134.
38. Ibid., 175.

The missionary discourses of savage eloquence were not supplanted by a Lockean discourse of lexical clarity; rather, the characterization of savage language as lexically unambiguous developed alongside a second linguistic theory developed by thinkers who adapted the missionary account of energetic savage eloquence. Like Sheridan, they divested the missionary account of its oracular foundations and attributed the energetic and sincere eloquence of savages instead to the structure of primitive languages themselves.

Sir William Temple on Ancient and Modern Eloquence

The shift from missionary representations of savage eloquence as the mark of a divine inspiration to a more secular representation of it as resulting from the characteristics of a distinct type of language occurred toward the end of the seventeenth century. In the same place and in the same year as Locke published *An Essay concerning Human Understanding,* Sir William Temple (1628–1699) weighed in on the quarrel of the ancients and moderns with two essays: *Of Poetry* and *On Ancient and Modern Learning.* In *Of Poetry,* Temple asked whether or not eloquence results from a study of the rules of rhetoric. Like the missionaries before him and Sheridan after him, Temple argued that real eloquence does not come from a diligent study of the complex art of rhetoric. He wrote that the "elevation of genius" from which real eloquence derives "can never be produced by any art or study, by pains or by industry, [and] cannot be taught by precepts or examples."[39]

Temple's main concern in the essay *Of Poetry,* however, was to answer the question whether the source of poetry and eloquence is divine or natural. In answering this question, Temple directly challenged the idea that poetry and eloquence have their source in divine inspiration. Temple began this essay by noting that among the Greeks and Romans "the causes of poetry are...said to be divine, and to proceed from a celestial fire, or divine inspiration." Temple, however, rejected divine inspiration as the source of eloquence, insisting that he could only "allow it to arise from the greatest excellency of natural temper,...without exceeding the reach of

---

39. Sir William Temple, *Essays* (London: Blackie and Son, 1910), 160–161.

what is human, or giving it any approaches of divinity, which is...debased or dishonoured by ascribing to it any thing that is in the compass of our action." Temple therefore naturalized the origins of eloquence. He wrote that "the more true and natural source of poetry may be discovered, by observing to what god this inspiration was ascribed by the ancients, which was Apollo, or the sun, esteemed among them the god of learning in general, but more particularly of music and of poetry." For Temple, such mythological attributions must be interpreted allegorically as indicating that "a certain noble and vital heat,...especially of the brain, is the true spring of these two arts or sciences." The Greek myth thus represents a thermal psychological process involving the warming of the emotions that give rise to genuine eloquent expression.[40]

Temple wrote his *Essay upon Ancient and Modern Learning* in reaction to Bernard Le Bovier de Fontenelle's (1657–1757) attempts to argue for the superiority of the "moderns" just two years earlier. One of Fontenelle's main arguments had been that the creative force of nature was constant, and thus the moderns had been able to improve on the models left by the ancients.[41] Temple's attempt to refute Fontenelle's modern claim was consistent with his claim that genuine eloquence resulted from a natural psychological process. Temple insisted that certain significant natural circumstances did affect people's creative capacities and so influence, among other things, the way they spoke. Consequently, languages might improve or decline over time depending on the influence of circumstances. He compared the mind to a tree and insisted that this tree would fare better or worse in different types of soil and climate. Temple asked, "[M]ay not the same have happened in the production, growth, and size of wit and genius in the world, or in some parts or ages of it, and from many more circumstances that contributed towards it, than what may concur to the stupendous growth of a tree or animal?"[42] In making his case for the superiority of the ancients, Temple included what he took to be certain important nonpsychological factors that shaped the distinct qualities of ancient and modern expression. Temple thus linked his psychological account of the source of eloquence to a historical account of the cultural and

---

40. Ibid., 153, 154, and 160.
41. Ibid., 200–201.
42. Ibid., 222.

material factors that shaped verbal expression. Temple claimed that "of most general customs in a country there is usually some ground from the nature of the people or the climate." Temple applied this belief in the influence of climate on the way people expressed themselves to argue that the true source of English "humour," for example, proceeded "from the native Plenty of our Soil, the Unequalness of our Climate, as well as the Ease of our Government, and the Liberty of professing Opinions and Factions."[43]

Along with climate and forms of government, Temple also included the structure of a language as one of the circumstances that could contribute to making a people's expression eloquent. For Temple there was a correspondence, or "rapport," between a speaker's "thoughts and words" or between the "conceptions and languages of every country." Temple noted that even if he could concede that modern "wit and eloquence" deserved greater praise than those of the ancients, "our languages would not." Temple characterized "the three modern tongues most esteemed,...Italian, Spanish, and French" as "all imperfect dialects," and he distinguished them from "the noble Roman" from which they in part derived. "'Tis easy to imagine," Temple wrote, "how imperfect copies these modern languages...must needs be of so excellent an original....[W]hereas the Latin was framed...by the thoughts and uses of the noblest nation that appears upon any record of story, and enriched only by the spoils of Greece, which alone could pretend to contest it with them." Temple thus anticipated a series of primitivist reflections on the relation between the structure of primitive language and the supposed energetic eloquence of American Indians. Temple's observations on "the antiquity, the uses, the changes, the decays, that have attended this great empire of wit" represent an early conjectural history of literary expression that would go on to have many eighteenth-century followers. Temple began his history of literary expression by noting that poetry is "the first sort of writing that has been used in the world; and in several nations [has] preceded the very invention or usage of letters." He followed this assertion with the following significant claim: "This last is certain in America, where the first Spaniards met with many strains of poetry, and left several of them translated into their language, which seems to have flowed from a true poetic vein, before any letters were known in those regions."[44]

---

43. Quoted from Robert C. Steensma, *Sir William Temple* (New York: Twayne, 1970), 94.
44. Temple, *Essays,* 238, 239, and 167.

Dubos: The Poetic Structure of Primitive Languages

Historians have not always been fair to Temple and have sometimes unjustly cast his admiration of the ancients in the terms used by his "modern" critics. Thus one historian judged that "all in all his discussion is unfair, prejudiced, and superficial."[45] And yet it is clear that his influence was profoundly felt in many intellectual circles in the eighteenth century. One individual who felt this influence was the French thinker Jean-Baptiste Dubos (1670–1742). Dubos, like Temple, was a diplomat in Holland before retiring to literary pursuits, and he traveled widely, encountering and establishing connections with many prominent thinkers of his day. Among his early correspondents and acquaintances were Boileau, Malebranche, Huet, Bayle, Locke, Le Clerc, Hennepin, and Chardin. During a visit to England, he met with Locke, and they became close friends. When the French translation of An *Essay concerning Human Understanding* appeared in 1700, Dubos received the proofs, and he may in fact have been the first in France to see this famous work.[46] Historians have noted this connection with Locke and suggested that Dubos was most deeply influenced by Locke when he published his *Réflexions critiques sur la poésie et sur la peinture* (1719). While it is certainly true that Locke's psychological sensationism played some part in the development of Dubos' literary theory, by focusing exclusively on this one influence, historians have neglected Temple's contribution to Dubos' historical, anthropological, and linguistic thinking.[47]

In his *Réflexions*, Dubos developed Temple's conjectural historical framework into a protoethnological program to explain how modern poetic expression had taken on a very different character from that of the ancients. Dubos' contemporary, the Abbé Goujet, for example, characterized his

---

45. C. S. Duncan, *The New Science and English Literature in the Classical Period* (Chicago: University of Chicago, 1913), 60.
46. Ibid., 73.
47. See, for example, Ulrich Ricken, *Linguistics, Anthropology and Philosophy in the French Enlightenment: Language Theory and Ideology* (London: Routledge, 1994), 53–54, and *Grammaire et philosophie au siècle des lumières: Controverse sur l'ordre naturel et la clarté du français* (Lille: Publications de l'Université de Lille III, 1978), 80–81. More recently John C. O'Neil has also emphasized the Locke-Dubos connection in his *Changing Minds: The Shifting Perception of Culture in Eighteenth-Century France* (Newark: University of Delaware Press, 2002), chap. 2. There is no mention of Sir William Temple in either Ricken's or O'Neil's studies.

Réflexions as "a history of the human mind."⁴⁸ Dubos' modern biographer describes the work as "Geography and ethnography come to the aid of history."⁴⁹ Although much has been made of Locke's influence on Dubos, his name in fact never appears in the *Réflexions*. Dubos, however, did cite explicitly Temple's argument that climate shapes a people's character or genius.⁵⁰ Dubos thus adopted and developed Temple's method for studying the historical development of culture in order to distinguish ancient and modern literature.

Dubos' *Réflexions* is generally important because of its broad influence on eighteenth-century literary and artistic theory, and it did have a specific influence on the fate of the theory of savage eloquence. Dubos placed the passions more directly at the center of his theory of rhetorical invention than had Temple. He wrote that "the agitation in which the passions take hold of us, even during moments of solitude, is so vivacious that any other state is a state of languor next to this agitation…; but men in general suffer still more in an existence without passion than the passions make them suffer."⁵¹ The positive function of passion thus made the persuasive effects of the Christian grand style, with which savage eloquence had been associated, a central element in Dubos' theory. Like Temple, and like the Puritan and the Jesuit missionaries who preceded him, Dubos maintained that inspiration was essential to artistic success. However, like Temple, Dubos naturalized this inspiration and held that the inspiration, or genius, was merely a gift of nature.

Like Temple, Dubos also held that genius was not merely an individual inspiration but also a function of the "cultures" from within which people spoke. Dubos followed Temple in trying to show how the structure of the Latin language itself made Roman oratory and literary productions superior to those of modern French writers and speakers.⁵² While Temple had offered only a brief discussion of the role of linguistic evolution in the shift

---

48. Abbé Claude-Pierre Goujet, *Bibliothèque française, ou histoire de la literature française* (Paris: Chez P. J. Mariette et H.-L. Guerin, 1740–1756), 3:138.
49. A. Lombard, *L'Abbé Dubos: Un initiateur de la pensée moderne (1670–1742)* (Paris: Hachette, 1913), 263.
50. Abbé Dubos, *Réflexions critiques sur la poésie et sur la peinture* (Paris: Ecole Nationale Supérieure des Beaux-Arts, 1993), 264.
51. Ibid., 4.
52. Ibid., 101.

from ancient to modern eloquence, Dubos presented a more expansive account of the changes between what he called "mother languages" and "derived languages." Dubos marked the distinction between the two in terms of the degree of emotional "energy" that expressions in these languages possessed. The factors that Dubos argued played a role in the degrees of linguistic energy can be described as essentially phonotactic and syntactic.

In terms of the sounds that prevailed in expressions of a language, Dubos held that in "mother languages," by which he meant the first languages that humans invented, there was "a greater number of imitative words than in the derived languages." Dubos argued that as languages developed over time, they lost "the energy that was given to them by natural connection of their sounds with the things of which they were the instituted signs. That is the derivation of the advantage that mother languages have over the derived languages." Dubos therefore argued that French, a derived language, was far less energetic than Latin, a mother language. In other words, in contrast to the Lockeans, who argued that a multiplication of abstract words led languages to become potentially less clear, Dubos argued that as sounds became less aspirated and guttural over time, languages became less energetic.[53]

Dubos also argued that the mother tongues possessed distinct syntactic advantages over the derived languages. Dubos wrote that "the genius of our language [i.e. French] is very timid, and rarely does it dare to undertake to perform against the rules [of composition] to attain beauty." Thus the syntactic rules required for correct speech, according to Dubos, actually became so restrictive in a derived language that they destroyed its passionate energy. He also claimed that the mother languages allowed for lexical inversion more easily than derived languages and thus that in Latin it was possible to "reverse the natural order of words and to transpose them."[54]

Dubos distinguished between mother and derived languages in the context of the famous quarrel of the ancients and moderns. He was thus concerned mainly with accounting for the literary differences between modern French and classical Latin poetry. But Dubos applied his argument about declining linguistic energy beyond Latin to suggest that a similar primitive linguistic energy characterized the languages of the peoples he called "les

---

53. Ibid., 104.
54. Ibid.

Sauvages." He described these savages as "men, in whom Nature has not yet been made to sit up straight" and who speak an "imitative language." By arguing that in modern languages, then, "it is often necessary to sacrifice either harmony to the energy of meaning, or the energy of meaning to harmony," Dubos developed Temple's account of the decline in modern poetic composition, and in so doing, he also provided a framework that later thinkers could apply to explain the uniquely energetic character of Indian languages.[55]

Charlevoix: From Savage Oracles to Savage Languages

Exactly twenty-five years after its first appearance, Dubos' *Réflexions* played a specifically significant role in the further development of the theory of savage eloquence. In 1744, the Jesuit François-Xavier Charlevoix (1682–1761) explicitly cited Dubos' distinction between mother and derived languages in attempting to account for the eloquence of Indian speech. According to one of his fellow Jesuits, contemporaries "nicknamed [him] the Herodotus of the missions of the Society of Jesus."[56] And yet Charlevoix also has been called "a pedestrian compiler of facts" who borrowed more from his contemporaries and predecessors than perhaps any other observer.[57] The tension implicit in these contrasting estimations of Charlevoix's writings on the Indians—that they were original on the one hand and derivative on the other—is a fair characterization of how he approached Indian languages in the sense that he explicitly tied earlier missionary descriptions of these languages to Dubos' account of how languages change their character and lose their capacity to eloquently communicate emotional energy over time. Charlevoix was original, therefore, in explicitly applying a poetic, rhetorical, and linguistic theory to his description of Indian languages.[58]

---

55. Ibid., 106.
56. See Camille de Rochemonteix, *Les Jésuites et la Nouvelle-France au XVIIIe siècle* (Paris: A. Picard et fils, 1906), 1:178.
57. J. H. Kennedy, *Jesuit and Savage in New France* (New Haven: Yale University Press, 1950), 181–182.
58. This is not to say that Charlevoix was not selective in his use of the linguistic information to which he had access. He criticized Jacques Cartier, Gabriel Sagard, and the Baron de Lahontan for their word lists. His criticism of Lahontan's writings on languages likely had much to do with

Charlevoix leaned heavily on the linguistic descriptions of his fellow Jesuit missionary to the Iroquois and protoethnologist Joseph-François Lafitau (1681–1746). Charlevoix, who had returned to France in 1722 and was then assigned to the editorial staff of the *Journal de Trévoux* while Lafitau was composing his *Mœurs des sauvages américains comparée aux moeurs des premiers temps* (1724), was responsible for the extensive review articles that notified readers of the book's importance. Lafitau had described "the Huron Language" as "noble" and "majestic." "The pronunciation," he added, "is unpolished, highly guttural, & the accent is difficult to acquire."[59] Charlevoix also twice cited Dubos' distinction between the energy of "the Mother Languages" and the weakness of "those which are derived from them" to show that "the Sioux, the Huron, and the Algonquian are rather the Mother languages" of the North American continent.[60]

Charlevoix, like the Jesuit missionaries before him, trained in rhetorical theory and in fact was sent to New France in 1705 to teach grammar at the Jesuit college in Québec. It is clear that Charlevoix was influenced by Dubos' reflections on the idea of primitive language and Lafitau's descriptions of the Iroquoian languages, yet Charlevoix said more than either of them about the linguistic energy of savage eloquence. Like Lafitau and others who preceded him in describing Indian languages, Charlevoix used rhetorical and paralinguistic categories to characterize and distinguish the Iroquoian and Algonquian language families. Thus, "the Huron Language is of an abundance, of an energy, and of a nobility, that we find reunited in perhaps none of the most beautiful [languages], that we know."[61] Charlevoix thus followed Temple and Dubos in taking the energetic eloquence of the savage orator to be a function of certain features of the Iroquoian and Algonquian languages.

---

his perception of Lahontan as an irreligious libertine. See his comments in his "Projet d'un corps d'Histoires du nouveau Monde, par le Pere de Charlevoix, de la Compagnie de Jesus" (1735), in *Journal de Trévoux, ou Mémoires pour servir à l'histoire des sciences et des arts* (Geneva: Slatkine Reprints, 1968), 35:165.

59. Joseph-François Lafitau, *Mœurs des sauvages amériquains, comparées, aux mœurs des premiers temps* (Paris: Saugrain l'aîné, Charles Estienne Hochereau, 1724), 2:479. Charlevoix also relied on Lafitau for his dismissal of the suggestions that the languages of America were corrupted forms of either Hebrew or Greek. See ibid., 2:463–474.

60. François-Xavier Charlevoix, *Histoire et Description générale de la Nouvelle-France* (Paris: Pierre-François Giffart, 1744), 38.

61. Ibid., 196.

More remarkable still is the way in which, in the middle of his discussion of the properties of Indian languages, he raised the issue of the eloquence of the speakers of these languages. "Among Barbarians, whom we never see studying to speak persuasively," Charlevoix wrote, "there is never introduced an infelicitous word, an improper term, a vicious construction, and... even the Children conserve, even as far as in their familiar speech, all this purity." Charlevoix subscribed to Dubos' vision of a gradual decline in a language's capacity for eloquence where he wrote that these Indian languages "are fallen" into "scarcity and sterility." For Charlevoix, this linguistic and therefore rhetorical decline had been accelerated by the infectious influences of European languages. "When we started to frequent these People," Charlevoix noted, "they ignored almost everything... which did not fall under their senses, they lacked the terms to express them," such that "when it was a question of speaking to them of any other things, we found a great emptiness in their Languages, and it was necessary, in order to make ourselves intelligible, to fill [their languages] with cumbersome circumlocutions."[62]

Charlevoix's discussion of Indian languages thus developed and reinforced the European belief that the primitive structure of their languages, rather than divine inspiration, was responsible for the Indians' energetic eloquence. In the thirty or so years following the publication of Charlevoix's *Histoire et Description,* several protoethnographic descriptions of the Indians appeared with discussions of the Indians' languages. Although one might question the accuracy with which Charlevoix and these others characterized the Iroquoian and Algonquian languages, Charlevoix's linguistic discussion is nonetheless significant, for it explicitly linked real descriptions of Indian languages to Dubos' theory of the primitive linguistic foundation for eloquent speech.

Civilized Language as the Corrupter of Savage Eloquence

Charlevoix's discussion also had a significant influence on French and British, and particularly Scottish, theories of the historical development of

---

62. Ibid., 196–197, 197, and 198.

linguistic communication. Dubos's and Charlevoix's writings, though they did have some notable influence in France during the second half of the century, were much more closely read by a number of Scottish university professors who attempted to account for the presumed historical transformation of all human societies from a primitive to a civilized state. One of the most prominent figures among the Edinburgh literati, the Reverend Hugh Blair (1718–1800), for example, cited Dubos' *Réflexions* in his *Lectures on Rhetoric and Belles Lettres*.[63] In his lecture titled the "Rise and Progress of Language," Blair developed an argument resembling Dubos' regarding "the style of all the most early languages, among nations who are in the first and rude periods of society."[64] Blair thus attempted, like Charlevoix, to incorporate available linguistic information into a theory of linguistic and cultural evolution that presented speakers of primitive languages as preeminently eloquent, if intellectually immature. Although Blair did not cite Charlevoix, he did cite Dubos as well as Cadwallader Colden, who, like Charlevoix, had argued that the Indians had "a certain...*Atticism,* in their language" that contributed to the eloquence of Indian oratory.[65] If Blair did not directly cite Charlevoix's *Histoire et Description,* that work was probably the most influential one in eighteenth-century discussions of the energetic and sincere language of the savage. Many of the Scottish enlightenment historians, like Adam Ferguson (1723–1816), for example, used it extensively as a source of information about the presumed savage stage of human development.[66] Among the sources besides Colden and Dubos that Blair did cite was another important Scottish moral philosopher of the late eighteenth century named Thomas Reid (1710–1796). Reid himself had relied on Charlevoix to draw a distinction between so-called natural and artificial languages and to construct a linguistic theory of cultural decline. In his *An Inquiry into the Human Mind* (1764), Reid made

---

63. Hugh Blair, *Lectures on Rhetoric and Belles Lettres* (Philadelphia: Troutman and Hayes, 1853), 17n.

64. Ibid., 66–67.

65. Cadwallader Colden, *History of the Five Indian Nations of Canada* (London: Printed for Lockyer Davis, 1755), 15.

66. Ferguson also used Colden's *History of the Five Indian Nations of Canada*. See Adam Ferguson, *Essay on the History of Civil Society* (Edinburgh: Printed for A. Millar and T. Caddel), 132. Lord Monboddo cited Charlevoix in his *Of the Origin and Progress of Language* (Edinburgh: Printed for J. Balfour and T. Cadell, 1774), 1:269.

what may have been the most explicit eighteenth-century British argument that there was a significant difference between energetic savage languages on the one hand and cold civilized languages on the other.

Reid attended the University of Aberdeen from 1722 to 1726, not long after another linguistic primitivist, Thomas Blackwell (1701–1757), had become professor of Greek there. Just as Temple and Dubos had argued that language was both a product of its speakers' environment and a source of the distinct character of its speakers' expressions, so Blackwell had insisted that *"true Poetry*... depends upon the *Manners* of a Nation, which form their Characters and animate their Language."[67] More significantly, Blackwell explicitly linked passionate eloquence, primitive language, and sincerity. In a passage that echoed Dubos' argument, he wrote, "The *primitive Parts* of the Languages reputed *Original,* are many of them rough, undeclined, impersonal Monosyllables; expressive commonly of the *highest Passions*... that present themselves in...savage Life."[68] "While a Nation continues simple and sincere," he wrote, "whatever they say has a weight.... Their Sentiments are strong and honest; which always produce fit words to express them."[69] Blackwell insisted that "what we call *Polishing* diminishes a Language...; it coops a Man up in a Corner, allows him but one Set of Phrases, and deprives him of many significant Terms and strong beautiful Expressions."[70]

During the period when Blackwell was principal of Marischal College, the regents of King's College at the same university elected Reid professor of philosophy. While there, he helped found the Aberdeen Philosophical Society, as a member of which Reid attended many discussions and debates concerning the question of the historical development of language and society. Reid devoted a whole section of his *Inquiry* to showing how by means of the elements of a primitive "natural language" "two savages...can communicate." Reid mentioned that his characterization of the languages of savages could "be confirmed by historical facts of undoubted credit, if it were necessary."[71] Reid's only reference to another work in his writings on the development

---

67. Thomas Blackwell, *Enquiry into the Life and Writings of Homer* (London, 1735), 57.
68. Ibid., 40. Although he never explicitly mentioned Dubos in his *Enquiry,* he did cite Temple's essay "On Poetry" on one occasion (71).
69. Ibid., 55.
70. Ibid., 58–59.
71. Thomas Reid, *An Inquiry into the Human Mind, on the Principles of Common Sense* (Edinburgh: Printed for A. Millar, 1764), 105.

of language, however, was to Charlevoix. In a letter to Dr. James Gregory (1753–1821), dated August 26, 1787, Reid wrote, "Charlevoix has given a very full account of some of the Canadian languages. I quote him from memory, having read his history of Canada, I think, about forty years ago; but, as it first led me into this speculation, I remember it the better."[72]

For Reid, linguistic changes were directly linked to mental and moral developments in societies. He argued that the so-called natural language essentially communicated passions and therefore contributed to making speakers energetically eloquent. He wrote, "It is by natural signs chiefly that we give force and energy to language; and the less language has of them; it is the less expressive and persuasive." For Reid, such primitive or natural languages contributed to the cultural well-being of the societies that used them. "A man that rides always in a chariot," Reid wrote, "by degrees loses the use of his legs; and one who uses artificial signs only, loses both the knowledge and use of the natural.... And for the same reason, savages have much more of it than civilized nations." While many of his contemporaries were ambivalent about the shift from a savage to a civilized language, Reid was not. He presented his readers with the following evidently rhetorical question: "[I]s it not a pity that the refinements of a civilized life, instead of supplying the defects of natural language, should root it out and plant in its stead dull and lifeless articulations of unmeaning sounds, or the scrawling of insignificant characters?" Since for Reid "the perfection of artificial language" was "surely the corruption of the natural" and "the fine art of...the orator" was "nothing else but the language of nature," the perfection of artificial language that had proceeded in tandem with the civilizing process had led to the corruption of energetic eloquence itself. Not only that, but according to Reid, the movement over time from primitive to civilized language represented the replacement of a language that facilitated the energetic communication of passion with what he called "a frigid and dead language."[73]

Reid's hypothetically proposed remedy to this corrupting process involved nothing other than that people "abolish the use of articulate sounds and writing among mankind for a century." If this were attempted, "every man,"

---

72. Thomas Reid, *Philosophical Works* (Hildesheim: G. Olms Verlag, 1983), 70.
73. Reid, *An Inquiry into the Human Mind,* 107, 106, 107–108, 108, 107.

Reid wrote, "would be...an orator."⁷⁴ For Reid, as for Sheridan, so-called civilized languages might "signify, but they do not express; they speak to the understanding, as algebraical characters may do, but the passions, the affections, and the will, hear them not."⁷⁵ Although Sheridan's *A Course of Lectures* had just recently appeared in print and Rousseau's *Essai sur l'origine des langues* would not be published for almost another twenty years,⁷⁶ all three had come to similarly ambivalent conclusions concerning the place of communicative transformations in the shift from a savage to a civilized state.

Rousseau agreed that language had an essentially social and therefore communicative rather than individual and representational function and that it was used to persuade others or to "act on someone else's sense."⁷⁷ Although all three authors were concerned with the loss of a capacity to communicate emotional energy in the move from a savage to civilized language, Rousseau's *Essai* best echoed the seventeenth-century missionaries' concerns with authenticity in speech and with the potential for counterfeit conversions among the Indians. His *Essai* distinguished between primitive languages that originated in warm climates and those in cold climates by associating them with either energy or clarity. He wrote that "southern languages must have been lively, resonant, accentuated, eloquent, and often obscure because of their vigor; northern languages, must have been muted, crude, articulated, shrill, monotone and clear, more because of their words than because of good construction."⁷⁸ In his later discussions of the move from "primitive" to "perfected" languages Rousseau tended to subordinate this distinction between southern languages of warm energy and northern languages of cold clarity. In his attempts to distinguish primitive and perfected languages, his descriptions of the former took on many of the characteristics of southern rather than northern languages. In the concluding chapter to the *Essai*, titled "The Relation of Languages to

---

74. Ibid., 109.
75. Ibid., 108.
76. Rousseau's *Essai* was first published three years after his death in a volume that gathered his writings on music under the title *Traités sur la musique* (Geneva, 1781).
77. Rousseau, *The First and Second Discourses*, 241.
78. Ibid., 274–275. Rousseau argued that modern languages "still retain something of these differences," so that "French, English, and German are the private languages of men who help one another, who argue with one another in a deliberate manner, or of excited men who get angry; but the ministers of the God's proclaiming the sacred mysteries, wise men giving laws to their people, leaders swaying the masses must speak Arabic or Persian" (275).

Governments," Rousseau insisted that, in their first stages of development, both types of primitive language were languages of authenticity in which deception, dissimulation, or counterfeiting was impossible. In this way, when a primitive northerner first uttered *aidez-moi* (help me), this speaker made just as sincere an emotional appeal as when the primitive southerner first uttered *aimez-moi* (love me).[79] Rousseau argued that those who spoke the civilized languages of Europe, however, rarely communicated their desires sincerely. "In ancient times," he argued, "when persuasion served in lieu of public force, eloquence was necessary. Of what use would it be today," he rhetorically asked, "when public force replaces persuasion?"[80] "Popular languages," he insisted, "have become as thoroughly useless as has eloquence. Societies have assumed their final forms."[81] Rousseau argued that as eighteenth-century European speakers had "nothing left to say...but *give money*," they need only say this "with posters on street corners or with soldiers in private homes."[82] In this linguistic shift, the authentic communication of energetic passion was replaced by counterfeit claims that masked a desire for power and wealth.[83]

Conclusion

The social, cultural, and political implications of this alternative to the Lockean theory of primitive speech, one that emphasized the sincerity of an energetic communication of emotion over the introspective representation of clear ideas, was put to use not only in representations of North

---

79. Ibid., 274.
80. Ibid., 293–294.
81. Ibid., 294.
82. Ibid.
83. Rousseau's concluding comments about the authenticity of primitive languages and the insincerity of civilized speech suggest an interesting intersection of early modern ideas about language and money. In an interesting article, Richard T. Gray has explored "the metaphorical field circumscribing analogies between language and money" in the eighteenth century. See his "Buying into Signs: Money and Semiosis in Eighteenth-Century German Language Theory," *German Quarterly* 69, no. 1 (Winter 1996): 1–14. The monetary crisis in the first quarter of the eighteenth century in Britain and France, particularly the collapse of the *Système Law* in France and the bursting of the South Sea Bubble in Britain in 1720 no doubt influenced this concern with communicational counterfeiting that lay behind the interest in the supposed energetic eloquence and sincerity of savage speech.

American Indians; it also had its place in representations of the newly encountered South Sea savages. Nicolas Bricaire de la Dixmerie's *Letter from a Tahitian Savage to the French* (1770), for example, attributed differences in Pacific Islander and French sociability to the differences between the primitive languages of the former and the civilized languages of the latter. "You kill reason with the force of your arguments," the imaginary Tahitian tells his French correspondent; "you decompose that which should only ever be felt; you set up as an art the odious secret of tricking reason itself. That's what you call, I believe, eloquence." In other words, the civilized French speaker uses cold analytical representations to deceptive and potentially villainous ends. In an act of moral redescription, the Tahitian savage turns the tables on his civilized and rational interlocutor. "You never tire of trying to obscure truth," he tells him, adding that the French do this "everywhere with a barbarous language." The Tahitian savage indicts this civilized French form of verbal villainy and linguistic barbarism because "everyone" who speaks a civilized language "cloaks himself and disputes. One opinion becomes the source of a thousand disasters, of a thousand heinous crimes." "In the end," the imaginary Tahitian asks, "what is reason, if its voice never makes itself heard; if instead of commanding us, it obeys us? Such a reason would never be worth the same as feeling, which never allows itself to be mistaken. You will grant this to us, no doubt, this feeling; for your indulgence would not go so far as to believe us to be reasonable beings. I will stick with my lot; it suffices to render me happy."[84] "Our Island," the Tahitian argues, "is home to different Nations, directed by different chiefs. Each communicates with all the others without deceptions or errors. They have never known discord, fraud, or the wish to spread confusion, or even the means to harm themselves."[85] De la Dixmerie used Tahiti, representing it as a concert of different nations living in harmony, as an allegory for what Europe might become. In the end, the imaginary savage Pacific Islander begs his civilized French correspondent, "My dear *Philosophe,* leave us our Language such as it is, and do not look at all to enrich it."[86]

---

84. Bricaire de la Dixmerie, *Le Sauvage de Taïti aux Français; avec un envoi au philosophe ami des sauvages* (London: Chez Le Jay, 1770), 64–66.

85. Ibid., 110.

86. Ibid., 149. For an extended discussion of the ways that eighteenth-century explorers fit the languages of Pacific Island societies into earlier treatments of primitive languages see Jim Hollyman, *Études sur les langues du Nord de la Nouvelle-Calédonie* (Paris: Peters, 1999).

Early modern theorists of savage eloquence insisted that this eloquence—and the sincerity and social harmony it implied—depended on the characteristics of a savage language. The idea of an energetically eloquent savage language emerged out of the context of the Puritan and Jesuit missionaries' emphasis on the eloquent discourses spoken at the moment of gracious inspiration as a way of guarding against counterfeit conversions. As these missionary descriptions of savage eloquence entered more secular accounts of language, notably Temple's, Dubos' and Blackwell's contributions to the quarrel of the ancients and the moderns, primitive eloquence became a function of language rather than divine inspiration. As a particular type of communication, the savage language was held to have distinct characteristics. Travel narratives, rhetorical treatises, and ethnographical descriptions of so-called savage cultures stressed the syntactically inverted, tonal, accented, oral, figurative, gestural, guttural, and aspirated characteristics of energetic savage languages.[87] Indians could thus be described as having uncultivated primitive languages and yet as also being supremely eloquent. The key to understanding this apparent tension lies in recognizing that certain early modern thinkers married their discussions of Indian languages to a linguistic concern with emotional energy, sincerity, and social harmony that allowed them to see the Indians as supremely eloquent without their having had any apparent talent or training in the rhetorical arts.

Early modern thinkers, therefore, idealized so-called savage languages for much more than their presumed semantic transparency. In fact, many of those who idealized primitive language did so for reasons having little to do with representation and clarity. In this respect, some historians

---

87. For a fuller account of the linguistic and paralinguistic characteristics of so-called primitive communication see my "Savage Eloquence in America and the Linguistic Construction of a British Identity in the 18th Century," *Historiographia Linguistica* 23, nos. 1/2 (1996): 123–158. In her study of French enlightenment interests in gestural or sign language, Sophia Rosenfeld has emphasized the visual quality of Condillac's, Rousseau's, and Diderot's conceptions of primitive language. See Rosenfeld, *A Revolution in Language* (Stanford: Stanford University Press, 2001), 36–56. While it is true that these thinkers and others insisted that gesture and facial expressions played a key role in savage speech, this was generally only one of a variety of characteristics they associated with primitive communication. Ultimately, the key virtues of savage eloquence and primitive language were their capacity to communicate emotional energy and consequently to guarantee the sincerity of speakers and really move their audiences. The sincerity and energy of primitive communication was typically supposed to have as much to do with the sonic qualities of their utterances as with the somatic transparency of their gestures.

who have discussed the early modern fascination with primitive language as a type have overinvested in the Lockean discourse of representational and semantic clarity and consequently have neglected certain widespread concerns about communication that had little to do with visual technologies of textual and gestural or pantomimic representation. As I suggest in chapter 1, this is not to say that certain early modern thinkers were not deeply invested in trying to guarantee lexical clarity and representational transparency—even to an extent that led some to fantasize that beasts might communicate more effectively than people. But the concern for semantic clarity hardly exhausts the set of early modern communicative preoccupations. The discourses of savage eloquence and primitive language were a strand of early modern linguistic anthropology that was at least as prominent as the Lockean discourse on language, if not more so. Historians have made so much of Locke and his influence on later thinkers like Condillac, however, that they have largely missed the fact that early modern concerns with communication frequently had more to do with guaranteeing the sincerity of speakers and with moving audiences than they did with semantic ambiguity and the abuse of words.[88]

---

88. See, for example, Lionel Trilling, *Sincerity and Authenticity* (Cambridge, MA: Harvard University Press, 1972).

Part III

CIVILIZED TONGUES

5

FRENCH LEVITY

> Minds are formed by languages; the thoughts take on the color of the idioms.... In each language the mind has its particular form. This is a difference which might very well be a part of the cause or the effect of national characters.
>
> JEAN-JACQUES ROUSSEAU, *Émile* (1762)

> If an uncultivated jargon, like that of the American savages, has so many natural advantages, how many acquired beauties must a cultivated language like ours have? French national gaiety and gallantry have made it appropriate for epigrammatic flashes of wit.... The flashes of French wit are brilliant meteors whose beams of light always astonish and please.
>
> BARET DE VILLENCOUR, *Discours public sur les Langues* (1780)

The claims that animals communicated with greater clarity and that savages communicated with greater energy than did speakers of European languages could be described as fantasies that projected certain early modern European thinkers' wishes and worries about their own speech communities. In fact, the concerns about clarity, wit, and energy that the preceding chapters have sketched played important, if frequently overlooked, roles in the ways that early modern French and British thinkers thought about their own languages. Early modern French and English speakers sought to redescribe certain classic linguistic defects as being in reality the properties that contributed to making their respective languages better than any other.

French and British thinkers both developed arguments that their languages were especially clear. French thinkers, however, also sought to argue that the facts that their language had especially soft sounds and that their lexicon was comparatively small were virtues that contributed to distinctly enviable forms of French communicational levity. British thinkers, by contrast, insisted that the rough and guttural sounds of their words and the comparative frequency of their syntactic inversions contributed to making English speakers both enlightened and energetically sincere. In these ways, French and British thinkers celebrated their respective languages and accused the other's speakers of being insincere flatterers and frivolous chatterers or verbal barbarians and uncivil savages.

In the quarrel of the ancients and moderns, a number of the moderns agreed with the ancients, like Temple and Dubos, in equating ancient and primitive. The strategy of the moderns, however, was to associate modern European vernaculars with linguistic refinement and cultural progress. A number of French thinkers, beginning in the 1670s, adopted this position in order to redescribe certain supposed defects of the French language as being in fact the source of the preeminence of the French language. They focused on properties that, not surprisingly, were the ones that would distinguish French from animal as well as savage forms of communication. While maintaining that French syntax made the language especially clear, they also insisted that the language lacked the rough sounds associated with savage energy and the lexical precision associated with animal clarity. In other words, they developed a discourse about the French language that presented it as being simultaneously clear, sweet, and equivocal and as contributing to distinctly French forms of salutary, sociable, and witty communication.

The *Querelle de l'Arc de Triomphe*

The idea that linguistic differences reflect and at the same time reinforce differences in the character of cultures was by no means new to the late seventeenth century. The Renaissance *questione della lingua*, which asked whether Latin, Greek, or the European vernaculars were preferable languages has been thoroughly studied by historians.¹ A striking number of French thinkers from the middle of the seventeenth to the end of the eighteenth century revived and reinvigorated this question of "the respective merits of languages," as Nicolas Beauzée (1717–1789) put it in the *Encyclopédie*.² The question flared into a full-blown quarrel in 1670, when Jean-Baptiste Colbert (1619–1683) was making plans to erect a triumphal arch to commemorate one of Louis XIV's military victories. During the planning, Colbert asked members of the Académie Française whether the inscriptions on the monument should be in French or Latin.³ Although the monument was never completed, Colbert's question set off a dispute, which, though related to the more famous quarrel of the ancients and moderns, took on a life and significance of its own during the following century.

This question of the superiority of the French language, like the monument and the quarrel of the ancients and moderns, was never fully resolved during the eighteenth century. Be that as it may, this *querelle de l'arc de triomphe* generated a fairly consistent set of characteristics that several eighteenth-century thinkers used in their attempts to judge the relative merits of languages. Although the quarrel had largely fizzled out by 1703, when Jean Frain du Tremblay (1641–1724) published his *Traité des Langues*, it left a sufficiently deep impression that he could cite it in the first chapter as the occasion for his composing his treatise. "It is not long ago since a controversy," he wrote, "became famous upon the subject of Inscriptions on public Monuments."⁴ Frain du Tremblay insisted that "what ordinarily causes disputes to be without end, is that everyone only takes a side out of prejudice, humor, or any other reason than justice and truth. This is because they do not take care to establish principles that both parties will be

---

1. See, among others, Sarah Stever Gravelle, "The Latin-Vernacular Question and Humanist Theory of Language and Culture," *Journal of the History of Ideas* 49, no. 3 (1988): 367–386; Cecil Grayson, *A Renaissance Controversy: Latin or Italian* (Oxford: Clarendon Press, 1960); Robert Hall, Jr., *The Italian Questione della Lingua* (Chapel Hill: University of North Carolina Press, 1942); and Richard Foster Jones, *The Triumph of the English Language* (Stanford: Stanford University Press, 1953).

2. Nicolas Beauzée, "Langue," in *Encyclopédie, ou Dictionnaire Raisonné des Sciences, des Arts et des Métiers,* ed. Denis Diderot and Jean le Rond d'Alembert (Stuttgart-Bad Cannstatt: Frommann, 1966), 9:264.

3. Ferdinand Brunot gives a good overview of this *querelle de l'arc de triomphe* in his *Histoire de la Langue Française des origines à nos jours* (Paris: Librairie Armand Colin, 1966), 5:10–20.

4. Jean Frain du Tremblay, *Traité des Langues* (Paris: Chez Jean-Baptiste Delespine, 1703), 2.

obliged to accept and by which we can know with assurance on which side to find reason." He intended his treatise to establish "the first principles that are necessary to judge this dispute."[5] The principles that he laid out in the book, therefore, summarized the terms of the querelle de l'arc de triomphe and established an explicit set of criteria for comparing and ranking different languages. The criteria that he laid out in his treatise—some of which have to do with the meanings of the words in a language's lexicon, some with its predominating sounds, and some with the language's syntax—fall into three main categories: clarity, energy, and elegance.

French Clarity

Those who took up the question of the relative merits of the French language between 1670 and the awarding of the Berlin Academy Prize in 1784 were very consistent in arguing that it had a particular facility for both clear conceptualization and clear communication. By far the longest treatise to emerge during the querelle de l'arc de triomphe was a work of over eleven hundred pages, titled *De l'excellence de la langue françoise,* by the French academician François Charpentier (1620–1702). In this work he took for granted, as he put it, that "the beauty of a language testifies to the beauty of the spirit of the people who speak it, and...we can...conclude that the people whose tongue is the most perfect is the one whose minds are the clearest and the noblest." Charpentier insisted that obscure works in Greek and Latin become much clearer simply by virtue of their being translated into French. "Do we count for nothing," Charpentier asked, "that admirable quality of the French language, which possesses par excellence Clarity and Neatness?...It is this Clarity, inseparable from the French language, which makes it much more difficult to translate the Greek authors into French than into Latin." He added that "by applying the maxims of philosophers and rhetoricians to the French language..., we easily see that it is a language that comes closest to the Idea of a perfect language. It possesses par excellence Neatness and Clarity, which are

---

5. Ibid., "Avertissement."

the principal beauties of discourse...because we never speak except to be understood."⁶

Charpentier argued that the French language's syntax in particular promoted clear communication more than did that of the classical languages. The very title of his thirtieth chapter, "That the Direct Construction, like That of French, Is Incomparably Better Than the Inverted Construction of Latin," indicated that he had in mind one of the linguistic issues that Dubos and others insisted was involved in making savage languages more energetic and therefore superior to civilized ones: the ability to rearrange or invert the order of words in a sentence.⁷ Charpentier argued that the so-called natural order of words (subject-verb-object) in French was superior to an inverted, or transposed, order. He wrote that the natural order was evidence of "Order and Neatness in the mind of the speaker; there is no way to deny that the [indirect construction] is evidence of Disorder and Confusion." Charpentier insisted that "those who admire the Latin language have taken this confusion for an ornament."⁸ Twenty years later, Frain du Tremblay discussed word order in his chapter "Of Neatness." There he related syntactic word order very explicitly to clarity in communication by reflecting on the meaning of the term "neatness." "This word," he wrote, "comes from the Latin, *nitere,* which signifies *shining,* which is to say, *reflecting a good deal of light.* And we use this term to denote the impression that polished and spotless bodies make on our eyes, when, because of the polish of their surface, they reflect a great deal of the light that hits them." "A discourse in which all the words are in their natural place and of a regular construction," he concluded, "cannot but reflect all its light."⁹ "If there are languages that are preferable in point of neatness to other languages," Frain du Tremblay added as he explicitly characterized the French as being superior to the Latin language, "they are those that require that the words be in their natural order; i.e. make them follow, in discourse, the same order that ideas have in the thought."¹⁰ Frain du

---

6. François Charpentier, *De l'excellence de la langue françoise* (Paris: Chez la Veuve Bilaine, 1683), 118–119, 462–463, and 610.

7. See Ulrich Ricken, *Grammaire et philosophie au siècle des lumières* (Lille: Publication de l'Université de Lille III, 1978).

8. Charpentier, *De l'excellence de la langue françoise,* 658–660.

9. Frain du Tremblay, *Traité des Langues,* 127.

10. Ibid., 124–125.

Tremblay concluded that "the fitter any tongue is for clarity of discourse, the more perfect it is."[11] Despite ostensibly claiming that no language was inherently better than another, Frain du Tremblay also insisted that the specific communicational virtue of "clarity is one of the prime characteristics of our [French] language."[12]

In his *Encyclopédie* entry on "Language," Beauzée argued that although all people share the same capacity for thought, different languages are like "different ways of painting the same object."[13] Beauzée asserted that *clarity* was "the quality that is most essential to any enunciation" and suggested that the tendency to arrange words in either natural or inverted orders contributed to making a language more or less "luminous."[14] He concluded that since what he called the "analogous languages" followed the "analytical order"—i.e., the order of ideas before they were translated into any given language—they were clearer than the transpositive languages.[15] In the article that follows Beauzée's, the Chevalier de Jaucourt (1704–1780) perpetuated the myth of French clarity in writing that "clarity, order, justness, and purity of terms distinguish French from other languages."[16]

Of all those who argued for the superiority of the French language during the eighteenth century, none captured this idea that French was preeminently clear with such aphoristic brilliance as Antoine de Rivarol (1753–1801) did in his essay that won the Berlin Academy's prize in 1784. His argument concerning the universality of the French language in large part simply reiterated the by then commonplace idea that the analogous languages were clearer and more rational than transpositive ones. "What distinguishes our language from the ancient and other modern languages," Rivarol wrote, "is the order and construction of the sentence. This order must always be direct and necessarily clear." He argued that "inversion has

---

11. Ibid., 108–109.
12. Ibid.
13. Beauzée, "Langue," 9:257.
14. Ibid., 258.
15. The abbé Gabriel Girard (1677–1748) was the first to use the terms "analogous" and "transpositive" to describe languages. Gabriel Girard, *Les Vrais principes de la langue françoise, ou la parole réduite en méthode, conformément aux loix de l'usage* (Paris: Chez Le Breton, 1747), 23. Girard claimed that the transpositive languages followed the order suggested by "the fire of the imagination," which suggested their greater energy (24).
16. Louis, Chevalier de Jaucourt, "Langue françoise," in Diderot and d'Alembert, *Encyclopédie*, 9:266.

prevailed around the world, because man is more imperiously governed by the passions than by reason." According to Rivarol, the French language "has been alone in staying faithful to the direct order, as if it were pure reason...; and it is in vain that the passions try to disrupt us and to solicit us to follow the order of sensations: the French syntax is incorruptible. It is from this, that such an admirable clarity, the eternal basis of our language, results." With this, Rivarol could boldly and famously assert, *"That which is not clear is not French;* that which is not clear may be English, Italian, Greek, or Latin."[17]

By characterizing French as the language that most faithfully reproduced the natural order of thought, Rivarol insisted that it was also the most rational or, in other words, the language in which the passions had the least influence. Of course, this was precisely the way other early modern thinkers tended to portray the language; but the negative consequences that some, like Temple, Dubos, Sheridan, Rousseau, or Reid, might have drawn from this characterization were entirely absent from Rivarol's argument. In fact, Rivarol suggested that French was superior to all other languages precisely because it was both clear and not overly energetic.

While a growing number of French thinkers argued that primitive languages were emotionally energetic if semantically opaque, others continued to insist that, despite its lack of emotional energy, one of the virtues of the French language was that, as the most civilized and refined of languages, it was especially clear. Beauzée, for example, characterized the transpositive languages as being abandoned "to the fire of the imagination, and to the interest, so to speak, of the passions."[18] He noted that, for this reason, transpositive languages allowed speakers to escape the necessity of having "invariably to follow the monotonous march of a *cold* analysis."[19] De Jaucourt also followed Beauzée in complaining that "the French language lacks...energy."[20] Some, like Frain du Tremblay, who complained that "those who boast of the energy of languages express themselves in

---

17. Antoine de Rivarol, "L'Universalité de la langue française," in Académie de Berlin, *De l'universalité Européenne de la langue française,* ed. Pierre Pénisson (Paris: Librairie Arthème Fayard, 1995), 162.
18. Nicolas Beauzée, *Grammaire générale...* (Stuttgart-Bad Cannstatt: Friedrich Frommann Verlag, 1974), 2:468.
19. Ibid., 481.
20. Chevalier de Jaucourt, "Langue françoise," 9:267.

mysterious terms," simply dismissed the criterion of energy outright as being a meaningless mystification.[21] Others, like Charpentier and Denis Diderot (1713–1784), simply rejected the argument that speakers of primitive languages were more sincere than speakers of the syntactically clear civilized languages. Charpentier, for example, argued that languages that permitted inversions lent themselves to dissimulation precisely because, as he put it, such constructions displayed an "all too apparent art."[22] Diderot, for his part, insisted that French "is of all languages the most refined, the most exact, and the most estimable; the language, in a word, that has retained the fewest of those defects that I would call the vestiges of primitive *stammering.*" Like most of his contemporaries, Diderot considered syntactic inversions to be one such primitive vestige. "By having no inversions in our language," he insisted, "we have gained in exactness, in clarity, and in precision…and by the same token, we have lost in warmth, in eloquence, and in energy." Unlike many of his contemporaries who believed that this energetic eloquence guaranteed a speaker's authenticity, however, Diderot, like Charpentier, described languages retaining this supposed primitive syntactic structure as "the languages of fiction and lies."[23] Beauzé actually accepted that French was not especially passionate and energetic but he also suggested that the lack of energy in analogous languages was not at all difficult to overcome and that this lack was more than made up for by what French speakers gained in syntactic clarity. In this way, for many in the eighteenth century, French qualified for the status of an especially virtuous language because it was especially clear rather than especially warm.

The Sweetness of Soft Sounds

While early modern thinkers tended to agree that the French language's syntax made it both distinctly clear and cold, they also tended to agree that on the basis of its prevailing sounds and an important peculiarity of its lexicon, the language should also be characterized as especially sweet, soft, and light. Beauzée argued that while all languages shared a set of fundamental

---

21. Frain du Tremblay, *Traité des Langues,* 147.
22. Charpentier, *De l'excellence de la langue françoise,* 648.
23. Denis Diderot, *Oeuvres complètes de Diderot* (Paris: Garnier Frères, 1875), 1:371.

sounds, each of which was linked to or motivated by specific ideas, there was also another set of sounds that characterized each language's "specific genius." Like Temple, Dubos, and others, Beauzée argued that certain physical and moral causes, among which he listed "the climate, air, locations, waters, the way of life and kind of food," produced a "considerable variety in the fine structures of the body." Beauzée held that while these physiological differences might not be apparent to the anatomist, they "can be easily noticed by a philosopher who...has only to notice which ones each nation uses the most in the words of its language and of how they use them." In this way, Beauzée added a phonotactic argument to the syntactic one to characterize a language as being especially primitive and energetic or as being especially civilized and clear. He held that each language's "accents," or prevailing sounds, "paint the manner in which those who speak are affected by those thoughts." Beauzée allowed that all languages were to some extent accented, but he insisted that some languages were more so than others. Beauzée argued that by examining the prevailing sounds of different languages, one could draw legitimate conclusions not just about the character or genius of those languages and their speakers but also about "their respective merits." The conclusions he drew from his cursory discussion of the contrasting sounds of different languages were that "the habitual use of rough articulations designates a savage and uncivilized people, while the liquid articulations are, in the nation that uses them frequently, a mark of nobility and delicacy."[24]

After laying down these phonotactic principles, Beauzée sketched the characteristics of several languages. He linked, for example, what he called "the Chinese nation's well-known softness of character" "to the fact that it does not make any use of the rougher articulation of [the phoneme] 'r.'" "The Italian language," he continued, "has softened its pronunciation of Latin words, to the proportion that the people who speak it have gradually lost the vigor of the ancient Romans." Beauzée characterized the Latin language in favorable terms noting that it was "candid [*franche*], having pure and neat vowels, and but few diphthongs." He added that consequently the genius of Latin language "is similar to that of the Romans themselves, which is to say appropriate for things that are firm and masculine." As

---

24. Beauzée, "Langue," 9:260 and 262. He characterized English as the language of a "nation with great depth, a lively apprehension, an impatient humor, and strong ideas" (264).

favorable as this characterization was, however, he quickly contrasted Latin to both Greek and French and argued that these two languages were especially appropriate "for subjects demanding charm and light graces." He attributed this character of the French language to its being "full of diphthongs and moist letters [*letters mouillées*]." After allowing that in regard to "the simple enunciation of thought," every language might have merits and be well suited to the circumstances of its speakers, he argued that there were other linguistic ends than this, such as "to flatter the ear and to touch the heart, as well as to enlighten the mind."[25]

Beauzée's claim that the French language's moist letters made it charming and gracefully light and therefore suited for delicate but enlightened communication was largely a reiteration of a conventional early modern characterization of the French as the most highly civilized of all languages. Charpentier, who stated that "there is a strict connection between the spirit of a people and the language they speak" and that "there are some languages that are more excellent than others," explicitly contrasted, for example, the civilized French language with savage American Indian languages. He depicted the Indians as being savages who were completely without civilization. "As one approaches the parts of the world that Europeans have not yet cleared," he wrote, "one encounters people who go about naked and live only by hunting.... One finds men whose only dwellings are huts of leaves and moss in the thickest forests; men... who are incapable of society, and who are as ferocious as the beasts they hunt." He insisted that "one must not look among such people for discursive elegance." "It is remarkable enough," he suggested, "that they are not mutes and it is too much to ask that they should be eloquent." By contrast, he noted that the French, like "all peoples who are skilled and have cultivated reason to a great degree, have never failed to embellish their Elocution and with it their politeness."[26]

Charpentier argued that "regarding Sound or pronunciation," "one can draw many consequences to the advantage of the French tongue." He argued that French abounded in vowels. "Most of our words," he wrote, "are terminated by two or three vowels, such as *la Vie, la Joye, l'Oüye*; as well as those with vowels that come together in the middle such as *Priere, lueur,*

---
25. Ibid., 264.
26. Charpentier, *De l'excellence de la langue françoise*, 84–86.

nuage, pieté." Charpentier argued that this abundance of vowels gave the French language a distinct sweetness. He added that French had countless words with the letters *l* and *n* but few that ended with the letters *um*, the sound of which, he argued, "resembles the mooing of a cow." Charpentier argued that this demonstrated that "the French tongue is an enemy of all harshness." The centerpiece of Charpentier's phonotactic argument was the "feminine *E*, which has but a soft sound, which one encounters very often, and which agreeably disrupts that equality and renders the harmony of the French language more varied and sweet." According to Charpentier, the '*e muet*' had an especially "brief" sound "that touches the ear less than the other vowels. It does not press the syllable; instead, it glides lightly above it and imitates something like what Musicians do in instrumental concerts, when after having forcefully touched the cords of the lute, they soften the sound all of a sudden and make it seem that the harmony is moving away. Charpentier therefore concluded that "this sweetness and this flexibility of the feminine *E*" was the reason "that the greater part of our words are incomparably sweeter to pronounce, than those of the Latins from which they derive." Charpentier thus developed the argument that even the sounds of spoken French gave it a less energetic but more charming or light quality.[27]

A few years earlier, in a dialogue about the French language in his *Entretiens d'Ariste et d'Eugène* (1671), the Jesuit Dominique de Bouhours (1628–1702) argued that "French is infinitely removed from the rudeness of all the Northern tongues, most of which flay the throat of those who speak it and the ears of those who hear it." He singled out "those double *uu*, double *ss*, double *kk*, that dominate those tongues, all those consonants jumbled one on top of each other are horrible to pronounce and make a frightening sound." He argued that by contrast, "the mix of vowels and consonants" in French "has an entirely different effect." He insisted that the fact that the French language had "neither strong aspirates, nor any of those letters scholars call *Gutturals*" made it an especially agreeable tongue. "There is nothing more agreeable to the ear," he added, "than our silent *e*... It facilitates the feminine rhymes, which gives a singular grace to our poetry. We pronounce the *u* softly and as a simple vowel.... We have difficulty

---

27. Ibid., 404, 405–407, 410–412, 418, and 434.

bearing the encounter of vowels that do not elide and produces a shocking effect.... In pronouncing many words, we change *oi* into *e,* to render the pronunciation easier and more fluid."[28]

These characterizations of French sounds as lacking in energy but as being especially elegant, graceful, and sweet were widely accepted and promoted by a number of other early modern French thinkers.[29] Indeed, although Rivarol's essay is remembered almost exclusively for its claim that the peculiarities of French syntax made the language preeminently clear, he also insisted that "the pronunciation of the French tongue has the mark of its character: it is more varied than that of Southern languages but less brilliant; it is much sweeter than Northern languages because it does not articulate all its letters. The sound of the silent *e,* ever resembling the final vibrations of sonorous bodies, gives it an exclusively light harmony."[30]

The Lightness of the Lexicon

The importance of the idea of linguistic lightness, levity, or *légèreté,* like the idea of linguistic warmth or energy, has largely been ignored by historians of this period. An especially interesting passage in *The History and Present State of Discoveries relating to Vision, Light, and Colours* (1772) by the British dissenting scientist and later radical Joseph Priestley (1733–1804) suggests, however, the significance of the multiple meanings implied by the English word "light" in the eighteenth century. In discussing Fontenelle's account of certain French experiments with light, Priestley wrote, "These experiments, [Fontenelle] says, agree very well with others which prove the *weight* of the particles of light. This he advances not ironically, but very gravely."[31] What is so interesting in this passage is Priestley's

---

28. Dominique de Bouhours, *Entretiens d'Ariste et d'Eugène,* ed. René Radouant (Paris: Editions Bossard, 1920), 63–64.

29. See, for example, Mayet's argument that French "softens foreign words." Etienne Mayet, "Est brevitate opus...," in Académie de Berlin, *De l'universalité Européenne de la langue française,* 98.

30. Rivarol, "L'Universalité de la langue française," 168.

31. Joseph Priestley, *The History and Present State of Discoveries relating to Vision, Light, and Colours* (London: Printed for J. Johnson, 1772), 385. Since Newton had argued that light must be

recognition that to say light has weight or gravity has the appearance of an amusing irony. He recognized the contradiction in the phrasing and so had to insist that his readers should take the phrase literally and seriously, or as he put it, *gravely,* with gravity. With this advice to his readers, Priestley not only noted the irony that light has weight but also coded seriousness and literalness as heavy (grave) and implied that what is ironic and not serious, or at least not overly serious, is light. If one is to follow the poststructural precept to begin acts of interpretation with discursive tensions it would be difficult to find a better passage than this one that played on the semantic instability of the English word "light," which can suggest not only clarity and, to Newton's followers, weight but also levity.

David Bell has drawn attention recently to eighteenth-century French investigations of lightness as a national characteristic. "To be French," he writes, "was to be particularly social, particularly refined and polite, and particularly cheerful or flighty (*léger,* implying a mix of vivaciousness, inconstancy, and perhaps also superficiality)."[32] The *Encyclopédie* article for "Nation," for example, noted that "it is a sort of proverb to say, *léger* like a Frenchman."[33] To the extent that this quality of légèreté was meant to be distinct to human sociability, a number of French thinkers agreed with Rica, a character in Montesquieu's *Persian Letters* (1721), who commented, "On this score it seems to me that a Frenchman is more human than anyone else."[34] Indeed, it was precisely at the point in his essay where Rivarol argued that the prevailing sounds of French gave it a quintessentially "light harmony" that he added that French, more than other languages, "is made for conversation, the bond between men and the charm of the ages.... Sure, sociable, reasonable, it is no longer the French language; it is the language of humanity."[35] In this way, Rivarol argued that French was an ideal language not just because it was especially clear but also because it was an especially light language that promoted polite sociability in the form of private conversation.

---

composed of particles, his scientific followers concluded that these particles must have mass or weight.

32. David A. Bell, *The Cult of the Nation in France: Inventing Nationalism 1680–1800* (Cambridge, MA: Harvard University Press, 2001), 147.
33. "Nation," in Diderot and d'Alembert, *Encyclopédie,* 11:36.
34. Montesquieu, *Persian Letters* (Indianapolis: Bobbs-Merrill, 1964), 146.
35. Rivarol, "L'Universalité de la langue française," 168.

This suggestion that French was the most fully human of languages also went hand in hand with the idea that it was the most highly cultivated, polished, or civilized tongue. Despite their concessions that French lacked the emotional energy of savage tongues, a number of early modern French thinkers insisted that this lack of energy was more than made up for by the civilized and civilizing quality of légèreté. David Bell notes, for example, that the French used their claim to being *léger* above all because they presented themselves as standing "at the end point of that long historical evolution which had taken them away from their 'savage' or 'barbarian' origins and rendered them steadily more 'polite,' 'policed,' or 'civilized.' Sociability, légèreté, and politeness were all closely linked to the concept of 'civilization,' which...depended on a vision of historical progress and cosmopolitan exchange between civilized people."[36] For many who developed this claim for lightness as an especially French national characteristic, its foundation was a linguistic one. Baret de Villencour therefore rhetorically asked readers of his *Discours public sur les Langues* (1780), "[I]f an uncultivated jargon, like that of the American savages, has so many natural advantages, how many acquired beauties must a cultivated language like ours have?"[37] Similarly, André Morellet (1727–1819) claimed that the difference between the sociability of the "civilized peoples of Europe" and the barbarism of the "savage nations of America" resulted from a fundamental difference between civilized and savage languages. Unlike Europeans, "these savages," he wrote, "have a language limited to a small number of words that relate to the objects of the first necessity.... The character of this people would be just as limited as its language.... It would ignore a ton of delicate sentiments, which generate so much sweetness in life and which perfect and complete civilization."[38]

If the fundamental difference between the civilized and the savage character is a consequence of the copiousness or size of a language's lexicon, however, this presented a particular challenge to those who believed that the French language was *the* language of légèreté and civilization. The reason for this was that many of those who discussed the French language

---

36. Bell, *The Cult of the Nation in France*, 149.
37. Baret de Villencour, *Discours Public sur les langues en general, et sur la langue françoise en particulier* (Paris: Chez l'Auteur, La Veuve Duchesne, Durand, et Cellot, 1780), 63.
38. André Morellet, *De la conversation* (Paris: Éditions Payot et Rivages, 1995), 39.

admitted that it had a comparatively small lexicon. In attempting to redescribe this linguistic defect as a special virtue of the French language, certain theorists argued that despite the comparatively restricted French lexicon, many French words managed to contain a surprising semantic abundance, which contributed to a special kind of equivocation that made the French tongue especially light.

Bouhours explicitly linked levity, language, and the French character in his *Entretiens* when one of the characters, Eugène, argued, "[T]he change that has occurred in our language [i.e. French] is an effect of the légèreté of which we stand accused."[39] Eugène's interest in this part of the dialogue, however, was to insist that "what strangers call a defect of the French language is in reality the mark, or rather the cause, of the perfection to which it has arrived."[40] In general, Bouhours' account of linguistic development resembled that of other early modern thinkers who held that languages were rough and energetic in their primitive stages, growing less energetic as they developed but more polished, delicate, and light.[41] Bouhours, however, saw little to regret in this exchange of energy for levity. After listing a number of changes in the history of the French language, Eugène tells Ariste, "You can see clearly that the change has spoiled nothing and that they are wrong who reproach our inconstancy when it comes to language."[42] Bouhours thus linked the notion of légèreté with what he took to be a distinctively French type of inconstancy, which allowed change but only for the sake of refinement.

When Charpentier waded back into the querelle de l'arc de triomphe twelve years later, he argued that what contributed to the French linguistic virtue of légèreté was a special quality of the French lexicon. Like Bouhours, he responded to the accusation that the French nation suffered from an excess of légèreté or inconstancy. He wrote, "After all, when I see that our

---

39. Bouhours, *Entretiens d'Ariste et d'Eugène*, 104. Michel de Marolles (1600–1681) attributed the accusation originally to Caesar but more immediately to Paolo Giovio (1483–1552) and Pietro Riccio Crinito (1465–1505). See Michel de Marolles, *Suitte des Mémoires de Michel de Marolles* (Paris: Chez Antoine de Sommaville, 1642), 30–31.

40. Ibid.

41. Although Bouhours is short on specifics, among the changes he listed were the introduction of articles, the transformations in the endings of words of Latin derivation, and the abolishing of "terms that seemed too rough." Among these changes was also the invention of the "feminine *e*" (110).

42. Ibid., 117.

Adversaries complain of the instability of our language, I cannot help but think that what leads them into a sentiment so contrary to the truth, is the vulgar opinion about the French Nation, which they accuse of being Inconstant in all things." Charpentier at first vehemently objected to this reproach of inconstancy. "I see nothing but proof," he wrote, "that the French Nation is incomparably more constant than the Roman one, which must be sufficient to cover us from this reproach of Legereté." Although he thus initially argued that the French were not particularly inconstant, he did suggest that if understood in a certain special way, the accusation was in fact correct. He wrote, "[L]et us do them one better, and concede this point. We are indeed lighter than most of our neighbors. We have no Hatred so Constant; we have no desires for Vengeance so obstinate; we forgive more easily.... It is the facility for forgetting injuries and for suffocating a righteous resentment, which proves our Inconstancy." "If this humor must be our fault," he added, "we are more than happy to be incorrigible." Charpentier thus associated the claims about French légèreté with a national inclination to self-effacement, diplomacy, and politeness. In a chapter devoted to discussing the "excellence," "delicacy," "modesty," and "courteousness" of the French language, Charpentier asserted that French "is sweet, meaningful, sonorous, eloquent, and numerous.... Above all, it is scrupulously Chaste and has an almost infinite Delicacy of taste." Of these linguistic virtues, Charpentier elaborated his claim that French was chaste and delicate by arguing that "when it comes to explaining oneself on some delicate issue, it does not have to be done with obscene expressions.... Such things must be said in a manner that they are wrapped in a delicate turn of phrase and in a way that one can always allow that the speaker wanted to say something else." What was special about the French language, in Charpentier's view, was that its words permitted a kind of equivocation that could defuse the potential for disputes. "This," he wrote, "is to have taken the Speech to the final degree of Nobility: it is to have introduced Courteousness into taking Liberties, and to have made a familiar habit of Modesty and Discretion."[43]

Charpentier thus presented the French language as being clear while also being ambiguous or equivocal in a very special way. The French language, he suggested, was so delicate and courteous (he might well have

---

43. Charpentier, *De l'excellence de la langue françoise*, 747–748, 755–757, 610–611, 612–614.

written *légère*) that it was able to express potentially offensive thoughts clearly enough without having to use words the meaning of which would be strictly offensive. It thus managed to subtly criticize without overtly offending sensibilities. Charpentier concluded, after citing a number of examples of indiscretions permitted by the Latin language, that "the French language has this Perfection above Latin: it is more courteous and more temperate.... And if... we can judge Nations by their Languages...; we can be sure that the Romans were very depraved, very coarse, very discourteous, and that the French are incomparably more civil and elegant."[44] This notion that French words contained an abundance of meaning that could be deployed in favor of polite, graceful, and diplomatic forms of sociability was developed through the eighteenth century by a number of other French thinkers. In fact, this idea helped such thinkers to specifically answer the charge that one of the greatest defects of the French language was that its lexicon was insufficiently copious.

Thirty-five years after Charpentier's long defense of the French tongue, the grammarian Gabriel Girard (1677–1748) published a little dictionary of synonyms that argued for their importance in sociable speech. In his preface, Girard insisted that this dictionary would contribute to a "subtle and agreeable way of expressing things."[45] Girard's dictionary could, however, be described as an antithesaurus inasmuch as he argued that there were, in fact, no such things as genuine synonyms in the sense of words having exactly the same meaning.[46] Behind Girard's project lay the idea

---

44. Ibid., 623–624.
45. Gabriel Girard, *La justesse de la langue françoise, ou les differentes significations des mots qui passent pour synonimes* (Paris: Laurent D'Houry, 1718), xi.
46. In his "Preliminary Discourse," Girard anticipated the following reaction to his work: "Do we not understand by *Synonyms,* they will ask me, the words that differing only by the articulation of the voice, resemble one another by the idea that they express? And if this is the case, either their meanings are not different, or they are not synonyms." To which Girard responded, "This term [synonym] can be understood in two senses; one more extensive and the other more narrow. One can take it for a resemblance of meaning that nonetheless exhibits some variety; which is to say that the synonymous words all present a single principal idea, but each of them adds nevertheless certain accessory ideas, which diversify the principal one in such a way that it appears in these different words as the same color appears under diverse nuances. One can also understand by *synonym* such an entire and perfect resemblance that the meaning, taken in all its force and all its circumstances, is always and absolutely the same; such that one of the synonyms signifies nothing more or less than the other; that one can employ them indifferently on every occasion; and that there is no more choice to make between them, when it comes to meaning, than there is between

that although certain words might share a single principal idea, they could be distinguished on the basis of what he called their "accessory ideas."[47] Girard argued that the richness, or copiousness, of a language must be judged "by the number of thoughts that it can express, and not by the number of articulations of the voice that it can make heard." Girard argued that a "truly rich" language would have words that distinguished not only principal ideas but also the delicate nuances of accessory ideas. A language "could not be more impoverished," he wrote, "even if it had a great quantity of words, if it could only express a small number of ideas." "We need only expressions and not sounds." Girard argued that many languages that were more copious than French merely abounded in such genuine synonyms, i.e., words with *exactly* the same meaning. Such languages, he wrote, "are better suited to tire the memory than to facilitate the art of speaking." People who thought this kind of lexical copiousness was a virtue, according to Girard, simply "confound[ed] abundance with superfluity."[48]

In making this distinction between real and apparent synonyms, Girard was thus providing a response to the common charge that French was not as copious as other languages. He circumvented the criticism by arguing that, while French admittedly had a smaller lexicon, it could, in the hands of an artful speaker, nevertheless capture delicate and fine nuances of meaning that other, more superfluous languages missed. Girard noted that even the same word could have slightly different meanings when used in different contexts or circumstances. "That which displeases in the repetition of words," he wrote, "is the repetition of ideas, not sounds. It is even sometimes good to use the same word over again rather than another when the context in which we use it introduces a contrast, however slight, in the

---

drops of water from the same spring, when it comes to taste." Girard, *La justesse de la langue françoise,* xxvi–xxix. Girard concluded that "if one takes the term *synonym* in the [narrow] sense, I do not believe that there are any synonymous words in any language" (xxx). He added that "to convince ourselves, we must only reflect attentively, as I have done, on all that we call synonyms, on the different circumstances and the different places where they can be used. I doubt not that people who will have taste sense very well that there is a choice to be made in the use of these words; that it is sometimes one word that has more grace, and sometimes the other one; and consequently this cannot come from anything besides the difference of their meaning" (xxxi–xxxii).

47. Antoine Arnauld and Pierre Nicole had discussed the semantic importance of such "accessory ideas" in 1662. See their *La logique ou l'art de penser* (Paris: Flammarion, 1970), 129–139.

48. Girard, *La justesse de la langue françoise,* xxxv–xxxvii.

French Levity   153

meanings."⁴⁹ Girard's semantic project was therefore to distinguish and untangle the nuances of meaning between words *esteemed* synonymous. Girard's dictionary of synonyms was very popular, especially among Enlightenment thinkers, went through several editions, and gave rise to many imitators.⁵⁰ His project directly influenced the eighteenth-century concern with the abuse of words and in clarifying their meanings.⁵¹ Unlike the very similar Lockean project for clearing up the semantic confusion of words, the synonymy project that Girard and his imitators undertook tended to revel in words with equivocal meanings. It also reflected many early modern thinkers' belief that the words of certain languages lent themselves better than those of others to finely nuanced and amusingly witty uses that promoted polite and sociable conversation.

An essay by François Thomas Chastel that competed against Rivarol's for the Berlin Academy's prize in 1784 repeated this claim that French words contained such an abundance of meaning that they could mean one thing while saying another. Given this characteristic, he argued, they lent themselves to precisely those lighter modes of polite sociability that

---

49. Ibid., xli–xlii

50. Voltaire wrote, "[T]he book of Synonyms will be around as long as the language and will even serve to keep the language alive." Quoted from Pierre Swiggers, introduction to *Les Vrais Principes de la Langue Françoise,* by Gabriel Girard (Genève: Librairie Droz, 1982), 15. Girard's dictionary had a direct influence on, among others, Duclos, Jaucourt, d'Alembert, Condillac, Rivarol, and Mauvillon. See ibid., 15. The only book-length study of the history of synonymy to date is Werner Hüllen's *A History of Roget's Theasurus: Origins, Development, and Design* (Oxford: Oxford University Press, 2004).

51. This project, though closely related to Locke's, also was not inspired by it, as some have suggested. In fact, Jacques Proust argues that it was Girard's project, rather than Locke's, that inspired much of the eighteenth-century interest in the "abuse of words" and in clearly defining words. He writes that Diderot "dreamed of a second *Encyclopédie,* one where the materials dispersed in the first one would be taken up anew from top to bottom." Proust quotes Jacques-André Naigeon (1738–1810), who wrote, "Diderot had conceived early on the plan of a work of which he never lost sight, and whose project even took on some importance in his head as experience...came to confirm what reflection had taught him. He wanted to produce what he called the *Universal and Philosophical Dictionary of the Language:* he even dispersed in the *Encyclopédie* a great many materials that were to serve one day in the composition of this vocabulary by which he had resolved to finish his literary career." See Jacques Proust, *L'Encyclopédie* (Paris: Collection Armand Colin, 1965), 177–178. According to Jeanette Gefriaud-Rosso, while Diderot was extremely interested in ideas about language in general, it was "especially that domain of grammar belonging to synonyms that he placed well above the others." See Jeanette Gefriaud-Rosso, "L'Encyclopédie, la femme et la grammaire," in *Éclectisme et cohérences des Lumières: Mélanges offerts à Jean Ehrard,* ed. Jean-Louis Jam, 79–89 (Paris: Librairie Nizet, 1992), 79.

guarded against violent disputes. He wrote, "The words that have double entendres are the causes of French gaiety.... No nation has so many words whose meanings are almost the same; the Englishman finds our language rich because the same word, having almost the same pronunciation, can signify opposite things." To this abundance of meaning contained by individual French words Chastel attributed the special French tendency to "word plays that are so pleasant" and "puns." He argued that this linguistic levity "decorates pleasantry, maintains the conversation of Frenchmen, and, during dinner parties produces courteous gaiety." Chastel concluded that "the French owe a great deal of their affability to their language; the one who speaks it is deliciously aroused by an agreeable idea, which is what the different meanings of each word produce."[52]

In making this claim in his essay on the universality of the French language, Chastel was merely repeating remarks made earlier in the century by the Marquis de Bièvre (1747–1789) in his article "Kalembour" in the *Supplément à l'Encyclopédie* (1777). In this entry, Bièvre wrote that although "all the languages of the world necessarily furnish an ample material for ambiguities," "there is no other language, either living or dead, that lends itself more to the pun than the French language." "The French," he added, "pun every day without even realizing it."[53] In his *Dissertation sur les jeux de mots*, which was not published until 1799, as part of his *Biévriana, ou Jeux de mots de M. de Bièvre*, Bièvre explicitly linked the French facility for wordplay and double meaning that many believed so essential to polite conversation and sociability to the French language's lack of copiousness. "Of all the languages of Europe," he wrote, "the French lends itself best to conversation, because the words follow the order of ideas; but it is also the most abundant in homonyms. This vice, joined to the taste of a refined wit [*bel esprit*], has given rise to all the wordplays with which our talk swarms."[54]

---

52. Franz Thomas Chastel, "Les Peuples du Nord Réfléchissent la lumiére," in Académie de Berlin, *De l'universalité Européenne de la langue française*, 20.

53. Marquis de Bièvre, *Calembours et autres jeux sur les mots d'esprit,* ed. Antoine de Baecque (Paris: Éditions Payot et Rivages, 2000), 43.

54. Ibid., 53.

One of the earliest French dictionaries of homonyms, a work that Louis Philipon-de-la-Madelaine (1734–1818) published at the very end of the eighteenth century, repeated the claim that the French owed their national tendency to witty sociability to the restricted lexicon of their language.[55] While he admitted that the comparatively small lexicon of the French language could be "an inconvenience," Philipon-de-la-Madelaine also insisted that "on the other hand, it generates those felicitous plays on words that the French seize so promptly and repeat with so much pleasure. Our language owes to homonyms its puns...: for the secret of the pun consists almost uniquely in decomposing the expression, or in reconstructing it in another meaning."[56] Philipon-de-la-Madelaine argued that when puns are used appropriately, "they vary, they animate, and they brighten up any conversation; they bring out that kind of big laugh, for which the philosopher may have a greater need than the common people."[57] According to one prominent discursive tradition, then, the French language, as Jaucourt wrote, spread "a charming amusement that is pleasing to all peoples."[58]

Bel Esprit

This common characterization of French as a language that contributes to the légèreté of the national character, laid a foundation for, or at the very least reinforced, claims about the distinctive ways in which French speakers communicated. Many agreed that French facilitated a special kind of semantic polyvalence or equivocation that made the language especially suited to gallantry, wit, and *esprit*. In her study of the stylistic tensions between *le goût moderne* and *le grand goût* in eighteenth-century France, Elena Russo shows how the increasingly controversial figure of the *bel esprit* was defined by precisely the kind of witty and

---

55. See Louis Philipon-de-la-Madelaine, *Homonymes Français, ou Mots qui dans notre langue se ressemblent par le son et diffèrent par le sens* (Paris: Capelle et Renand, 1806), 12.
56. Ibid., 12–13.
57. Ibid., 14. In this discussion of punning, Philipon-de-la-Madelaine explicitly referred to Bièvre (13).
58. Chevalier de Jaucourt, "Langue françoise," 9:266.

light communication for which many claimed the French language was especially suited.[59]

According to Russo, from the mid-seventeenth to the early eighteenth century, "the *bel esprit*...successfully embodied the synthesis between worldliness and verbal virtuosity." A bel esprit, like Pierre Carlet de Chamblain de Marivaux (1688–1763), rejected overtly serious topics and was preoccupied with surprising his audiences by communicating subtle and delicate nuances of meaning, even to the point of reveling in apparent antitheses, oxymorons, and paradoxes. Although the eighteenth century saw a growing ambivalence in some circles, particularly in the *partie philosophique,* the group of thinkers most closely identified with the high Enlightenment, toward the figure of the bel esprit, a great many persisted in celebrating the witty and light character of French speakers in general and the French language in particular.

The bel esprit's witty communication preeminently took the form of amusing polite conversations that, according to many, both brightened and enlightened sociable gatherings. Etienne Mayet's essay for the Berlin Academy's prize in 1784 argued that over time "the natural Courtesy and politeness of the French" had embedded itself in the very structure of the French language. He argued that the French language had taken on the polite, affable, courteous, and witty quality of its speakers to such a degree that the French nation had come to be admired by other nations for "the finesse of its expressions." Mayet concluded that French had earned a permanently preeminent place among the European languages, "by the great richness of its words,...the sweetness of its pronunciation, the harmony of its diction, its facility for...a polite and sociable wit that is the instinctive share of the French. This is a merit...and a pleasure that other nations know they lack. The French language more than any other is the one that expresses with the greatest facility, neatness, and delicacy, all the objects of the civilization of a polite people, and in this way it contributes across Europe to the great pleasures of life." Predominant among these great pleasures of life was

---

59. Russo characterizes the *goût moderne* as a gallant, playful, witty, self-referential, and frequently dissonant use of contrarieties and contrasts. Some of its most representative exemplars were Fontenelle, Marivaux, Montesquieu, and Voltaire. The partisans of the *grand goût* rejected this kind of witty discourse in favor of a sublime, serious, and energetic patriotic grand style. See Elena Russo, *Styles of Enlightenment* (Baltimore: Johns Hopkins University Press, 2007), 9.

the polite and sociable conversation that some French thinkers believed to be at the very core of learning.[60] Claims about the légèreté of the French language, therefore, also grounded the frequent claims, such as Voltaire's, that the language was suited above all to conversation.[61] Sharing Voltaire's growing ambivalence about the language's character as light and clear but also weak, de Jaucourt wrote that French was "a language made for men who are more agreeable than sublime, more sensual than passionate, and more superficial than profound."[62]

One of the central themes of Voltaire's *Siècle de Louis XIV* (1752) is the contrast he drew between the barbarous ferocity and violence of the sixteenth and early seventeenth centuries and the triumph of a polite sociability during the second half of the seventeenth century. He wrote that "all the previous stages had been recognizable by the defects that characterized them." By the end of Louis XIV's reign, however, "politeness triumphed in all conditions." Voltaire concluded one of his chapters on progress in the arts by noting that "the spirit of sociability is the natural lot of the French." "The French language is of all the languages," he wrote, "the one that expresses with greater facility, neatness, and delicacy, everything in the conversation of polite people; and as such it contributes throughout Europe to one of the greatest charms of life."[63]

In answering the question, "[W]hat must one do to speak and write well?" Eugène says that "by frequenting polite people, one without noticing it takes I-know-not-what tincture of politeness that books cannot provide; it is only in fine conversations that one learns to speak both nobly and naturally."[64] Bouhours thus argued that "those who do nothing but read and who never encounter high society are not sufficiently polished and usually do not have that easy and natural appearance that is so much

---

60. Etienne Mayet, "Est brevitate opus…," 79, 79–80, and 102.

61. Voltaire, *Œuvres complètes de Voltaire,* ed. Louis Moland (Paris: Garnier Frères, 1879), 19:245.

62. Chevalier de Jaucourt, "Langue françoise," 9:266. Jaucourt complained about the French language's lack of energy: "Let us admit the truth; the speech of polite Frenchmen is nothing but a weak and gentle singing; let us admit it, our tongue…does not have a noble boldness of images, nor pompous cadences, nor those grand movements that could represent marvels; it is not epic; its auxiliary verbs, its articles, its uniform march, its lack of inversions are a hindrance to the enthusiasm of poetry."

63. Voltaire, *Oeuvres Complètes,* 14:534, 547, and 554–555.

64. Bouhours, *Entretiens d'Ariste et d'Eugène,* 124.

in fashion." In his essay on conversation, Morellet argued that "if, among all the nations of Europe, the French nation is the one where we find the greatest sociability, this is because we converse more in France than in any other country in the world."[65] This polite conversation and the forms of civilized sociability that it generated, he argued, represented one of the "powerful causes of the perfecting of the human species."[66] Morellet, like Voltaire and many of his French contemporaries, argued that the polite and witty conversation that contributed to French sociability was facilitated by the virtues of the French language. In Morellet's idealization of civilizing conversation, he compared speakers to butterflies who moved lightly from one flower to another. An ideally enlightened and civilized conversation, he therefore argued, would display "a light rapport and a slightly marked tie between the ideas." This lightness, he added, would "be sufficient to render the conversation reasonable without being grave and light without being foolish."[67] In this little tract on conversation, Morellet summarized in a very short compass a thoroughly developed conception of the mutually reinforcing links among the French language, French wit and learning, and the French national character, each of which was both clear and light.

In his essay for the Berlin Academy's prize, Friedrich Melchior Grimm (1723–1807) directly quoted Voltaire's *Siècle de Louis XIV* to argue that the "beauty" of the French language proceeded in tandem with the cultural changes that had occurred since the seventeenth century: "the extreme easiness in the commerce of the polite world, the affability, the simplicity, and the culture of wit, have made Paris a city which is, for the sweet life, better than Rome and Athens in the days of their greatness." Grimm, like many others, argued that the violent European wars of the previous centuries should be considered civil wars that had been facilitated, if not entirely caused, by the misunderstandings and disputes generated in part by problems of communication.[68] Grimm argued that "there is nobody who cannot see that, when the different peoples of Europe had begun to learn and to speak our language, they had the following motives: for some

---

65. André Morellet, *De la Conversation*, 36.
66. Ibid., 37.
67. Ibid., 69.
68. Ibid., 112.

it was charming amusement, which is to say that joy, that pleasure, that drunkenness, which foreigners feel in the company of Frenchmen and of our performances, where a certain *je ne sçais quoi,* which is easier to experience than to define, seems to carry away and ravish our neighbors." Although Grimm introduced these cultural characteristics as external ones that made people want to learn the language, he went on to argue that these characteristics were in reality only the *products* of speaking the French language itself. He wrote that "simplicity of manners and affability" "are the necessary effects of a pure language"; that "if we consider the French language along with the manners of the nation, we will see that the proprieties of the language and those of the manners have such a connection and such an affinity, that they, so to speak, lend a hand to each other." To develop this argument, Grimm pointed to the shared fate of Latin and Rome. "This mutual bond of language and manners is so certain," he wrote, "that even Rome, once the capital of the world, so polite and so admired in the century of Augustus, did not witness the degeneration of manners...until the purity of the language...began to change." Grimm could therefore suggest that other European princes, "admirers of Louis and of Frederick, who know the nobility, the sweetness, and the elegance of the French tongue, will always glory in being able to understand and to speak it."[69]

These links among learning, conversation, and language had important implications for the way many late-seventeenth- and eighteenth-century French thinkers conceived of certain cultural practices. Many suggested, for example, that learning could best be promoted through oral conversations rather than written texts. These conversations, moreover, should neither be too pedantic and heavy nor exclude articulate women. As Michèle Cohen points out, "the most consummate expression of *politesse* was in conversation. Women were seen as the natural means to the achievement of this ideal because of their refined and delicate manners, their 'natural aversion to coarseness' and, according to Vaugelas, the purity of their French."[70]

---

69. Friedrich Melchior Grimm, "Sublata causa tollitur effectus," in Académie de Berlin, *De l'universalité Européenne de la langue française,* 110, 112, 113–114, 117, and 121.

70. Michèle Cohen, *Fashioning Masculinity: National Identity and Language in the Eighteenth Century* (London: Routledge, 1996), 13. Cohen rightly cautions against drawing anachronistic conclusions about women's status or "feminism" in old regime France. She notes, "While [women] clearly had a crucial role bearing in important ways on the cultural life and manners of the nobles

Although he was among those who complained most bitterly and most famously about women's roles as participants in French salon conversations, Rousseau also remarked in his *Émile* (1762) that women's tongues were more flexible than men's, that girls began to speak at a younger age, and that they did so more easily and agreeably than boys.[71]

In Voltaire's account of French linguistic refinement, the aristocratic Parisian women who established their famous salons, which he called "schools of politeness," were the main agents of linguistic and cultural refinement. He wrote that "decency, for which they were obliged principally to the women who gathered high society around them, made *les esprits* more agreeable."[72] As Bell notes, "for most French authors, the civilized traits of sociability, *légèreté*, and politeness reflected the extraordinary influence of women...to whom vivaciousness and love of society came naturally [and who] ruled French *moeurs*, obliging men to strive to please them."[73] Rivarol, like many others, formally contrasted British and French conversation by noting that women were excluded from the former. "In England," he wrote, "men live very much with one another; also the women who have not left the domestic space, cannot be seen on the tableau of the nation; but one would only be painting the French from profile if they were to paint the tableau without [the women]."[74]

In his essay that shared the Berlin Academy's prize in 1784, Johann Christoph Schwab noted that "what contributes more than anything else to giving French its playful and light character, is the liberty that

---

and the ways these were produced, we should not allow the importance of the role to obscure its nature: it was oriented not to the women's production of her self, but to the production of the...honnête homme....These women's conversation...was ultimately productive of gender difference, not power" (14).

71. Jeanette Geffriaud-Rosso, "L'*Encyclopédie,* la femme, et la grammaire," in Jam, *Écclectisme et cohérences des Lumières,* 81. In his *Letter to d'Alembert on the Theater* (1758), after he applauded the ancients for their having kept men and women in strictly separate spheres, Rousseau commented, "As for us, we have taken on entirely contrary ways; meanly devoted to the wills of the sex which we ought to protect and not serve, we have learned to despise it in obeying it....Every woman at Paris gathers in her apartment a harem of men more womanish than she." Jean-Jacques Rousseau, *Politics and the Arts: Letter to M. d'Alembert on the Theatre,* trans. Allan Bloom (Ithaca: Cornell University Press, 1968), 101.

72. Voltaire, *Oeuvres Complètes,* 14:546.

73. Bell, *The Cult of the Nation in France,* 148–149.

74. Rivarol, "L'Universalité de la langue française," 146.

exists between the sexes."⁷⁵ In fact, in her *British Synonymy*, a dictionary inspired by Girard's work, Hester Lynch Piozzi (1741–1821), a friend of the famous English lexicographer Samuel Johnson, suggested that "while men teach to write with propriety, a woman may at worst be qualified— through long practice—to direct the choice of phrases in familiar talk."⁷⁶ Piozzi added that "although the final cause of definition is to fix the true and adequate meaning of words…; yet *here* we must not suffer ourselves to be so detained, as synonymy has more to do with elegance than truth—And I well remember an observation made by my earliest, perhaps my truest friend, Doctor Arthur Collier, that women should learn rhetorick in order to persuade their husbands, while men studied to render themselves good logicians, for the sake of obtaining arms against female oratory."⁷⁷ Thus, the eighteenth-century conception of French as a language that promoted elegant manners and light sociability while perfecting the mind through polite conversation also necessarily included certain women speakers.

To the extent that eighteenth-century French communication was carried on in print, the preferred genres were often what French thinkers called *oeuvres badines, feuilles volantes,* and *pièces fugitives:* playful, short, fleeting and witty writings that mirrored and facilitated the light sociability of conversation. In fact, Chastel argued that French "novels" and "light stories" helped "the French language to acquire an Empire like that of [French] fashions by its frivolity." "Our novels and light stories," he wrote, "have attracted to us the superficial people…; let us admit it, it is to the soft manners, to the congeniality of the French and to the superiority of their theaters that their language owes its universality, just as it is to their good taste, to their elegance, to that superiority in the design employed for amusement that the fashions of France owe their being so widespread."⁷⁸ While Chastel saw the popularity of the French language as resulting from a national tendency to légèreté, Johann Christoph

---

75. Johann Christoph Schwab, "Dissertation sur la langue françoise," in Académie de Berlin, *De l'universalité Européenne de la langue française,* 429 n. 47.
76. Hester Lynch Piozzi, *British Synonymy* (London: Printed for G. G. and J. Robinson, 1794), 1:ii.
77. Ibid., 1:v–vi.
78. Franz Thomas Chastel, "Les Peuples du Nord Réfléchissent la Lumière," in Académie de Berlin, *De l'universalité Européenne de la langue française,* 18.

Schwab argued that the French language promoted what he called "that part of literature designated under the denomination 'light genre' or fugitive pieces."[79] Rivarol similarly argued that French lent itself especially well to "fugitive works that fly from mouth to mouth and give wings to the French language." "The first newspapers that circulated in Europe were French," he added in pointing to a quintessentially modern genre of fugitive writing, "and they related nothing more than our victories and our masterpieces. We kept in touch through our academies and the language spread itself with their correspondence."[80] Bièvre noted that "severe critics" complained that puns suffered when they were written down. He argued, however, that "it is in no way a genre that finds itself more at home in conversation than in a book.... It is always sure of its effect, even in spite of the spelling, when it is seasoned with some salt, or it presents to the mind a really pleasant contrast."[81]

Claims about the légèreté of the French tongue seemed thus to suggest also that it lent itself to the pointed epigrams, or *inscriptiones argutae*, that had been used commonly for the temporary monuments that Colbert and others had criticized as being too transient to timelessly transmit royal glory.[82] Baret de Villencour argued that "France's gaiety and gallantry have made [its language] appropriate for epigrammatic flashes of wit.... These flashes of French wit are brilliant meteors whose beams of light always astonish and please."[83] As early modern treatises on the epigram almost never failed to point out, the "epigram is a descendant of the inscription."[84] Theorists of the epigram, furthermore, insisted that French epigrams in particular should always have a "conceit" or "point."[85] The supposed

---

79. See Schwab, "Dissertation sur la langue françoise," 422.
80. See Rivarol, "L'Universalité de la langue française," 156.
81. Bièvre, *Calembours et autres jeux sur les mots d'esprit,* 39–40.
82. According to John Sparrow, around the beginning of the sixteenth century, some inscriptions took the character of witty writing, or *argutezza*. "Composers had begun to infuse into their imitations of classical inscriptions unclassical strains of feeling and turns of expression." John Sparrow, *Visible Words: A Study of Inscriptions in and as Books and Works of Art* (Cambridge: Cambridge University Press 1969), 103. Sparrow notes that by the end of the 1670s the modern form of witty inscriptions had transformed the epigraphic scene (106).
83. Villencour, *Discours Public sur les langues en general,* 63.
84. See, for example, Guillaume Colletet (1596–1659), *Traité de l'épigramme* (Paris: Antoine de Sommaville, 1658), 13.
85. As James Hutton noted, by the end of the seventeenth century in France, "point" "mostly assume[d] the form of a play on words, if this expression be taken to include not merely puns, but

légèreté of the French tongue, which made its words so abundant in subtly contrasting meanings, thus made it especially suited to the pointed wit required for the specifically French form of epigrams.

The linguistic claims that French légèreté facilitated wordplay thus laid a linguistic foundation for the belief that French speakers excelled in composing epigrams to wittily commemorate fleeting events, ranging from lovers' quarrels and quarrels in the republic of letters to controversies in the political sphere. Perhaps no French writer captured this belief better than Louis-Sebastien Mercier (1740–1814), who complained that "there is no event which, among this mocking people, is not 'recorded' by vaudevilles. Its character is always turned to the epigram." Mercier noted that "in Paris everything is subject to a little ditty; and anyone, be he a general in the French army or a condemned man, who has not been made the subject of such a ditty will remain forever unknown among the people [*au peuple*]."[86] Thus Colbert's failed project to build permanent monuments animated by French inscriptions to persistently inform posterity was superseded by claims that the French language should be celebrated for facilitating the playful delights of epigrammatic and fugitive commemoration that were the calling card of the bel esprit.

As Russo notes, the bel esprit came under increasingly hostile attack beginning around the middle of the century by thinkers associated with the high Enlightenment. These thinkers frequently criticized the French language for lacking either the lexical linearity that Locke intended his project to correct or the capacity for an energetic eloquence of the kind frequently identified with savage speech. And yet the celebration of the sonic sweetness and lexical lightness of the French language persisted well into the late eighteenth century. In fact, the relative merits of the language became one of the significant issues that divided the philosophes and their enemies. While some philosophes complained that it was inadequately clear or energetic, other thinkers argued that, as a preeminently soft, sweet and light language, it had the qualities that had given France a greater share of civilized communication than any other nation.

---

also, for example, a clever discrimination of synonyms." James Hutton, *The Greek Anthology in France* (Ithaca: Cornell University Press, 1946), 54 n. 11.

86. Louis-Sebastien Mercier, *Tableau de Paris* (Amsterdam, 1782–1788), 1:301; 6:42.

Rivarol "On the Universality of the French Language"

Among the most representative of the antiphilosophes to develop this argument was Rivarol, who won the Berlin Academy's prize awarded in 1784 for the essay that best answered the following questions: "What has made French the universal language of Europe? What has earned it this preference? Can it be presumed that it will keep this same preference?"[87] Rivarol, like most who competed for the Berlin Academy's prize, surveyed the European "nations" and their languages and insisted that in doing so "one can see the character of peoples and the genius of their language keeping pace with one another and the one is always the guarantor of the other." He added that "if we can judge a man by his words, we can also judge a nation by its language." After sketching what he took to be the inferior geniuses of the German, Spanish, and Italian, Rivarol turned to "the two people...for whom everything differs, climate, language, government, vices and virtues; these neighbors and rivals, who, after having disputed for three hundred years, not who would rule, but who would exist, who continue to dispute the glory of letters, and who have shared for the past century the attention of the universe." Rivarol meant, of course, the English and the French, and he wrote, "[L]et us oppose the [English] language to our own, their literature to our literature, and let us justify the choice of the universe."[88]

Rivarol thus set out to judge linguistic excellence by comparing the French and English languages and the national characters they reflected

---

87. Antoine de Baecque has argued that "the Enlightenment is an *age of laughter*, for a specific culture constituted itself around the fact of laughter, with all its practices and its representations." De Baecque recognizes, however, that Bièvre was among the enemies of the so-called *partie philosophique:* "Fighting against the party of the philosophes in the name of the tradition of French wit, the marquis de Bièvre inscribed himself into a merciless fight, that which the satirists, the 'satirical faction,' carried on against the philosophes." Among the members of this anti-philosophe faction de Baecque includes Rivarol. Bièvre's quarrel with the philosophes resulted from his belief that this gay Enlightenment was being threatened by an ironically overheated enthusiasm for the coldness of clarity. De Baecque quotes Bièvre: "A century where everything fades under a cold analysis, where wit, by the force of reasoning, decomposes itself, denatures itself, and is left without any character even by the mania of having one. But this last one is that of *seriousness*." Antoine de Baecque, "Un chevalier du bel esprit," in Bièvre, *Calembours et autres jeux sur les mots d'esprit,* 11, 14, and 15. De Baecque characterizes this tension between Bièvre's witty punning and the philosophes' cold clarity as one of "the contradictions of the Enlightenment" (12).

88. Rivarol, "L'Universalité de la langue française," 141, 143, and 148.

and reinforced. Like other eighteenth-century French thinkers, Rivarol characterized English as more energetic than French. He wrote, "[W]e can say...that if English has the audacity of the languages of inversion, it also has their obscurity, and its syntax is so bizarre that the rule sometimes has fewer applications than exceptions." If Rivarol merely captured with greater aphoristic flare a commonplace of characterizations of the French language as being especially clear, he did not stop there. Besides being exceptionally *clear*, Rivarol argued, French is also exceptionally *light*. He claimed that "the pronunciation of the French language...is...sweeter than [that of] the languages of the North." Rivarol also rejected the claim that the commonplace of French légèreté or inconstancy should be understood as a defect. While he accepted that the French were especially inconstant, like others before him, he interpreted this lightness in purely positive terms by connecting it to the superiority of French civility, refinement, and politeness. "The Englishman, being dry and taciturn," he wrote,

> adds to confusion and timidity..., an impatience and a dislike of everything...; the Frenchman, however, has a spark of gaiety that never leaves him.... The Frenchman seeks the pleasant side of life; the Englishman seems always to be attending a tragedy.... France has politeness and grace; and... it furnishes the models in customs, manners, and appearances.... It is to always please others that the Frenchman always changes; it is to not be too displeasing to himself that the Englishman is forced to change.... Finally, if it is possible that the Frenchman has only bought so much grace and taste at the expense of his manners, it is even more possible that the Englishman has lost his without acquiring either taste or grace.

For Rivarol, the especially light and reasonable French national character was reflected in and reinforced by the peculiarities of the French tongue.[89]

Light for the World: Raising France's Commercial Empire

Rivarol's essay is also interesting in the way it linked the character of the language to what he argued was the unique character of the French

---

89. Ibid., 160, 168, and 145–147. The connection between linguistic energy and savagery that was the subject of part 2 is suggested by Rivarol's claim that England was slower than France "in emerging from barbarity" (159).

Empire and in the way that it reflected his understanding of his own individual relationship with the French language. Rivarol's essay explicitly linked linguistic perfection and the success of France's commercial empire. From the outset of his essay, he compared and contrasted the Roman and French empires, writing, "The time seems to have come to say the *French world,* just as once we said the *Roman world.*" He drew a sharp distinction between the French and Roman worlds, however, by noting that the French world was a "uniform and peaceful empire of letters that extends itself over the variety of peoples and which [is] more durable and stronger than the empire of weapons." Rivarol contrasted the Roman Empire, as an empire of violent conquest, with the French Empire, as an empire of peaceful and emulative cultural dissemination. Discussing the "explosion" of French commercial culture, he noted that it gave "a theater, clothes, taste, manners, a language, a new art of living and previously unknown pleasures to the states that surround [France], a sort of empire that no people has ever exercised before." This new type of empire, he argued, was entirely unlike "that of the Romans, who planted their language and slavery everywhere, who fattened themselves with blood and destroyed until they were themselves destroyed!"[90]

As Rivarol pointed out toward the beginning of his essay, however, he was interested in comparing the French language and empire not so much with Latin and the Roman Empire as with the English language and the British Empire. As Rivarol characterized the foundation of the British Empire, however, it closely resembled that of the Roman Empire as predominantly built on military conquest and selfish gain. Rivarol characterized the British people as exhibiting a "spirit of anxiety and impatience" that easily turned to violence. This spirit, he argued, led the British to be inwardly violent. He cited as evidence the bloody English civil wars that led to the execution of Charles I. Rivarol added that when this coarse and violent character "[burst] outwardly," Britain imperially and imperiously imposed itself and its language on the world. British commerce, "which has branched itself out into the four corners of the globe, has resulted in the fact that [Britain] can be hurt in a thousand different ways, and the reasons for war will never be missing for her. Thus to all the esteem that

---

90. Ibid., 129 and 157.

one cannot refuse to a powerful and enlightened nation, people always join a little hatred, mixed with fear and envy." Rivarol thus cast the British as being threatened because their empire, as he understood it, was predicated upon the necessity to import foreign goods and with them the cultural and linguistic character of the peoples who produced them.[91]

Rivarol did not only point to the nature of the French language as a guarantor against commercial corruption. He argued that France's commercial empire operated in a very different way from Britain's. Ignoring the fact that France had overseas territories, Rivarol wrote that the "spirit of conquest" was incompatible with France's "interests" and "genius." This was because "the whole world needs France, while England needs the whole world.... France has attracted more by its charms than by its wealth; ... her empire has been that of taste." "When one reigns by opinion," he asked, "does one need any other empire?"[92] France, in other words, was able to export its culture because it reflected the charming, sweet, and light character of the French language, which made it so attractive to everyone, while Britain had to force itself on the world to import goods and with them words to enrich its language.

After discussing the "productions of the mind," the literature that France produced from the Renaissance to his own day, Rivarol noted how these were joined with the "productions of industry." He wrote that French "pompons and fashions accompanied our books to foreign countries, because people everywhere have wanted to be reasonable and frivolous as in France. Consequently, our neighbors, while constantly receiving our endlessly changing fashions, furniture, fabrics, lacked terms with which to describe them; they were so overwhelmed by the exuberance of French industry that..., in order not to be separated from us, others studied our language from all sides." For Rivarol, then, the French commercial empire was to be distinguished from the Roman and British empires, which were founded on military conquest and the despoilment of foreign countries for their riches and their words. Again, comparing the French and British commercial empires, Rivarol wrote that "England always goes to do its commerce among different peoples, and no one ever goes to [England] to do theirs. Thus the one who travels never gives his language; he rather

---

91. Ibid., 143–144.
92. Ibid., 144–145.

would take that of others: yet it is almost without ever leaving home that the Frenchman has extended his [language]." Rivarol thus attributed the French language's greater universality over that of English to what he perceived to be differences between their respective commercial empires. In his view, while the British, like the martial Romans before them, were interested only in acquiring what others possessed, the French were content to offer the world the best of what they produced.[93]

Rivarol supplemented his argument that the unique form of the French commercial empire resulted in the extension of the French language with an argument that the structural properties of the language contributed to its universality. He wrote that "if we supposed that, by its location, England did not find itself relegated to the Ocean and that it could attract its neighbors, it is nonetheless likely that its language and its literature would not have been able to be chosen by Europe, for there are no objections against the German language that are not also applicable against English." According to Rivarol, these linguistic characteristics of the English language "render it less appropriate for conversation than the French language, which has a pace that is so easy and so disengaged."[94]

Rivarol's Rise: Proper Names in Their Proper Places

The conception of the French language as contributing to the levity and therefore perfection of sociable conversation may also have affected the way Rivarol viewed his own rise to literary prominence from relatively modest circumstances in a provincial corner of France. Whether we see Rivarol, as his enemies did, as the poor son of a provincial innkeeper trying to write his way into the pantheon or, as he truly was, the son of a successful bourgeois father who had himself climbed from the status of innkeeper to that of tax farmer, Rivarol was among those who were not recognized as noble.[95] When he arrived in Paris from the Midi, he was perceived as being

---

93. Ibid., 156–157 and 159. Rivarol also wrote that "toward the end of the [seventeenth] century,... England disengaged itself from France's rays and shined with its own light.... Its language had enriched itself, as did its commerce, from the spoils of nations" (158–159).

94. Ibid., 160.

95. His grandfather, Antoine-Roche, though he may have been noble, when he fled from Italy to the south of France to take up the role of innkeeper, described himself as a "marchand boutonnier." Rivarol's father, Jean-Baptiste, thus joined "the ranks of the provincial bourgeoisie."

the son of a modest innkeeper. As such, Rivarol attempted to make his name in the conversational world of the Parisian salons, and within a short time he was being sought out precisely for his art of conversation.[96] Rivarol has been described as "the marvelous *chatterer* of his day." He once declared in a letter to a friend that "he [did] not like 'texts.'"[97] Rivarol turned to the conversable world of the salons, where he could make his name as a wit. In these salons he no doubt encountered some of the bright lights of the enlightened Parisian literati, like Buffon, Sieyès, Condorcet, Diderot, Grimm, and Rousseau.

Rivarol explicitly linked the polite, sociable, and enlightened world of Paris to conversation and contrasted it with the bookish and pedantic tedium of provincial life. He described Paris as "the city in which people most ignore...the existence of a crowd of books." "One must have lived in the province," he noted, "to have read a great deal. In Paris, the mind maintains and enlarges itself in the swift sphere of events and of conversations; in the provinces, it can only subsist on readings: also a person selects people in the capital whereas in the provinces one merely chooses books."[98] Given Rivarol's penchant for the world of salon conversation, it is not surprising to find that he insisted that the French language was suited more than any other for polite conversation. Italian and German had too many "ceremonious forms, enemies of conversation," while English, Rivarol insisted, was "less adequate for conversation than the French language."[99]

Although he inherited his father's inn, Jean-Baptiste worked as an innkeeper for only about four years. Besides being an innkeeper for this short period, Jean-Baptiste also worked in the silk industry. See Michel Cointat, *Rivarol (1753–1801): Un écrivain controversé* (Paris: L'Harmattan, 2001), 25–31 and 75–78.

96. The apocryphal story of Rivarol's appearance on the Parisian scene in 1777 is that one day soon after his arrival in Paris, he wandered through the Jardin de Luxembourg. Curious visitors to the garden happened to be looking at the renovations to the Palais Médicis. After hearing a good deal of nonsense from this group, Antoine spoke up and gave a discourse on gnomonic theory. Afterwards he received an ovation, and an old man tapped him on the shoulder, telling him, "That was very good.... Are you planning to be a scientist?" "Sir," Rivarol responded, "I have come to Paris hoping to make a name for myself in the world. I admit, however, that my mind leans somewhat more toward literature than to the exact sciences." "Come to see me.... I am the one who had this sundial constructed. I am d'Alembert." See Cointat, *Rivarol*, 41.

97. Ibid., 46.

98. Quoted from Bernard Faÿ, *Rivarol et la Révolution* (Paris: Librairie Académique Perrin, 1978), 48.

99. Rivarol, "L'universalité de la langue française," 140, 160.

In contrast to these others, Rivarol claimed that French, "free of all the protocols that the contemptible and low have invented for vanity and that the weak have invented for power, is more suited to conversation, the bond of men and the charm of all ages."[100]

Rivarol also took the special characteristics of the French language to be the guarantor of a stratified speech community. Rivarol placed a gap between higher and lower strata in the community of French speakers. He wrote that "when in the capital an immense mass of people can constantly mingle without ever becoming the same as one another, then we can begin to distinguish as many nuances in the language as in the society; the delicate nature of proceedings leads to that of propositions;... such is what occurred during the first years of the reign of Louis XIV. The weight of the royal authority put every person in his place." He also argued that "if it is the laboring part of a nation that creates all the words and all the expressions with which the arts and trades have enriched languages, it is the leisured part that chooses and that reigns." "Work and rest," he added, "are for the former, while leisure and pleasure are for the latter.... It is to the boredom of a leisured people, that art owes its progresses and its finesses.... Anything is good enough for men of study and labor who seek nothing more in the evening than a relaxing escape in spectacles and art; but, for the souls that are exasperated by pleasures and weary of rest, there is a constant need for new attitudes and for ever more exquisite sensations." Rivarol's distinction between those who worked and sought rest on the one hand and those who rested and sought flashes of amusement on the other hand, corresponded to the distinction between the life of the bourgeois and artisan on the one hand and the life of the aristocrat on the other. Rivarol suggested that the French language separated these two groups into their appropriate respective places. Indeed, he went on to link this issue to "that reproach of poverty and of extreme delicacy that is often made against the French language." Rivarol responded to this reproach by writing that "no doubt, it is difficult to express everything with nobility; but there you have precisely that which in a sense constitutes its character. Styles are ranked in our language, just like the subjects are in our monarchy... and it is by way of this hierarchy of styles that good taste operates."[101]

---

100. Ibid., 168.
101. Ibid., 150, 171, and 171–172.

Rivarol therefore suggested that precisely because of the supposed abundance of meaning in words in the French lexicon, its speakers could be ranked into classes. In a note to this argument, Rivarol wrote, "We can divide the French into two classes, in relation to their language: the first class is of those who know [not only their language but also] the sources from which it has taken its riches; the other is of those who know only French. These two classes do not see the language from the same perspective, and do not have, as far as style is concerned, the same data."[102] Rivarol's belief that the character of the French language allowed the leisured and aristocratic language virtuoso to be ranked at the top, conformed to his own attempt to fashion himself as a noble Parisian salongoer. In 1777, when d'Alembert helped him gain entry into Parisian polite society, Rivarol adopted his grandmother's cousin's name, Deparcieux, and gave it a noble twist, calling himself the Chevalier de Parcieux. Rivarol gave up this title when the real Antoine Deparcieux forbade him from using the title and name.[103] Rivarol could, however, return to his grandfather's nobility and reclaim the status for himself. He did this very self-consciously, as the following remark of his to his father shows: "The crown that you leave at the bottom of an old trunk—and you have good reason to do so, it does not become you—I am reclaiming it. Does it not suit me perfectly? One might say it was made for me, all the more proof that it is mine. The eclipse is finished. Rivarola will be reborn."[104]

Rivarol's later opposition to the French Revolution's social leveling was thus prefigured in his prize-winning essay on the universality of the French language.[105] Rivarol believed, however, that the Revolution would lose its popular support and collapse under its own weight. "The

---

102. Ibid., 184 n. 31.
103. Cointat, *Rivarol (1753–1801),* 40. The real Antoine Deparcieux (1703–1768) was a mathematician and member of the academy. The practice of adopting a noble title was not uncommon. D'Alembert had done the same, as did Voltaire and several others. Indeed, Voltaire, who disliked the real Antoine Deparcieux, seemed to find nothing wrong with Rivarol's title when he joked, "Has it not been said that you are the nephew of Mr. Deparcieux? To be able to believe it, it would be necessary for one neither to see nor hear you." Quoted ibid., 42.
104. Quoted ibid., 43.
105. Uppermost among the factions that Rivarol blamed for the French Revolution were the philosophes. "These are the most dangerous," he wrote, "for they never keep any sense of reality and their adventurous speculations would lead us into republicanism." Quoted from Faÿ, *Rivarol et la Révolution,* 96.

National Assembly," he wrote, "cannot fail to 'depopularize' itself by its hesitant, contradictory, and partial measures.... More dangerous are the Jacobin clubs that stir the deepest sludge of the population and federate the local discontentments in order to turn them into a coherent opinion."[106] Rivarol argued that the Parisian commoners would never succeed in their Revolution and could never achieve enlightenment. "The errors of the *Capital*, or rather its crimes, are too evident: it has already furnished tragic subjects for posterity and terrible arguments to the enemies of liberty.... A curse on those who stir the depths of a nation! There is no century of enlightenment for the populace."[107] The social and political ramifications of this strand of early modern thinking about the French language are significant. Rivarol's characterization of the virtues of the French tongue contrasted sharply with inclusive conceptions of language that saw it as a vehicle for making enlightenment universal. This strand of early modern linguistics led Rivarol inexorably to embrace an exclusive conception of the French language, one that corresponded to the stratifications of ancien régime society in which there could be, as he wrote, no popular enlightenment.

Light Balloons: The French Character Weighs Itself

Rivarol ended his essay with a comment on the successful French invention of the balloon.[108] He wrote that "it is in France...that two men have found themselves between the heavens and the earth, as if they had succeeded in breaking the eternal contract that all bodies have made with it [the earth]; they have voyaged in the air, followed by shouts of admiration and the alarms of recognition. The commotion that such a spectacle has left in everyone's minds will last a long time, and, by such discoveries, physics follows in this way the imagination into its last refuges."[109] This comment suggests interesting parallels between his understanding of the French language, French intellectual culture, the French national character, and his

---

106. Ibid., 97.
107. Cointat, *Rivarol (1753–1801)*, 265.
108. On the French invention of the balloon and its deployment as a cultural icon, see Charles Coulston Gillispie, *The Montgolfier Brothers and the Invention of Aviation, 1783–1784* (Princeton: Princeton University Press, 1983).
109. Rivarol, "L'universalité de la langue française," 175.

own experience of using this especially light language to rise from modest beginnings to the heights of an amusing commercial refinement and polite sociability. In the first place, the balloon, like Rivarol's language, helped a select group of people raise themselves to great heights. Rivarol imagined the French speech community as a stratified one divided between those above and those below. Rivarol was successful in using the language to lift himself from his humble provincial origins to the rarefied heights of the sociable stratus of polite salon conversation.

More than this, the balloon represented learning as a process that resisted monotonous, ponderous, and grave investigations and communications. Learning was frequently celebrated not just as the introspective clarification of ideas but also as the communication of these ideas in an atmosphere of gay sociability, with a degree of amusing levity. This characterization of the language as one that contributed to learning through conversation reflected a common French conception of science as something that should be pursued in an atmosphere of gay sociability. Fontenelle, the doyen and popularizer of French science in the late seventeenth and early eighteenth centuries—whom Priestley cited in reporting on the experiments to weigh light particles—explicitly insisted that the *new science* should be practiced in what he called "a very unphilosophical manner." He characterized his many reports of discoveries as attempts "to bring [science] to the point where it's neither too dry for [sociable and courteous] men and women, nor too playful for scholars."[110] And, of course, it is hardly insignificant that he composed his *Conversations on the Plurality of Worlds* (1686) as a *pièce fugitive,* a conversation carried on between a courteous man and a courtly woman.

Ballooning very rapidly came to symbolize all that was best in French science and intellectual culture. Though there were not many immediately obvious scientific implications to the balloon, balloon launchings after 1783 quickly became occasions for men of letters, scientists, and other cultural elites, male and female, to gather in fields and enjoy the scientific enterprise as a kind of *fête champêtre,* or garden party. Significantly, the early reports of experiments in ballooning noted that they were carried on in just such a sociable atmosphere of gaiety. The *Histoire de l'académie royale des*

---

110. Fontenelle, *Conversations on the Plurality of Worlds,* trans. H. A. Hargreaves (Berkeley: University of California Press, 1990), 3.

sciences reported the first successful flight in 1783: "We should add for the honor of the Sciences, that never was an experiment carried out with such cheers and such pomp, and never did it also have such illustrious Spectators, nor so many."[111]

Indeed, the balloon was an oft-used symbol of French gaiety. In 1790, for example, during a revolutionary festival there was an attempt to raise a balloon, "decked in the three colors, set to lift off at the beginning of the military revue, and to unfurl the flag of liberty in the heavens." The attempt failed before the balloon ever got off the ground, and one reporter noted that the crowd "cheered at its collapse." This revolutionary reporter had to search for an explanation for the joy that this failure inspired in the revolutionary crowd. In the end, he argued that "we must not see in this an ominous presage." Instead, he pointed out that the French crowd cheered because the balloon was understood to have "*lost its vigor,* witty words [that describe] an occasion which always inspires French gaiety. In fact, a big balloon that collapses while trying to lift itself up resembles closely enough something at which it is not difficult to guess."[112] The reporter thus noted that the French crowd's ability to use its language in such a way as to lift its spirits by recognizing the figure of a failed phallus in this balloon's collapse was representative of a distinctly French lightheartedness. The Marquis de Bièvre, writing about the Revolution in 1799, would offer the following reflection: "[T]he revolution that is now producing so many changes has had almost no effect on the French character. [It has] the same frivolity, the same taste for refined wit. Paris, this country so fertile in contrasts, offers in this genre some excesses of extravagance. While everything is in flames, the Parisian plays on words, and consoles himself with puns."[113]

---

111. Le Roy et al., "Rapport fait à l'Académie des Sciences, sur la Machine aérostatique, de MM. de Mongolfier," in *Histoire de l'académie royale des sciences avec les mémoires de mathématique et de physique tirés des registres de cette Académie* (Paris, 1783), 14.

112. *Confédération nationale, ou Récit exact et circonstancié de tout ce qui s'est passé à Paris, le 14 juillet 1790, à la federation* (Paris: Chez Garnéry, libraire, an II de la liberté [1790]), 154.

113. Bièvre, *Calembours et autres jeux sur les mots d'esprit,* 56. Among the few British writers who celebrated puns was one essayist who claimed that puns could defuse potential crises of communication. He wrote that one "advantage in punning is, that it ends disputes.... How often have Aristotle and Cartesius been reconciled by a merry conceit! how often have whigs and tories shook hands over a quibble! and the clashing of swords been prevented, by the jingling of words!" See *The Guardian,* April 22, 1713, reprinted in *The British Essayists,* ed. James Ferguson (London: Printed by J. Haddon for G. Offer, 1819), 16:184–185.

Other writers, particularly those across the Channel, would have agreed in finding amusing parallels between collapsing balloons, failing phalluses, the French character, and the French language, but they would not have been such favorable ones. Instead, as the next chapter will show, they took the "balloonomania" of the times to be an indication of the lack of energy or potency in the French language and national character. The French language became for many in Britain, a potentially dangerous source of insincerity, empty formalism, hot air, or what they frequently called "false politeness."

6

ENGLISH ENERGY

> If the English language is poor, and, if I may say so, even a little savage, when it comes to the primitive character of its elements and their grammatical disposition, it has, on the other hand, a great richness and a great energy, because of the abundance of its signs and the very original boldness of its expressions.
>
> J. H. MEISTER, *Souvenirs de mes voyages en Angleterre* (1795)

Rivarol shared his Berlin Academy essay prize with Johann Christoph Schwab, who also ended with a note on the French invention of ballooning. Schwab's remarks, however, were markedly different from those by Rivarol, who saw the invention as a shining example of French levity. Schwab, by contrast, insisted that "whatever honor it gives to the French," Germans had a "superior talent for invention."[1] After noting that the French invention was as much the result of luck as it was "the work of wisdom and calculation," Schwab insisted that the invention of the aerostatic machine was much less significant than many other inventions over the previous millennium. The invention of ballooning could not be ranked, Schwab added, among the "sublime" discoveries, like gunpowder,

---

1. Johann Christoph Schwab, "Dissertation sur la langue françoise," in Académie de Berlin, *De l'universalité Européenne de la langue française,* ed. Pierre Pénisson (Paris: Librairie Arthème Fayard, 1995), 441 n. 61.

firearms, and printing, which had clear practical applications. "What use have we derived from it so far?" Schwab asked; "What changes has it produced?... And will we ever travel more securely and less expensively by hot-air balloon?" "In a word," he concluded, "the invention of the hot-air balloon is nothing...but a lovely and shiny discovery."[2]

Schwab thus dismissed the hot-air balloon as too superficial and frivolous to be considered a sublime discovery. He closed his note by proposing a more sublime invention than the balloon: "Let us suppose," he wrote, "that we discover how to travel easily under water, how to voyage, for example, at the bottom of the sea...; would this invention...cause as great a splash?"[3] Like Priestley, who played on the ironies of the Newtonians, who gravely claimed that light must have weight, Schwab played on the ironies of the shininess and lightness of the French discovery. He insisted that a graver and therefore more sublime discovery would have been that of a machine that helped people to sink to the depths of the seas.

Schwab's contemporaries in Britain similarly took the Montgolfiers' invention to be, in the words of the *Critical Review*, little more than a "childish spectacle" or, as Horace Walpole put it, a "philosophical plaything."[4] Among the more interesting British reactions to ballooning was *London Unmask'd: Or, The New Town Spy* (1785), which, as Paul Keen notes, "gave the last word to...Sir Gravity, who urged [people] to 'dismiss this frothy topic.'"[5] These were just a few of the many British responses to ballooning that treated it as having little to do with the notion of science as a grave enterprise that was being promoted by British practitioners like Priestley. These moves to cast ballooning as an overly frivolous French confection reflect an attitude that also lay at the foundation of commonplace British comments on the French language.

Many British writers admittedly embraced and promoted the French language, particularly before the Glorious Revolution (1688), as either a model to emulate or an instrument for acquiring social grace and courtly polish. Increasingly, however, eighteenth-century British writers came to

---

2. Ibid., 441–443 n. 61.
3. Ibid.
4. Quoted from Paul Keen, "The 'Balloonomania': Science and Spectacle in 1780s England," *Eighteenth-Century Studies* 39, no. 4 (Summer 2006): 530.
5. Ibid.

see the language and those who spoke it as a source of potential linguistic and cultural infection. Most of the language's admirers and critics did agree with the estimation that it was especially refined and witty. Indeed, Mandeville's dialogue on language, which cast animals as communicating more clearly than humans and savages as communicating more clearly than the civilized, recapitulated the issue by contrasting the French and English languages. In the sixth dialogue, Horatio insists that "if the chief Design of [Speech] is to persuade, the *French* have got the start of us a great way; theirs is really a charming Language." When Cleomenes resists this conclusion, Horatio presses him: "But without Banter, don't you think that the *French* Tongue is more proper, more fit to persuade in, than ours?" Finally, Cleomenes responds to Horatio that while "nothing is more difficult, than to compare the Beauties of two Languages together, because what is very much esteem'd in the one, is often not relish'd at all in the other," all the "favourite Expressions in *French* are such, as either sooth or tickle; and nothing is more admired in *English,* than what pierces or strikes.... The *French* call us Barbarous, and we say, they are Fawning." The dialogue ultimately leaves the question of linguistic superiority undecided, but what Cleomenes does insist upon is that while the French tongue lends itself to a refined and light form of communication, this may not be preferable to the barbarous energy of English sincerity.[6]

Those who were critical of the language followed Mandeville's lead and redescribed the French ideal of communicational *politesse* as what they called a "false politeness." In fact, the problem with the French language, as they saw it, was that it was too often so successfully equivocal that French speech was meaningless. The language, they argued, promoted forms of sociability that were nothing more than an empty formalism, or hot air. Many in Britain explicitly rejected the ideal of linguistic levity associated with French and promoted English as an energetic language that guaranteed communicational sincerity. The very structure of the English language, they frequently argued, retained certain characteristics of primitive languages and so reflected and reinforced the British national characteristics of clarity, energy, sincerity, and gravity.

---

6. Bernard Mandeville, *The Fable of the Bees: Or Private Vices, Publick Benefits* (Oxford: Clarendon Press, 1924), 2:296 and 297.

In his study of early modern attitudes toward English, Richard Foster Jones noted that at the beginning of the seventeenth century a number of assumptions about English and its speakers "led inexorably to the conclusion that the language itself was rude, or barbarous."[7] In 1712, Swift wrote *A Proposal for Correcting, Improving and Ascertaining the English Tongue* because he held that English was "less Refined than [the languages] of *Italy, Spain,* or *France.*"[8] By 1724, the poet Leonard Welsted (1688–1747) could argue that English had been refined over the previous hundred years sufficiently for him to assert that it had reached "that *Standard* or Perfection, which denominates a Classical Age."[9] English had been brought to such a standard by those who worked "to refine the Savageness of the Breed;...the most beautiful Polish is at length given to our Tongue, and its *Teutonic* Rust is quite worn away."[10] For many at the turn of the eighteenth century, then, English either was too barbarous to qualify as a perfect language or could be characterized as perfect only to the extent that it had been refined and its primitive properties had been polished away.

A number of early modern commentaries on the English language thus positioned it within a commonplace theory of linguistic development that presumed that languages were savage and unrefined in their beginnings and became more refined and civilized as they developed. For many the properties of primitive languages were defects; however, for others, a language's primitive energy was a linguistic virtue that made their speech warmer, more effective and authentic. In this respect, a language that retained certain primitive characteristics would be preferable to an overrefined and cold tongue. In fact, a number of commentators on the English language argued that it had significant advantages over others in general and especially over the quintessentially polite French tongue. In fact, while Swift's belief that English was inferior to the more refined continental and

---

7. Richard Foster Jones, *The Triumph of the English Language* (Stanford: Stanford University Press, 1953), 168.

8. Jonathan Swift, *A Proposal for Correcting, Improving and Ascertaining the English Tongue* (London: Printed for Benj. Tooke, 1712), 9. Swift suggested, therefore, that the English should establish an academy, much like the Académie Française, to refine the language.

9. Leonard Welsted, "Dissertation concerning the Perfection of the English Language, the State of Poetry, etc.," in *Critical Essays of the Eighteenth Century,* ed. Willard Higley Durham (New York: Russell and Russell, 1961), 358.

10. Ibid.

classical (Latin and Greek) languages continued to find support throughout the century, an increasing number of thinkers argued that the English language not only was as clear as any other language but also had advantages over other languages when it came to its energy.[11] In fact, by the end of the eighteenth century, Jacob Heinrich Meister (1744–1826) could describe the English language as praiseworthy precisely because of its savage character. "If the English language is poor, and, if I may say so, even a little savage," he wrote, "it has, on the other hand, a great richness and a great energy, because of the abundance of its signs and the very original boldness of its expressions."[12] Over the course of the late seventeenth and eighteenth centuries, British attitudes toward the English language cast it as mixing the characteristics of clarity, energy, gravity, and elegance in such ideal proportions that it became for many the perfect language. This attitude was grounded on a set of linguistic characteristics that facilitated the contrasts between an energetic and savage English and an overly refined and light French. Many eighteenth-century British thinkers therefore argued that the English language was not only natively clear and had acquired a sufficient degree of elegant polish, but also that it had become so without losing to any significant degree those qualities associated with energetic communication. For such thinkers, the happy result was an almost ideal language that would promote learned communication, or "commerce", while guarding against the threats of luxuriant overrefinement, softening, and the false politeness with which it was frequently associated.

Tillotson, *The Spectator*, and English Sincerity

A number of the widely read essays by Joseph Addison (1672–1719) and Richard Steele (1672–1729) in *The Spectator* took up linguistic issues. Addison's essay number 135 for August 4, 1711, for example, begins, "I have somewhere read of an eminent Person who used...to give Thanks to

---

11. On the attempt to reform English on the model of the classical languages, see Adam R. Beach, "The Creation of a Classical Language in the Eighteenth Century: Standardizing English, Cultural Imperialism, and the Future of the Literary Canon," *Texas Studies in Literature and Language* 43, no. 2 (Summer 2001): 117–141.

12. Jacob Heinrich Meister, *Souvenirs de mes voyages en Angleterre* (Zurich: Chez P. F. Aubin, 1795), 101–102.

Heaven that he was born a *Frenchman:* For my own part, I look upon it as a peculiar Blessing that I was Born an *Englishman.* Among many other Reasons, I think my self very happy in my Country, as the *Language* of it is wonderfully adapted to a Man who is sparing of his Words, and an Enemy of Loquacity." In the essay, Addison set out to explore the connection between the English language and the character of its speakers. He noted that English "Discourse is not kept up in Conversation.... For, to favour our Natural Taciturnity, when we are obliged to utter our Thoughts, we do it in the shortest way we are able, and give as quick a Birth to our Conception as possible." Among the linguistic features facilitating this abrupt and nearly immediate communication, Addison included the comparative number of "Monosyllables, which give us an Opportunity of delivering our Thoughts in few Sounds." Addison noted that even words that were not monosyllables were pronounced so rapidly in English that, as he put it, "we often make them so." He noted that English speakers tended to contract the ending of words that ended in *ed,* to substitute *s* for *eth* at the end of certain words, and to adopt contractions that drew "two Words into one." Although Addison complained that "this Humour of shortning our Language," "indeed takes off from the Elegance of our Tongue" and makes it less "Tunable and Sonorous," he concluded that "it shows the Genius and natural Temper of the English, which is modest, thoughtful and sincere." In this way, Addison contrasted the modesty, thoughtfulness, and especially sincerity of English speakers to the "light" and "talkative" character of French speakers.[13]

Addison's argument was just one instance of a commonplace characterization of the language as reflecting and reinforcing English speakers' energy, simplicity, and sincerity. Steele's *Spectator* essay number 103 for June 28, 1711, cited a sermon by John Tillotson (1630–1694), the archbishop of Canterbury. In this 1694 sermon, which he delivered just months before he died, Tillotson had complained that, what he called "the old *English* plainness and sincerity,... is in a great measure lost among us." Tillotson blamed the apparent decline of plain and sincere English speech on what he called "a long endeavour to transform us to a servile imitation of none of the best of our neighbours, in some of the worst of their qualities." Although he did

---

13. Joseph Addison and Richard Steele, *The Spectator,* ed. Donald F. Bond (Oxford: Clarendon Press, 1965), 2: 32, 33, 35, and 36.

not make it explicit, there can be little doubt that the neighbors in question were the French. The qualities in question were those associated with French politeness. "The dialect of conversation," Tillotson lamented, "is nowadays so swelled with vanity and compliment and so surfeited... with expressions of kindness and respect, that if a man that lived an age or two ago should return into the world again, he would really want a dictionary to help him to understand his own language."[14] Tillotson linked English sincerity with a native lexicon and style that was being infected by French words and French styles to such an extent that "sincerity and plainness are out of fashion."[15] He characterized this infection in explicitly linguistic terms, writing "that our language is running into a lie, that men have almost quite perverted the use of speech and made words to signify nothing, that the greatest part of the conversation of mankind and of their intercourse with one another is little else but driving a trade of dissimulation." Tillotson therefore concluded that French words were without meaning, or as he put it, "they are meer Cyphers" that "signify nothing" and that English was in serious danger of being infected by this language suited above all for hypocrisy. The significance of Steele's *Spectator* number 103, which cited Tillotson's sermon approvingly, comes into sharper focus when read alongside Addison's *Spectator* number 165, which complained much more explicitly of the French infection of the English language. In this essay, the *Spectator* wished that "certain Men might be set apart as Superintendants of our Language, to hinder any Words of a Foreign Coin from passing among us; and in particular to prohibit any *French* Phrases from becoming Current in this Kingdom."[16]

In contrasting English and French speech by the degree to which they could be sincere, Tillotson, Addison, and Steele were merely drawing out an implication of what many in France took to be the légèreté of their own language, which suited its speakers to polite sociability and witty

---

14. John Tillotson, *Of Sincerity towards God and Man* (London: Printed by J. and T. Dormer, 1735), 21. See also Christina Lupton, "Sincere Performances: Franklin, Tillotson, and Steele on the Plain Style," *Eighteenth-Century Studies* 40, no. 2 (2007): 181.

15. Tillotson, *Of Sincerity towards God and Man,* 22.

16. Steele's essay begins as an approving report of a "Discourse against" "the excessive way of speaking Civilities." Addison and Steele, *The Spectator,* 1:429. See also ibid., 2:149, which focused particularly on the adoption of French military terminology during the period when the British were fighting the French in the War of the Spanish Succession (1702–1713).

conversation.[17] British sincerity was the contrasting counterpart to French légèreté; both had significant communicational implications, and so both were frequently explained in linguistic and stylistic terms.

Copiousness, Sound, and Structure

British sincerity was also linked to some of the same linguistic characteristics associated with so-called savage languages. Addison, for example, emphasized the English language's rough consonants, particularly its gutturals and aspirates and its monosyllabic character.[18] Although there had been earlier claims that the English language displayed certain perfections, most such claims were short and generally unsupported by much in the way of argument. As the linguistic ideas that emerged during the quarrel of the ancients and moderns made their way across the English Channel, they provided British thinkers with a framework for discussing the relative merits of languages. As a consequence, writings on the English language began to take a more consistent and extensive form. In 1731, Thomas Stackhouse (1677–1752) published an English translation of Frain du Tremblay's *Traité des Langues* and appended to it his own essay that characterized English as a language that was especially clear, grave, and energetic.

In terms of the characteristics generally associated with linguistic clarity such as perspicuity, purity, neatness, and copiousness, English was increasingly described by British thinkers as adequate if not excellent. In examining the debate over inkhorn terms, or loan words, and neologisms in sixteenth- and seventeenth-century England, J. L. Moore and R. F. Jones have shown that before the seventeenth century, loan words were generally

---

17. Many of the recent surveys of eighteenth-century ideas about English national character discuss the idea of the English as especially sincere, though none links it specifically to the language. See Gerald Newman, *The Rise of English Nationalism: A Cultural History 1740–1830* (New York: St. Martin's, 1987), 123–139. See also Paul Langford, *Englishness Identified: Manners and Character, 1650–1850* (Oxford: Oxford University Press, 2000), 85–135.

18. See my "Savage Eloquence in America and the Linguistic Construction of a British Identity in the 18th Century," *Historiographia Linguistica* 23, nos. 1/2 (1996): 123–158, and my "*A Language More Peculiarly Circumstanced Than Any That Has Yet Appeared*: English as a *Perfect* Language in Eighteenth-Century Linguistic Thought," in *History of Linguistics 1996*, ed. David Cram, Andrew R. Linn, and Elke Nowak (Amsterdam: John Benjamins, 1999), 175–182.

accepted as necessary only to the extent that people agreed that English was barren and deficient. There was a growing tendency, however, not only to accept these words but to embrace them as important to the copiousness of the English lexicon.[19] By the early eighteenth century, commentators argued that English had a very extensive lexicon and that it was more copious than most, if not all, other languages. In his *English Grammar* (1688), Guy Miege (1644–1718?), for example, wrote that English was especially copious. "For, besides the Treasures of the ancient *Dutch* which the *English* retains in the *Saxon* Monosyllables," he wrote, "the choicer Wits of this Nation have fetcht hither the very Quintessence of some forein Languages; who, like Bees, have gathered the best, and left the worst. By which means they have so happily improved their Mother Tongue.... And, whereas the *French* is stinted, and grown barren through its exceeding Nicety; the *English* on the contrary is grown mighty Copious."[20] The French language's restricted lexicon was thought to contribute to French levity because a French word must have an abundance of meanings and the French speaker was often able to say many things with a single word. With its copious lexicon, English was closer to the ideal of a language in which individual words conformed to particular things. This copiousness thus made saying one thing and meaning another more difficult to do in English than in French.

After surveying the influence of a variety of languages (old British, Latin, Saxon, Danish, and French) on English, Stackhouse wrote that "it plainly appears, what great Additions and Improvements, at least in Point of Copiousness, our Language must have received... making *English* one of the most copious of all modern Tongues." If Stackhouse was convinced that the English language met "the first great Requisite in any Language," which was "to have a sufficient Number of these Signs, whereby to express our Minds," he cautioned only against continuing to borrow too many French words. It was "much to be wish'd, that we would stop..., before the Strength and Sinews of our Language be impair'd by too close a Commerce with *one,* that visibly wants them." Stackhouse characterized the

---

19. J. L. Moore, *Tudor-Stuart Views on the Growth Status and Destiny of the English Language* (College Park, MD, McGrath, 1970).

20. Guy Miege, "A Prefatory Discourse," in *The English Grammar* (London, 1688; repr. Menston, UK: Scolar Press, 1969), no page no. During the sixteenth century, English authors generally saw loan words as necessary only because the English language was "barren" or insufficiently copious.

English lexicon as a source of the language's "Strength and Sinews." In this way he made copiousness, commonly taken to be a characteristic of a language's clarity, a mark also of the great energy of English.[21]

In taking up the issue of word order, Stackhouse noted that the English language, like the French, followed the natural order. He adopted the French theory that this natural order promoted clarity to argue that English syntax is also especially clear. Stackhouse, however, did not accept the corollary that the English language must therefore suffer from a deficient "cadence." Instead, he wrote that English did not follow the natural order "so strictly as the *French*." As a consequence, he could argue that when one evaluated the two implications of a language's word order, "*viz.* what Signification [it] convey[s] to the Mind; and what Pleasure [it] give[s] to the Ear," the English language, generally following a natural order but allowing inversion more than the French, combined the advantages of both. English thus represented a kind of happy medium between clarity and elegance. Stackhouse cited Samuel de Sorbière (1615–1670), who had written that "if it be in the Power of a Tongue to join the Sweetness of Harmony, and the natural Order of Ideas together…; such a Tongue deserves a Preference before one, that brings them out in Rank, one after another, and by the way of formal and dull Procession." Stackhouse could then conclude that the English Language "has all the Perspicuity that Particular can afford us; and yet we sometimes deviate a little form that Order, where…the Cadence of a Period, or the Force of an Expression seem to require it; which gives our Language no small Pre-eminence." Although Stackhouse had presented this as a simple question of the relative measures of clarity and elegance of expressions in a language, he ended by noting that inversions could lend "force" or energy to an expression. Stackhouse's suggestion that English grammar contributed not only to its clarity and elegance but also to its energy is especially interesting given that Frain du Tremblay's *Traité des langues,* to which Stackhouse appended his essay, not only had characterized energy and clarity as opposed to each other but had even dismissed energy as a meaningless criterion for evaluating languages. In seeing the English language's copiousness and grammatical structure

---

21. Thomas Stackhouse, *Reflections on the Nature and Property of Languages in General and on the Advantages, Defects, and Manner of Improving the English Tongue in Particular* (London: Printed for J. Batley, at the Dove in Paternoster-Row, 1731), 171 and 172.

as contributing to its energy, Stackhouse therefore disregarded Frain du Tremblay's claims.[22]

When he turned to consider the English language's "Strength and Significancy," or energy as a distinct category, Stackhouse wrote that it was in fact a "Quality, in the Excellency of any Language." After surveying various subjects, among them pulpit oratory, medicine, and history, and various authors such as Locke, Pope, and Milton, Stackhouse remarked "that there is something in the Tongue itself that gave a vast Help to their Fancy.... The Strength, the Life, the Vigour of our Tongue...and the rapid Concurrence of its harsher Consonants...are mightily assistant to the Poet's Passion."[23]

Stackhouse repeated this claim that English was especially energetic when he came to discuss Frain du Tremblay's third general set of criteria of linguistic excellence, those relating to a language's number and harmony. For Stackhouse, this category was a phonotactic one that had to do with, as he put it, "the Gratification of the Ear." He argued that the best languages would "avoid the frequent Concurrence of Vowels, which make the Tone languid, as that of Consonants, which make it too strong." In his analysis, Stackhouse noted that English "is loaded with Consonants indeed, and, in what we retain from our *Saxon* Ancestors, is very harsh and rough in its Pronunciation." Stackhouse thus admitted that English could "not then come up to the Softness and melting Tone of some of our Neigbours." Instead of recognizing the lack of elegance as the defect that the French theorists before him had made it out to be, Stackhouse criticized those languages of neighboring peoples "who," as he put it, "have spoil'd their Sinews to meliorate their Sound." "Our Language," he asserted, "is strong and masculine, bold and majestick.... Softness be not *its* proper Genius." In arguing that the English language's properties made it tend toward not only clarity but also energy and gravity, Stackhouse quoted Thomas Sprat's *History of the Royal Society* (1667): "[T]he *English* Genius is not so airy and discursive, as that of some of our Neighbours, (meaning the *French*)." Stackhouse's essay on the characteristics of the English language thus reworked and ignored some of the linguistic assumptions in Frain du Tremblay's text to which it was appended, and in doing so it

---

22. Ibid., 174, 175, and 175–176.
23. Ibid., 176 and 178.

presented the English language as being a language of clarity, gravity, and, above all, energy.[24]

From the English Dictionary to the Scottish Rhetoric

By the second half of the century, the theoretical foundation had been established for claims that the English language both reflected and reinforced the manly, energetic, warm, strong, bold, nervous, as well as clear and grave, character of its speakers. Samuel Johnson (1709–1784) commented in the preface to his famous *Dictionary:* "[W]hen I took the first survey of my undertaking, I found our speech copious without order, and energetick without rules." And, in fact, Johnson worried that the French language might insinuate itself and corrupt the English language and ultimately the character of its speakers. "Our language, for almost a century," he wrote, "has...been gradually departing from its original Teutonick character, and deviating towards a Gallick structure and phraseology, from which it ought to be our endeavour to recal it." Whether or not Johnson's *Dictionary* should best be described as a work of prescription rather than description, he claimed that he intended it to protect the energetic English language and in doing so to promote enlightenment.[25]

Fewer than twenty years later, Hugh Blair's *Lectures on Rhetoric and Belles Lettres* (1783) could confidently assert that since English was "a compound language," there were "advantages that attend it; particularly...the number and variety of words with which such a language is likely to be enriched." "Few languages," he continued, "are, in fact, more copious than the English." For Blair, not only did this copiousness aid in making English clear, but it also added to the gravity of English expressions. He wrote, "In all grave subjects especially, historical, critical, political, and moral, no writer has the least reason to complain of the barrenness of our tongue. The studious reflecting genius of the people, has brought together great store of expressions, on such subjects, from every quarter." Blair linked

---

24. Ibid., 179, 181, and 189. See Thomas Sprat, *The History of the Royal Society of London* (London: Printed for Rob. Scot, Ri. Chiswell, Tho. Chapman, and Geo. Sawbridge, 1702), 40.
25. Samuel Johnson, preface to *Johnson's Dictionary: A Modern Selection,* ed. E. L. McAdam, Jr. and George Milne (New York: Pantheon, 1963), 4, 18, and 27–28.

gravity more to energy than to clarity. "It is chiefly, indeed, on grave subjects," he wrote, "and with respect to the stronger emotions of the mind, that our language displays its power of expression. We are said to have thirty words, at least, for denoting all the varieties of the passion of anger." Thus he could conclude that "from the genius of our language,...it may be expected to have strength and energy.... By our abounding in terms for expressing all the strong emotions of the mind,... our language may be esteemed to possess considerable force of expression."[26] Blair identified the copiousness of English and its attendant emotional strength as the source of the "richness" of English poetry, which he contrasted with the poverty of French poetry. Copiousness, thus, became a feature that contributed just as much to the gravity and energy of English as to its clarity or perspicuity.

When he came to the conventional criticism that the English language had a "deficiency in harmony of sound," Blair argued that "this charge against our tongue has been carried too far." Though he argued that English was not as harsh and consonantal as people tended to assume, he wrote that "it must be admitted, that smoothness, or beauty of sound, is not one of the distinguishing properties of the English tongue." Not surprisingly, he sought to redescribe this vice as a linguistic virtue. Blair wrote, "Though not incapable of being formed into melodious arrangements, yet strength and expressiveness, more than grace, form its character.... The general effect...is to give a brisk and a spirited, but at the same time, a rapid and hurried, and not very musical, tone to the whole pronunciation of a people." In other words, Blair situated English between the fiery and energetic primitive tongues and the cold and languid overcivilized languages.[27]

Besides these lexical and phonotactic arguments in favor of seeing English as a distinctly energetic instance of a civilized language, Blair argued that the syntactic structure of the language made it both especially clear and energetic. He argued that, like "all the modern languages of Europe," English expressions exhibited the "order of the understanding...So that the

---

26. Hugh Blair, *Lectures on Rhetoric and Belles Lettres* (Philadelphia: Troutman and Hayes, 1853), 96, 97, and 97–98. Blair listed the following English terms for emotion: "Anger, wrath, passion, rage, fury, outrage, fierceness, sharpness, animosity, choler, resentment, heat, heart-burning; to fume, storm, inflame, be incensed, to vex, kindle, irritate, enrage, exasperate, provoke, fret; to be sullen, hasty, hot, rough, sour, peevish, etc."

27. Ibid., 98 and 99.

ideas are made to succeed to one another...according to the order of nature and of time.... Our arrangement, therefore, appears to be the consequence of greater refinement in the art of speech; as far as clearness in communication is understood to be the end of speech." While Blair lumped together all the modern European languages as following the natural order, he also noted that these tongues followed that order more or less rigidly. Blair insisted that "the French language is, of them all, the most determinate in the order of its words, and admits the least of inversion.... The English admits it more." Blair argued that "many observations, both curious and useful" could be derived from this "natural progress of language," which he summarized in the following terms: "[L]anguage was at first barren in words, but descriptive by the sound of these words; and expressive in the manner of uttering them, by the aid of significant tones and gestures: style was figurative and poetical; arrangement was fanciful and lively." Blair characterized the development as the replacement of warm imagination by a cold understanding, or as he also put it, a movement "from fire and enthusiasm to coolness and precision." What is striking is that, in some of his descriptions of the English language, Blair cast it as sitting somewhere closer to a golden mean in this development than other languages, particularly the French and Italian, which he presented as lying nearer to the corrupted end of linguistic history. According to Blair, English retained its vehement and rough sounds as well as some of its inverted idiom. As with his discussion of the copiousness of English, Blair argued that these syntactic properties contributed to making English an energetic modern tongue.[28]

This discourse on the English language was further developed later in the century by James Dunbar (1742–1798), who became regent at King's College, Aberdeen, just after Reid's departure for Glasgow, where he succeeded Adam Smith in the chair of moral philosophy. Although his appointment came too late for him to be considered Reid's colleague, Reid had probably taught him while Dunbar was a student at King's College. As a professor at the University of Aberdeen, Dunbar participated with many of the Aberdeen literati in the same Wise Club where Reid had presented some of his early writings. There was a clear correspondence between a number of the discourses and questions he presented to the club

---

28. Ibid., 70 and 72.

and the contents of his *Essays on the History of Mankind in Rude and Cultivated Ages*. Among those discourses, two that he delivered in 1768 and 1769 were especially related to the supposed historical development of languages from what he called "artless communities" to become "polished languages."[29] In the most primitive human languages, Dunbar believed, "there is a mechanical connection between the feelings of the soul and the enunciation of sound." Thus in this primitive stage of linguistic development, humans were "happy surely" because they "were not only devoid of the inclination, but unfurnished with the means of deceit."[30] Like many of his contemporaries interested in savage speech, Dunbar thus insisted that such primitive languages were remarkable in that they prevented dissimulation and hypocrisy.

Yet while Reid and others had argued that for this reason primitive languages were preferable to more developed ones, Dunbar insisted on the unqualified superiority of polished languages. He wrote that "as therefore the *analogical faculty* enlarges the sense of words, the *discriminating faculty* augments them in number. It breaks speech into smaller divisions, and bestows a copiousness on language by a more precise arrangement of the objects. Thus, by the distribution of our ideas, as well as by the enlargement of the fund, language is constantly enriched."[31] Thus, while some argued that "artificial" language supplanted and was therefore destructive of the features of a primitive language, Dunbar reworked the relation between the two such that the polished language could be an addition to rather than a corruption of the savage languages and the energetic eloquence and sincere speech they produced.

Dunbar's "Of the Criterion of a Polished Tongue" followed Blair and others in casting the English as ideally situated to benefit from the virtues of an energetically passionate primitive language and a rationally clear polished language. He, like Blair, argued that "the great excellence of a rude

---

29. James Dunbar, *Essays on the History of Mankind* (London: William Strahan and Thomas Cadell, 1781), 2. These essays dealt with the following questions: "What are the characteristics of polished language? And how is the comparative excellency of different languages to be estimated?" See James McCosh, "Appendix II: Questions in the Philosophical Society of Aberdeen," in *The Scottish Philosophy: Biographical, Expository, Critical, from Hutcheson to Hamilton* (London, 1875; repr. Hildesheim, Ger.: Georg Olms Verlagsbuchhandlung, 1966), 472.

30. Dunbar, *Essays on the History of Mankind*, 70.

31. Ibid., 96–97.

tongue consists, if not in *perspicuity,* at least in *vivacity* and *strength*.... And the advantages of a cultivated tongue, when opposed to these, will consist chiefly in copiousness of expression, in the grace of allusion, and in the combination of more melodious sound." Dunbar concluded that "an entire union of these qualities, with those others, would constitute the utmost perfection." "The one system," he suggested, "is more fertile of harmony and elegance, and even of strength; and by operating more successfully on the imagination, seems better adapted to the purposes of eloquence and polite literature. The other system, more allied to perspicuity and precision, is, on that account, more approved by the understanding, as a commodious vehicle for philosophy and the sciences." Although Dunbar suggested that these linguistic virtues of energy and clarity were "rather incompatible" with one another, he presented the English language as effectively combining them: "In perspicuity, the English tongue is perhaps superior both to the Greek and Latin, while it falls considerably short of the French. In elegance and force it is more perfect than the French, while infinitely inferior to the Greek and Latin." As the discussion in chapter 4 of ideas about savage eloquence showed, one of the greatest virtues of so-called savage languages was that, because of their energetic warmth, they guarded against dissimulation and guaranteed sincerity. In reworking the terms of linguistic evaluation that they borrowed from the French quarrels, Stackhouse, Johnson, Blair, and Dunbar further developed the linguistic basis for arguing that the English language was clear and energetic and its speakers rather more sincere and grave than witty and graceful. During the rest of the century, these terms were repeated many times to characterize and celebrate the English language and the character of its speakers.[32]

English in Smellie's *Encyclopaedia Britannica*

Among the Edinburgh literati, one figure in particular—the printer, editor, translator, and compiler of the first edition of the *Encyclopaedia Britannica*, William Smellie (1740–1795)—like Rivarol in France, used these linguistic

---

32. Ibid., 130, 131, 131–132, and 132.

arguments to make sense of his own experiences of the eighteenth century as an age of enlightened communication. Smellie, like many of his contemporaries, was fascinated by the differences between types of languages and argued that the English language was responsible for the intellectual, commercial, and imperial success of Great Britain. Smellie's most extensive discussion of language appeared in the first edition of the *Encyclopaedia Britannica*. In its article "Language" Smellie explored the linguistic characteristics that he claimed made the English language superior to all others.[33]

Smellie insisted on the distinction between primitive and civilized forms of language. "Hence the reason why the language of all barbarous and uncivilized people is rude and uncultivated," he argued, "while those nations which have improved their reasoning faculties, and made some progress in the polite arts, have been no less distinguished by the superiority of their language than by their preeminence in other respects." Having thus distinguished savage from civilized language, Smellie observed that there were some languages that had risen to what he called the "height of perfection." His article set out, as he put it, "to make some remarks on the advantage or defects of...some of those languages with which [he was] most intimately acquainted, as this may perhaps lead us to some discoveries of real utility to ourselves."[34]

Smellie divided his evaluation of types of languages into two sections that correspond to the distinction he made between a language's "idiom" and its "genius." In analyzing idioms, he followed Girard in distinguishing between "transpositive" and "analogous" languages based on whether or not they permitted syntactic inversions. Under the heading "genius," Smellie examined more broadly what he called "the particular set of ideas which the words of any language, either from their formation or multiplicity, are most naturally apt to excite in the mind of any one who hears it

---

33. There is every reason to think that Smellie was the author of the article. In a letter to the Dublin bookseller Thomas Ewing, the London publisher John Murray, an acquaintance of Smellie's, mentioned the article on language as original material in the *Britannica*. See John Murray to Thomas Ewing, 15 June 1772, from Murray's Copybook, Archives of the John Murray Publishing House, London, as quoted in William J. Zachs, "The Life and Works of Gilbert Stuart, 1743–86: A Social and Literary Study" (PhD diss., University of Edinburgh, 1988), app. 2.

34. William Smellie, "language," in *Encyclopaedia Britannica*, vol. 2 (Edinburgh: Printed for A. Bell and C. Macfarquhar, 1771), 863 and 864.

properly uttered." Under this heading, then, he included mainly phonotactic and semantic issues.[35]

Smellie set out to judge the merits of the two idioms according to the following three criteria: the better idiom would have "a greater variety of sounds, and consequently more room for harmonious diversity of tones"; "a greater freedom of expression [would be] allowed in uttering any simple idea...admitting of a greater variety in the arrangement of the words which are necessary to express that idea"; and the superior idiom would also have "a greater precision and accuracy in fixing the meaning of the person who uses the language."[36] Thus under what he presented as a syntactic analysis, he established three criteria that corresponded to the phonotactic, the syntactic, and the semantic levels of language. According to Smellie, each of these was closely related to the other two, since by allowing a greater variety of syntactic constructions, a language would also potentially lead to more variety of sounds and greater semantic precision.

The evaluation of the relative merits of classical and modern languages on the morphological level had become a well-worn path by the time Smellie composed his *Britannica* articles. More than many of his British contemporaries, though, he argued that English was structurally preferable to the classical languages. First, he argued that transpositive languages required speakers to use a small set of word endings over and over again to distinguish parts of speech. The similarity and repetition of these word endings in the transpositive languages, he argued, would significantly reduce the variety of sounds. Smellie commented that in the classical languages there was "such a jingle of similar sounds" that it was "most disgusting to the ear."[37]

When he turned to the question of which idiom promoted a variety of expression, Smellie argued again that "the method of conjugating by inflection seems to be deficient." He reasoned that in English not only could the order of the subject, auxiliary, and verb be rearranged, but also by emphasizing or "having the accent on the different words" the "power as well as the sound" of the expression could be varied. Regarding verbs, Smellie argued that the analogous idiom permitted a greater variety of sound,

---

35. Ibid., 864.
36. Ibid.
37. Ibid., 871.

expression, and consequently greater semantic precision. When he turned to the variety of expression offered by inflected nouns, however, Smellie ultimately agreed with his contemporaries that the inflected languages possessed an advantage. Smellie emphatically restricted the advantage, however, to "this single circumstance alone" because he argued that "it does not appear that any other of [a language's] cases [besides the accusative and nominative] adds to the variety, but rather the reverse." He concluded that "with respect to precision, distinctness, and accuracy in expressing any idea, the [analogous idiom] enjoys a superiority beyond all comparison" because "no single word can ever express all that variety of meaning which we can do by the help of auxiliaries and the emphasis." Smellie therefore agreed with others, like Rivarol, that the analogous structure of sentences in English and French made these two languages especially well suited to clear communication.[38]

After thus arguing for the superior clarity of the analogous idiom, the one most clearly exhibited by the English language, Smellie turned to the genius of various European languages. In this section, Smellie judged the merits of languages on the basis of "the particular set of ideas which the words of any language...excite in the mind" or "the effects" that languages "must naturally produce upon the people who employ them." In his evaluation of genius, as in that of idiom, Smellie presented the English language as having a decided advantage over all the others. He described a number of features of various European languages in order to suggest their comparative merits and defects. While he was clearly interested in demonstrating how English surpassed each of these languages, he noted that his contemporaries tended to take French to be the best language. Therefore his discussion of the comparative merits of the different geniuses focused mainly on English and French. He wrote, "It will perhaps, by some, be thought an unpardonable insult, if we do not allow the French the preference of all modern language in many respects." "But so far must we pay a deference to truth," Smellie continued, "as to be obliged to rank it among the poorest languages in Europe." Among the very first reasons, which Smellie offered for this judgment, was his claim that French "wants energy."[39]

---

38. Ibid., 866, 870, and 867.
39. Ibid., 864, 872, and 876.

Guarding against Assaults of Flattery: The Language of the Passions

If Smellie believed that French and the other refined languages were defective because they lacked energy, he argued that there was something peculiar in the structure of the English language that made it especially energetic and warm. In his discussion of French, Smellie objected to it on the grounds that appeals to emotion in that language often involved studied and therefore affected speech. In his description of the phonotactic character of English, Smellie noted that it was "bold, daring, and abrupt...admirably well adapted to express...great emotions." English was also "happy...in the full and open sound of the vowels...and in the strong use of the aspirate H." To this description of English sounds, he added that English interjections had "more of that fullness and unrestrained freedom of tones, in which their chief power consists, and are pushed forth from the inmost recesses of the soul in a forcible and unrestrained manner." Smellie commented not only on the English language's "nervous force which it derives from the accent" but also on its great "number of monosyllables." Smellie also noted that "although [English] can equal, if not surpass, every modern language in works of prose, it is in its poetical powers that our language shines forth with the greatest lustre." The article also observed that "in point of manly dignity,...intuitive distinctness, nervous energy of expression, unconstrained freedom and harmony of poetic numbers, [English] will yield the palm to none." Indeed, "these great and distinguishing excellencies," Smellie wrote, "far more than counterbalance the inconveniencies" of the language.[40]

Smellie's emphasis on the English language's interjections, on its aspirated, tonal, accented, and monosyllabic nature, and above all on its preeminence as a poetic language—all recurring features in eighteenth-century descriptions of savage languages—suggests that he was characterizing English as a language that can effectively communicate both civilized ideas and primitive passions. Smellie wrote, for instance, that "the artificial language does not debar the use of...the natural." Far from being an obstacle to the communication of ideas, a language of the

---

40. Ibid., 878, 877, and 879.

passions "tends to ascertain the meaning of these with greater precision, and consequently to give them greater power." Smellie therefore believed that unlike other so-called civilized languages that tended to supplant the primitive natural language, English incorporated this primitive energetic foundation of communication to guarantee greater somatic transparency and sincerity and to make English speech more energetically meaningful and moving.[41]

In a separate essay on the means of promoting public spirit, Smellie noted that "although infants are ignorant of artificial language, yet are they adepts in the natural language of the passions. An infant knows...[when] a person...is indulging a selfish passion."[42] Thus, while "every man lies open, at one quarter or other, to the assaults of flattery," it is children who are "so well skilled in the language of Nature, that if they but perceive your countenance, or hear the most distant sound in your voice, they see into the inmost recesses of thy soul."[43] Smellie thus adopted the claims of those who argued that primitive languages helped to promote the sincerity of their speakers. He found in English "a force and energy which conveys, in an irresistible manner, a most perfect knowledge of the situation of the mind of the speaker at the time."[44] For Smellie, English speakers could not appeal to the emotions in the studied and potentially dissimulating fashion of French speakers. In this respect, the energetic warmth of the English language was a fortuitous vestige of the passionate natural language that made deception difficult.

French as a Meaningless Language

In developing his claim that English surpassed all languages, especially French, Smellie presented a series of arguments concerning the relationship between languages and social forms. He characterized all other languages as promoters of social and political corruption because, unlike

---

41. Ibid., 863.
42. William Smellie, *Literary and Characteristical Lives*...(Edinburgh: Printed and sold by Alex. Smellie, et al., 1800; facs. repr. with introduction by Stephen Brown, Bristol, UK: Thoemmes Press, 1997), 340.
43. Ibid., 352.
44. Smellie, "Language," 867.

English, they did not facilitate what he called "private conversation." He argued, for example, that it was precisely

> in private conversation, where the mind wishes to unbend itself with ease, [that] these [the characteristics of the transpositive idiom] become so many cloggs which encumber and perplex. At these moments we wish to transfuse our thoughts with ease and facility...and wish to be freed of the trouble of attention as much as may be. Like our state-robes, we would wish to lay aside our pompous language, and enjoy ourselves at home with freedom and ease. Here the solemnity and windings of the transpositive languages are burdensome; while the facility with which a sentiment can be expressed in the analogous language is the thing that we wish to acquire. In this humble, though most engaging sphere, the analogous language moves unrivalled.[45]

Smellie therefore argued for the superiority of English over other languages on the same basis as those who praised French: it facilitated and promoted conversation, learning, and civility.

In describing his ideal of conversation, however, Smellie did not repeat Morellet's allegory of a butterfly gliding lightly from flower to flower; instead, he presented the ideal of conversation as having distinctly thermal characteristics. "It is by the enlivening glow of conversation," he wrote, "that kindred souls catch fire from one another, that thought produces thought, and each improves upon the other, till they soar beyond the bounds which human reason, if left alone, could ever have aspired to." Smellie insisted that the language that best promoted this kind of energetic conversation would be the most beneficial to society.[46]

As with the idea that French was the language that promoted light communication, certain significant implications followed from the idea that English was the language of energetic communication. Smellie recognized and therefore had to counter the more conventional claim that French was more suited to conversation than any other language. According to Smellie, the French were "gay and loquacious, and fond to excess of those superficial accomplishments which engage the attention of the fair

---
45. Ibid., 871.
46. Ibid., 872.

sex." He reiterated French claims that their language allowed speakers to say one thing while meaning another. He wrote that French had "such an infinity of words capable of expressing vague and unmeaning compliment, now dignified by the name *politeness,* that in this strain, one who uses the French [language] can never be at a loss... as it is easy to converse *more* and really say *less,* in this than any other language."[47] Smellie, however, hardly saw this as a genuine communicational virtue.

For Smellie, languages like French that were supposed to lend themselves to artful and polite though potentially meaningless utterances tended in the end toward the corruption of society. Smellie described French as a language suited to "the courts of princes, and assemblies of great personages;...In these circumstances, as the heart remaineth disengaged, conversation must necessarily flag; and mankind in this situation will gladly adopt that language in which they can converse more easily without being deeply interested—On these accounts the French now is, and probably will continue to be reckoned the most polite language in Europe, and therefore the most generally studied and known." Smellie insisted that the British should not "envy them this distinction." He saw French as a tongue of tyranny where a few courtiers who would have mastered the language could use "unmeaning phrases" for flattery and their own selfish interests at the expense of the public interest.[48]

This conception of French as a language without meaning that facilitated dissimulation was well diffused throughout eighteenth-century Britain. Many British writers contrasted the false politeness of French speakers to the genuine politeness or civility of English speakers. Smellie explicitly linked the idea of "expressing vague and unmeaning compliment" to the form of communication that he described as having been in his day "dignified by the name *politeness.*" In this sense, French politeness was opposed to British sincerity. The author of one essay, published in *The Mirror* in 1779, after commenting on the "force" and "energy" of savage oratory, noted that "in France, they contrive to throw over their greatest excesses a veil so delicate and so fine, as in some measure to hide the deformity of vice, and even at times to bestow upon it the semblance of virtue. But with us, less delicate and less refined, vice appears in its native colours, without concealment and

---

47. Ibid., 877.
48. Ibid.

without disguise." "If ease and politeness be only attainable at the expense of sincerity," the author commented, "I flatter myself, there are few of my readers who would not think the purchase made at too high a price."[49] In drawing the contrast between the energy of Indian oratory and insincerity of French politeness, he was warning his British readers of the threat of emulating French speech. John Brown (1715–1766), in his *Estimate of the Manners and Principles of the Times* (1757), similarly linked the corruption of British sincerity with the corrosive influence of vacuous French forms of speech and sociability, particularly the double entendre. Figuring vicious speech as an indecent woman, he wrote that "in ancient Days, *bare* and *impudent Obscenity,* like a common Woman of the Town, was confined to *Brothels.*" Brown then suggested that in his own day vicious speech had found a way of circulating publicly: "the *Double-Entendre,* like a modern fine Lady, is now admitted into the *best Company;* while her *transparent Covering* of Words, like a *thin* fashionable *Gawze* delicately thrown across, *discloses,* while it seems to *veil,* her *Nakedness* of Thought."[50] Brown characterized the double entendre as an indecent feminine importation of French insincerity.

It is hardly insignificant that Brown cast the French language as viciously deceitful and feminine. While the advocates of French as a language of sociable learning frequently insisted that some women, as refiners or lighteners of language, ought in principle to be included in conversations, British advocates of English tended to argue that women ought to be excluded from them. John Andrews (1736–1809), for example, insisted

---

49. "No. 18. Saturday, March 27, 1779," in *The Mirror;* reprinted in *The British Essayists,* ed. James Ferguson (London: Printed by T. C. Hansard, 1819), 34:95.

50. John Brown, *An Estimate of the Manners and Principles of the Times* (London: Printed for L. Davis, and C. Reymers, 1757), 45. Brown characterized the French as "insincere, yet honourable" (141). An essay published the year before in *The World* (November 4, 1756), began by praising the double entendre as having improved polite conversation. The essay's author noted that the double entendre "owes its birth, as well as its name, to our inventive neighbours the French." The comment that follows his attribution, however, suggests his critical irony: "[I]t is that happy art, by which persons of fashion may communicate the loosest ideas under the most innocent expressions." The author also complained that "it were heartily to be wished that the ladies could be prevailed upon to give fewer invitations in public places; since the most frugal of them cannot always answer for her own economy: and it is well known that the profusion of one single entertainment has compelled many a beautiful young creature to hide herself from the world for whole months after." See Adam Fitz-Adam, "No. 201, Thursday, Nov. 4, 1756," in *The World,* reprinted in Ferguson, *The British Essayists,* 29:237.

that "there is nothing, perhaps, wherein the Disparity between the English and French Men of Fashion, is more visible and striking than in their different Conduct towards Womankind." If the French excel the British in the domain of conversation, he wrote, "the misfortune is not so great when it is reflected that by indulging it in the same excess as they do, what we might gain in Delicacy and Refinement, we might lose in Manliness of Behaviour and Liberty of Discourse; the two Pillars on which...our national Character is mainly supported."[51] Although Smellie was a great advocate of the benefits of "private conversation," by defining French as a meaningless language, he could argue that it was "peculiarly well adapted for that species of conversation which must ever take place in those general and promiscuous companies, where many persons of both sexes are met together."[52] Smellie, however, insisted that "the attention of the fair sex" tended to be engaged only by "superficial accomplishments." In his biography of John Gregory (1724–1773), Smellie approvingly summarized Gregory's advice to his daughters: "Modesty naturally disposes young women to be rather silent in large companies."[53] Thus, even when Smellie allowed that women might attend conversations, he recommended that they do so as little more than silent spectators and not as genuine participants.

Two essays published in succeeding issues of the *World* in December 1754 also explicitly took up the question of the relationship between women and language. The author distinguished between "the polite" and "the grammatical part[s] of our language," arguing that while men managed the latter, it was women who managed the former. In a tone of irony, the author suggested that he was "always inclined to plead the cause of [his] fair fellow-subjects [i.e., women]." He noted that "language is indisputably the more immediate province of the fair sex: there they shine, there they excel." "If words are wanting," he claimed, an indignant woman "instantly makes new ones: and I have often known four or five syllables that

---

51. John Andrews, *An Account of the Character and Manners of the French* (London: Printed by C. Dilly, J. Robson, and J. Walter, 1770), 68.

52. Smellie, "Language," 877.

53. Smellie, *Literary and Characteristical Lives*, 99–100. Gregory had written, "[M]odesty, which I think so essential in your sex, will naturally dispose you to be rather silent in company." See John Gregory, *A Father's Legacy to his Daughters* (London: Printed for W. Strahan, T. Cadell, and W. Creech, 1774), 28. Smellie also followed Gregory in noting that "females cannot be possessed of a more dangerous talent than Wit."

never met one another before, hastily and fortuitously jumbled into some word of mighty import. Nor is the tender part of our language less obliged to that soft and amiable sex; their love being at least as productive as their indignation." According to the article's author, women not only invented neologisms but also misused existing words and by doing so created the kinds of ambiguous and equivocal words that many French commentators took as signs of the superiority of the French language. "Not content with enriching our language by words absolutely new," he wrote, "my fair country-women have...improved it by the application and extension of old ones to various and very different significations. They take a word and change it...to be employed in the several occasional purposes of the day." The author of the essay then called for the publication of "a genteel Neological dictionary, containing those polite, though perhaps not strictly grammatical words and phrases, commonly used, and sometimes understood, by the Beau Monde." The following week, another essay that appeared in the *World* explicitly attacked the previous week's essay as if it had not been a satire. The author wrote,

> Novelty is [the ladies'] pleasure: singularity, and the love of being beforehand is greatly flattering to the female mind....
>
> From hence only can we account for that jargon which the French call the *Bon ton,* which they are obliged to change continually, as soon as they find it prophaned by any other company but one step lower than themselves in their degrees of politeness. A lady armed with a new word, exults with a conscious superiority, and exercises a tyranny over those who do not understand her, like the delegates of the law.... But a word which has been a month upon the town, loses its force, and makes as poor a figure as the law put into English.

The author of this essay linked women's speech directly with ambiguity and insincerity. He argued that "though it is very grievous to be ignorant, it is much more terrible to be deceived or misled." He insisted that people were too often deceived or misled precisely because women had a tendency to fall into "the abuse of turning old words from their former signification to a sense not only very different, but often directly contrary to it."[54]

---

54. Adam Fitz-Adam, "No. 101. Thursday, Dec. 5, 1754," and "No. 102. Thursday, Dec. 12, 1754," in *The World;* reprinted in Ferguson, *The British Essayists,* 27:260, 262, 265, 266, and 267. The first of the two essays gave the example of the word "vastly" used to describe something small:

English as a Manly Democratic Language

Smellie's argument concerning the energetic warmth of the English language was replayed on the syntactic field, where he claimed that the idiom of the English language was "in concord" with its "natural genius and style."[55] Smellie referred to the transpositive idiom as a "contagion" from which English had remained free and retained, as he put it, the "primitive simplicity" of the analogous idiom.[56] This notion of the syntactic simplicity of the English language permitted Smellie to push even further his characterization of all English speakers, including the noneducated "vulgar," as intelligent and in no way hampered by their language. If the idea that French was a light language tended to encourage the inclusion of some women but the exclusion of the lower orders in conversations, the idea that English was an energetic language tended to encourage the exclusion of women but the inclusion of all men.

Smellie believed that the English language's analogous idiom was a manifestation of its primitive simplicity. He compared the English language to a well-constructed machine, the operation of which was "obvious to an ordinary capacity" and that could be "easily put in order by the rudest hand." He held that English was therefore the easiest language to use, and this idea grounded his belief that English-speaking nonelite men shared with their elite counterparts a fully developed capacity for communication. "Our language follows an order of construction so natural and easy," he wrote, that it is "within the reach of the most ordinary capacity…; and on this account we may boast, that in no nation of Europe do the lower class of people speak their language with so much accuracy, or have their minds so much enlightened by knowledge, as those of Great Britain." English thus stood in stark contrast to other European languages, which had less of its primitive simplicity and were less inclined to promote social equality. In considering other more refined languages, Smellie wrote that no matter "how perfect soever the language may be when spoken with purity, the bulk of the nation [who speak it] must ever labour under the

---

"I had lately the pleasure to hear a fine woman pronounce, by a happy metonymy, a very small gold snuff-box that was produced in company to be Vastly pretty, because it was so Vastly little."
   55. Smellie, "Language," 864.
   56. Ibid., 878.

inconvenience of...inaccuracy of speech and all the evils which this naturally produces." "It is sufficient to observe," he concluded, that an overly refined language "tends to introduce a vast distinction between the different orders of men; to set an impenetrable barrier between those born in a high and those born in a low station; to keep the latter in ignorance and barbarity, while it elevates the former to such a height as must subject the other to be easily led by every popular demagogue. Smellie thus argued that the English language gave men "born in a low station," the opportunity to be the intellectual equals of "those born in a high" station. Smellie denied the existence of an unbridgeable linguistic and mental divide between elite and nonelite English-speaking men. While for Rivarol there could be no century of enlightenment for the French-speaking masses, for Smellie the characteristics of the English language, its lack of "minute distinctions" and "nice grammatical rules," and its energetic character together helped to shield all those who spoke it, including "those born in a low station," from the tyranny of elites whose counterparts in communities speaking different languages could use speech to deceive and mislead audiences.[57]

The idea that, as the Scottish commonsense philosopher James Beattie (1735–1803) put it in *The Theory of Language* (1788), "elocution is not perfect, unless the artificial signs of thought are enforced by the natural," was central to a belief that English, as an energetic language, promoted sincerity. Beattie, like Sheridan and others, followed Horace in relating this natural and sincere eloquence to the success of orators and actors, who, as he wrote, "will never express naturally what they do not intensely feel." He argued that in "oratory, which is addressed to the passions,... the natural signs of thought must enforce the artificial with as strong an energy, as in the action of the theatre. But the publick speaker, whose aim is to instruct and persuade, gives scope to those natural expressions only, that imply conviction, and earnestness."[58] This idea that there was a natural language that presented a speaker's state of mind or attitude and therefore promoted communicational sincerity suggested that artificial languages might mask the natural language to a greater or lesser extent. Even Sheridan, despite his complaints against the coldness of refined tongues, keenly argued in his

---

57. Ibid., 878 and 872.
58. James Beattie, *The Theory of Language* (London: Printed for A. Strahan and T. Cadell, 1788), 12 and 13. For Horace's argument, see his *Ars Poetica* 1.101–103.

Rhetorical Grammar of the English Language (1781) that "whoever imagines the English tongue unfit for *oratory,* has not a just notion of it." "In oratory and poetry," Sheridan wrote, "there is no tongue, ancient, or modern, capable of expressing a greater *variety*...of passions, by its *sounds*...than the English....Nor is there, as far as I know, any language more *copious,* than the English; an eminent advantage for *oratory.*" "It is greatly to our shame," he insisted, "that, while *we* do so little for the improvement of our language, and of our manner of speaking it in public, the *French* should take so much pains in both these respects, though *their* language is very much *inferior* to *ours,* both as to emphasis and copiousness."[59] The energy and sincerity of English speech thus contrasted with commonplace descriptions of French as a vehicle for insincere and equivocal speech that facilitated false forms of politeness.

As the implications of ideas of French as a language of légèreté led many in France to argue that light conversations rather than grave books were the engines that promoted civilization and that only printed materials that reflected conversational lightness had much merit, so the advocates of English as an energetic language were led to conclude that print could be effective only if it managed to communicate the energy of spoken English. One common refrain in eighteenth-century British rhetorical and linguistic discourse was that while speech could energetically demonstrate its own sincerity and so move an audience, writing frequently failed to communicate this sonic energy. For this reason, print was often described as cold and lifeless and contrasted with warm and enlivening speech. Sheridan argued, for example, "that before you can persuade a man into any opinion, he must first be convinced that you believe it yourself. This he can never be, unless the tones of voice in which you speak come from the heart, accompanied by corresponding looks, and gestures, which naturally result from a man who speaks in earnest."[60] Sheridan presented English as a language that was well suited to sincere and energetic oral expressions of emotion, and so he concluded that the real problem was that writing destroyed this communicative energy.

---

59. Thomas Sheridan, *A Rhetorical Grammar of the English Language* (Dublin: Printed for Messrs. Price, W. and H. Whitestone, 1781), 161–162.

60. Thomas Sheridan, *British Education or, The Source of the Disorders of Great Britain*...(London: Printed for R. and J. Dodsley, 1756), 91–92.

On Saturday, August 18, 1711, Richard Steele's *Spectator* number 147 had taken up the related issue of how reading destroys English pulpit oratory. In discussing the importance of "Reading of the Common Prayer," Steele wrote that the inability to read and recite expressions that had been written down had resulted from the failure to give "due Observations" to "the proper Accent and Manner of Reading." Steele noted that in one service he attended the reading was performed "so distinctly, so emphatically, and so fervently, that it was next to an Impossibility to be unattentive.... I then consider'd I address'd my self to the Almighty, and not to a beautiful Face. And when I reflected on my former Performances of that Duty, I found I had run it over as a matter of Form, in comparison to the Manner in which I then discharged it. My Mind was really affected, and fervent Wishes accompanied my Words." Steele called for people to "be inform'd of the Art of Reading movingly and fervently, how to place the Emphasis, and give the proper Accent to each Word, and how to vary the Voice according to the Nature of the Sentence."[61]

Although Steele was mainly concerned with public pulpit oratory, Sheridan and the other British elocutionists—figures like John "Orator" Henley (1692–1759), John Mason (1706–1763), James Burgh (1714–1775), John Herries (?–1781?), and John Walker (1732–1807)—insisted that capturing the enlivening warmth of English speech was no less important at the bar and in the senate, theater, court, and camp, all domains in which speakers had to communicate with speech something that was written. These elocutionists sought to reform writing by suggesting ways that print might indicate how to read aloud with the appropriate energy of spoken English.[62] These projects took for granted that, as Mason indicated, "the End of a good Pronunciation is, to make the Ideas seem to come from the Heart." If written texts could be made to indicate also their appropriate emotions that would attend a sincere communication, "then they will not fail to excite the Attention and Affections of them that hear us."[63] Thus,

---

61. Addison and Steele, *The Spectator,* 2:78 and 79.
62. See John Mason, *An Essay on the Power and Harmony of Prosaic Numbers...* (London: Printed by James Waugh, for M. Cooper, 1749); Joshua Steele, *Prosodia Rationalis...* (London: Printed by W. Bowyer and J. Nichols: for J. Almon, 1775); and John Walker, *The Melody of Speaking Delineated...* (London: Printed for the author; and sold by G. G. J. and J. Robinson; and T. Cadell, 1787).
63. John Mason, *An Essay on Elocution, or, Pronunciation* (London: Printed for R. Hett; J. Buckland; J. Waugh; and M. Cooper, 1748), 5–6.

the British, no less than the French, believed that writing ought to more closely reflect speech. A significant difference, however, was that while many French thinkers looked for genres, like fugitive pieces, that could capture the lightness of spoken French, the British frequently were more concerned with finding ways to convey the energy of spoken English. The British elocutionary movement aimed, therefore, at teaching how to read print aloud in energetic ways or at developing textual marks to indicate to readers the energy of English speech.

Concerns about English energy and pulpit oratory also were closely linked to concerns about dramatic performances on the stage. One of Addison's *Spectator* essays, which took up the different national conventions for theatrical performances, quoted René Rapin's (1621–1687) comment from Thomas Rymer's translation of Rapin's *Reflections on Aristotle's Treatise of Poetry* (1694): "The *English* have more of *Genius* for *Tragedy* than other People, as well by the Spirit of their Nation which delights in Cruelty, as also by the Character of their Language which is proper for Great Expressions."[64] In his *Discours sur la tragédie à Mylord Bolingbroke,* with which he prefaced the publication of his *Brutus* (1731), Voltaire repeated this claim that the English language was especially well suited to communicating the energy required for tragic performances.[65] That same year, after surveying various subjects, among them pulpit oratory, and English authors, Stackhouse remarked that it was thanks to English linguistic energy that British "Tragedians have better succeeded in their Compositions than any other Nation. The Strength, the Life, the Vigour of our Tongue...and the rapid Concurrence of its harsher Consonants...give Grief and Rage their different Turns, and are mightily assistant to the Poet's Passion."[66] Smellie, after describing the energetic characteristics of the English tongue, similarly commented that English "is more peculiarly adapted for the great and interesting scenes of the *Drama* than any language....Nor has any other nation ever arrived at that perfection which the English may justly claim in that respect; for however faulty our dramatic compositions

---

64. See René Rapin, *The Whole Critical Works of Monsieur Rapin* (London: Printed for H. Bonwicke. T. Goodwin, M. Wotton, B. Tooke. S. Manship, 1706), 2:210 and 217–218. For Addison's essay, see *The Spectator,* 1:188 n. 1.

65. See Voltaire, *Le Brutus de M. de Voltaire, avec un Discours sur la tragédie; Seconde édition revue et corrigée par l'auteur* (Amsterdam: J. Ledet et Jaques Desbordes, 1731), 4.

66. Stackhouse, *Reflections on the Nature and Property of Languages in General,* 178.

may be in some of the critical niceties...,—in nervous force of diction, and in the natural expression of those great emotions which constitute its soul and energy, we claim, without dispute, an unrivalled superiority."[67] Though Sheridan, Johnson, Reid, and others might have worried about the corrupting influence of writing, of French, or of women's speech on the English language's energetic sonic properties, others saw the simplicity and energetic gravity of the English language as contributing to a remarkable rise of British theater.

The Scottish Smellie as an Exemplary English Speaker

Smellie's arguments that the English language was particularly well suited to meaningful communication reflected his own rise from a comparatively modest to a prominent position in eighteenth-century British Enlightenment circles. Like Rivarol, Smellie's beginnings were provincial and non-noble. Unlike Rivarol, who longed to move to the conversational center of the world of French communication, Smellie repeatedly passed up opportunities to move from his provincial Edinburgh to metropolitan London.[68] Like Rivarol, Smellie's socioeconomic standing in eighteenth-century Britain should have placed him in a position outside that class of elites who could easily participate in the polite world of letters. Smellie went to school until the age of twelve, when he was to have been apprenticed to a staymaker. In 1752, when the terms of this apprenticeship could not be agreed upon, he became an apprentice instead in the Edinburgh printing house of Hamilton, Balfour, & Neil. Thus from the age of twelve until he was nineteen, Smellie worked as an apprentice in the Edinburgh print trade. This proved advantageous for his education because his firm encouraged him to attend three hours of lectures a day at the University of Edinburgh.[69]

---

67. Smellie, "Language," 2:877–878. For a discussion of eighteenth-century debates about sincerity and representation on the stage, see Paul Friedland, *Political Actors: Representative Bodies and Theatricality in the Age of the French Revolution* (Ithaca: Cornell University Press, 2002), 20–21.

68. See Robert Kerr, *Memoirs of the Life, Writings, and Correspondence of William Smellie* (Bristol, UK: Thoemmes Press, 1996), 1:325–328.

69. Frank A. Kafker, "William Smellie's Edition of the *Encyclopaedia Britannica*," in *Notable Encyclopedias of the Late Eighteenth Century: Eleven Successors of the Encyclopédie*, ed. Frank A. Kafker, 145–182 (Oxford: Voltaire Foundation, 1994), 146–147.

In 1764, his last year as a relatively obscure journeyman printer working in the firm of Murray & Cochrane, Smellie drew up critical comments on the edition of Lord Kames's *Elements of Criticism* that he was then typesetting for the press. He sent his observations anonymously to Kames, who responded favorably and, after discovering the letter's authorship, became Smellie's patron.[70]

His formal education and Kames's patronage helped Smellie gain access to the relatively closed circle of Edinburgh literati.[71] Eventually, his rising reputation within that circle led the publishers Andrew Bell (1726–1809) and Colin Macfarquhar (1745?–1793) to ask him to compile and edit the first edition of the *Encyclopaedia Britannica*.[72] Smellie, however, remained a man of relatively low social status and even lower economic standing.[73] He suffered continually from shortages of money, and over the years his economic circumstances deteriorated. In one of his letters, Smellie wrote, "Here, therefore, moneyless and rich relationless, I have a better chance than any where else."[74]

Though he never claimed, as did Rivarol, an aristocratic title or to belong to an aristocracy of the tongue, Smellie might have understood Rivarol's argument that English was the only civilized language that did not generate and reinforce separate speech communities among speakers of a single language as explaining his own rise from the status of a typesetter to that of one who belonged to the small circle of prominent Edinburgh literati. In the introduction to a facsimile edition of Smellie's *Literary and Characteristical Lives,* Stephen Brown argues that Smellie had a "lifelong concern with the democratization of knowledge." Brown points out that

---

70. See Kerr, *Memoirs of the Life, Writings, and Correspondence of William Smellie*, 1:346–352.

71. While still working in the printing trade, Smellie had edited periodicals such as the *Scots Magazine* (1759–1765) and the *Edinburgh Magazine and Review* (1773–1776).

72. He also translated Buffon's *Natural History* in nine volumes (1780–1785), revised for publication several new books, such as William Buchan's *Domestic Medicine* (1770), and produced several political pamphlets on Scottish political subjects. He prepared a series of biographical sketches of prominent Scottish Enlightenment figures. He also wrote the *Philosophy of Natural History* (1790–1799), which remained a standard work well into the nineteenth century. Smellie's manuscript papers include more than forty unpublished works in his hand.

73. Kafker has suggested that his "low status both socially and in the world of letters,... which would not have recommended him to [the Britannica's] subscribers" was one of the reasons his contributions were anonymous. See Kafker, "William Smellie's Edition of the *Encyclopaedia Britannica,*" 148.

74. Kerr, *Memoirs of the Life, Writings, and Correspondence of William Smellie*, 1:165.

"in his earliest correspondence with fellow journeyman printer William Tod and with the Reverend Samuel Charteris, whom he had met at the University of Edinburgh, Smellie refers with near obsession to projects for promoting learning and disseminating knowledge among the general public." Brown also notes that in this correspondence, "Smellie distinguished between two choices for addressing the public, one responsible, instructive, and civil, the other controversial, ironic, and decidedly uncivil." Brown suggests that "in his work with newspapers, magazines, and the *Britannica*, Smellie wanted to enlighten his readers in order to empower them and to demystify the arts and sciences so that the knowledge of the doctors and the professors would be readily accessible to anyone who could read." While this is no doubt true, Smellie's article on language and its emphasis on the links between language, conversation, and enlightenment, demonstrate that this conception of an extensive and inclusive enlightened society was not to be restricted merely to those who read.[75]

Smellie's arguments concerning the particular character of English as a language suited to private conversation represent his reflections upon the specific communicative mode that facilitated his own rise among the Edinburgh literati. Smellie's ascent to literary respectability resulted not only from the formal university education he received as an apprenticing typesetter; his participation in the world of conversational exchange was largely responsible for his eventual standing in Edinburgh literary circles. Smellie helped found the Society of Antiquaries of Scotland, and he belonged to the Philosophical Society of Edinburgh. He therefore used the communicative modes of conversation and print to his advantage in order to enlighten himself and to share his enlightenment with others. As one of Smellie's biographers notes, he founded the Newtonian Club "out of a dissatisfaction with the University of Edinburgh's Philosophical Society and [it] was conceived around a set of rules that seem a parody of the older

---

75. Stephen Brown, introduction to Smellie, *Literary and Characteristical Lives*, ix, x, and xiii. This extensive and inclusive vision of enlightened society distinguishes Smellie from Hume, whose conception of conversation as a vehicle of refinement, like Rivarol's, was decidedly intensive and exclusive. Nancy Struever points to this aspect of Hume's notion of conversation in "The Conversable World: Eighteenth-Century Transformations of the Relations of Rhetoric and Truth," in *Rhetoric and the Pursuit of Truth: Language Change in the Seventeenth Centuries*, ed. Brian Vickers and Nancy Struever (Los Angeles: William Andrews Clark Memorial Library, 1985), 90–92.

association, which had its beginnings with David Hume."[76] These projects and beliefs correspond well to Smellie's claim that his native language encouraged learning among what he called the "lower class of people." He may have sincerely believed that he owed much of his own success among the Edinburgh literati to the English language's distinctly simple and energetic character.

Some early modern language theorists held that the introduction of abstract ideas and the loss of passionate speech, changes that they associated with modern polite and commercial sociability, had corrupted languages so that civilized Europeans used language in ways that corrupted society. Smellie's characterization of English as a language of private conversation, however, presented it not only as a guarantee against tyranny or demagoguery but also as a language that promoted the progress of civilization. Smellie wrote that "the genius of the analogous language is...favourable for the most engaging purposes of life, the civilizing [of] the human mind by mutual intercourse of thought."[77] It is in this energetic and conversational sphere of English communication that Smellie believed the refinement of society occurred. For Smellie, no English speaker was ever in principle excluded from or left untouched by this process.

In a significant sense, Smellie's ideal speech community resembled the picture of the speech communities in the rude stage of the history of civil society painted by one of his contemporaries, Adam Ferguson (1723–1816). Ferguson accounted for the fact that some of the greatest literary works were produced in primitive times by arguing that "in rude ages men are not separated by distinctions of rank or profession. They live in one manner, and speak one dialect. The bard...has not to guard his language from the peculiar errors of the mechanic, the peasant, the scholar, or the courtier, in order to find the elegant propriety, just elevation, which is free from the vulgar of one class, the pedantic of the second, or the flippant of the third."[78] For Smellie, so long as English continued to resist the "contagion"

---

76. Brown, "Introduction," xv. These rules are reproduced in Kerr, *Memoirs of the Life, Writings, and Correspondence of William Smellie,* 1:67–69. If they are read as a parody of the Philosophical Society's rules, as I think they should be, then they suggest that he intended the Newtonian Club to represent a contrast to the overly exclusive Philosophical Society.

77. Smellie, "Language," 2:872.

78. Adam Ferguson, *An Essay on the History of Civil Society* (New Brunswick, NJ: Transaction Publishers, 1991), 174.

of French linguistic lightness, English speakers would continue to refine one another indefinitely. According to Smellie, there were two essential forms that social relations could take, and these corresponded to the two fundamental types of language represented by English and French. On the one hand, a syntactically simple, phonotactically energetic, and therefore semantically clear language tended toward an institutionally disengaged and putatively inclusive sphere of private conversation. On the other hand, a grammatically complex, passionately detached, and lexically light language tended toward a hierarchical and demagogic society open to cultural corruption and political tyranny.

Luxury, the British Commercial Empire, and English

Smellie's linguistic discourse can also be read as an eighteenth-century reworking of a classical republican discourse that lamented the decline of eloquence and language as a consequence of luxury associated with commercial and imperial expansion.[79] "Roman eloquence," the elder Seneca wrote, "reached its peak in the time of Cicero. Since then, day by day, things have become worse, whether because of the luxury of the times...or by some...malign and eternal law...that whatever has been brought to the highest point falls again to the lowest more swiftly than it rose."[80] According to George Kennedy, Seneca was pointing to "the loss of interest in public life...in contrast to ambition for private wealth. He thus suggests, but does not elaborate, the possibility that political changes from republic to empire may be at the root of the decline."[81] Thus, while empire may have brought peace, it also entailed the corruption of language and the decline of eloquence.

Many of Smellie's contemporaries believed that the corrosive luxury associated with commercial imperial expansion and the decline of language would go hand in hand. Take, for example, the following comments from

---

79. For a discussion of the "decline of eloquence" as a symptom of political decline in early modern European thought, see Jean Starobinski, "Eloquence et Liberté," *Revue suisse d'histoire* 26, no. 4 (1976): 549–566.

80. Quoted from George A. Kennedy, *A New History of Classical Rhetoric* (Princeton: Princeton University Press, 1994), 187.

81. Ibid.

the preface to Johnson's *Dictionary*. He wrote that "commerce, however necessary, however lucrative...corrupts the language."[82] Like Rivarol, Johnson suggested that British commerce would eventually corrupt British speech. "They that have frequent intercourse with strangers, to whom they endeavour to accommodate themselves," Johnson continued, "must in time learn a mingled dialect.... This will not always be confined to the exchange, the warehouse, or the port, but will be communicated by degrees to other ranks of the people, and be at last incorporated with the current speech."[83] In the end, Johnson suggested that a language must decline dramatically in a commercially prosperous and polite society that was oriented toward luxury markets. With cultural development, Johnson wrote,

> a language is amplified, it will be more furnished with words deflected from their original sense....Copiousness of speech will give opportunities to capricious choice by which some words will be preferred, and others degraded; vicissitudes of fashion will enforce the use of new, or extend the signification of known terms....Pronunciation will be varied by levity or ignorance, and the pen must at length comply with the tongue; illiterate writers will at one time or other, by publick infatuation, rise into renown, who, not knowing the original import of words, will use them with colloquial licentiousness, confound distinction, and forget propriety. As politeness increases, some expressions will be considered as too gross and vulgar for the delicate, others as too formal and ceremonious for the gay and airy; new phrases are therefore adopted, which must, for the same reasons, be in time dismissed.[84]

For the most part, Smellie accepted this vision of commercial progress as eventually corrosive of languages, minds, and cultures. His critical remarks on the Italian language, for example, suggest that he believed that languages and cultures tend in general to decline over time. He argued that

---

82. Johnson, preface to *Johnson's Dictionary*, 25.
83. Ibid. Johnson added that only people who retained some of their primitive culture could be sure to keep their language unchanged for some time. He wrote, "[T]he language most likely to continue long without alteration, would be that of a nation raised a little, and but a little, above barbarity, secluded from strangers, and totally employed in procuring the conveniencies of life; either without books, or...with very few: men thus busied and unlearned, having only such words as common use requires, would perhaps long continue to express the same notions by the same signs." (25).
84. Ibid., 26.

in Rome, after the destruction of Carthage, "luxury began to prevail, and stem austerity of their manners to relax, and selfish ambition to take place of that disinterested love for their country.... Ambitious men... amused the mob with artful and seditious harangues."[85] According to Smellie, the first speakers of Italian, after invading Rome, had been "enervated by luxury...; they had become fond of... sensual pleasures...; and their language partook of the same debility as their body."[86] Smellie claimed that

> the unaccustomed flow of riches which they at once acquired... conspired to enervate their minds, and render them soft and effeminate.—No wonder then, if a language new moulded should at this juncture partake of the genius of the people who formed it; and instead of participating of the martial boldness..., should be softened and enfeebled by every device which an effeminate people could invent.... Thus the Italian language is formed flowing and harmonious, but destitute of those nerves which constitute the strength and vigour of a language.[87]

While Rivarol held that the French language, French conversation, French cultural refinement, and the French commercial empire built on the export of frivolous French luxury goods all worked in tandem to civilize humanity, Smellie, like many of his British contemporaries, worried about the potential corrosive influence of commercial luxury. By arguing that commercial and imperial expansion represented a serious threat to public virtue, Smellie was a rather typical eighteenth-century British thinker. Eighteenth-century Scots like Smellie particularly regarded their union with a commercially successful and imperially expanding England as a potential source of corruption. A number of the Edinburgh literati developed arguments to show that such fears concerning the British union were unfounded. Smellie offered his own version of this argument by insisting that the peculiarities of the English language would guard against the corrupting influences of commercial, imperial, and cultural progress. Thus while Rivarol argued that it was the luxuriant levity of the French language that would guarantee that everyone would speak frivolously in French and so

---

85. Smellie, "Language," 873.
86. Ibid., 875.
87. Ibid.

dismissed worries about the corrosive effects of commercial empire on language, Smellie argued that it was the energetic warmth of the English language that would guarantee the global spread of an energetic and sincere English commerce and communication.

While the structure of the English language guarded against corruption at the hands of tyrannical demagogues, other languages, like Latin, Greek, Italian, and French, lent themselves ultimately to the usurpation of political authority by courtiers or demagogues motivated by selfish rather than public interests. Smellie believed that the unrefined energy of the English language would guarantee that social and commercial refinement could proceed indefinitely. Smellie concluded his *Britannica* article with the claim that the "language of Great Britain" is "a language more peculiarly circumstanced than any that has ever yet appeared.—It is the language of a great and powerful nation, whose fleets surround the globe, and whose merchants are in every port; a people admired, or revered by all the world."[88] These words exhibit Smellie's deep faith that the peculiar circumstances of his language guaranteed that Britain's destiny was one of greatness.

Smellie's reply to those who held that the union would be a corrupting influence was to insist on the unique virtues of the English language. His discussion of these linguistic and cultural issues can also be read, then, as part of the story of the Edinburgh literati's agenda promoting commercial sociability through anglicization and the formation of a British national identity centered on the conception of a shared national language. By insisting that the peculiar circumstances of the English language would guard against the moral decline associated with the British commercial empire, Smellie presented Great Britain as a "Happy Union."[89] In his *Britannica* article "English," Smellie noted that "the English tongue...[has] become the most copious, significant, fluent, courteous, and masculine language in Europe, if not in the world."[90]

---

88. Ibid., 879.

89. For a discussion of Scottish attitudes to anglicization, see Janet Sorensen, *The Grammar of Empire in Eighteenth-Century British Writing* (Cambridge: Cambridge University Press, 2000); and my "Welsh Indians and Savage Scots: History, Antiquarianism, and Indian Languages in Eighteenth-Century Britain," *History of European Ideas* 34, no. 3 (September 2008): 250–269.

90. Smellie, "English," in *Encyclopaedia Britannica...*, 2:499.

Conclusion

Both William Smellie and Antoine de Rivarol argued not only that their respective languages were superior to the refined Greek and Latin but also that they were the most perfect of all the refined modern European languages. Each of them believed that his success in life had been, at least in large part, the result of the superiority of his respective language. Each tied his discussion of the particular characteristics that made his language superior to his discussions of polite and commercial sociability. In doing so, both men argued against those who insisted that over time their respective languages had (or would) become corrupt. In fact, Smellie argued, the peculiar virtues of English guarded against the vices of commercial luxury and an overly refined sociability that many in Britain associated with the French and their language. Rivarol and Smellie each insisted that the other's national language was defective. For Smellie, the simple, warm, and energetic English language generated a sincere, extensive, and inclusive speech community that used private conversation and print to refine and enlighten all English speakers. Rivarol insisted that the distinctly light French language was the one most suited to polite conversation but as such was a language that facilitate double entendres and generated an intensive and exclusive or stratified speech community in which the various social orders had their appropriate places. Smellie and Rivarol thus both presented their respective languages as the vehicles of enlightenment par excellence. The respective ways in which they conceived of the processes of enlightenment, however, were fundamentally different. For Rivarol enlightenment and the language that best promoted it must be clear but also not be too grave, serious, or pedantic. An ideal language must promote social levity as it amusingly refined its speakers' minds. While Smellie could agree that an ideal language must be clear, he was critical of the meaningless social levity and dissimulation that he believed the French language promoted. Instead, Smellie argued that an ideal language should be energetic and warm. He believed that because of its peculiar qualities the English language promoted the spread of clear ideas but in a way that also guarded against the kinds of socially corrosive dissimulation that he and many other in Great Britain associated with the false politeness promoted by French.

Coda

French Levity and English Energy in the Revolutionary Wake

> The Americans avoided using expressions like "you speak English well"; "you understand English well." Instead, I often heard them say: "you speak American well"; "American is not difficult to learn."...If nothing else, we can conclude at least that the Americans could not express in a more energetic manner their aversion for the English.
>
> François-Jean de Chastellux, *Voyages dans l'Amérique septentrionale* (1785)

> France no longer laughs and French gaiety has passed away and become a shadow.... We have those writers who have given our language an English accent to thank for our state!... If France has become grave and serious, it is now also quiet.
>
> Rivarol, *Le Petit Almanach de Nos Grands Hommes pour l'année 1788* (1808)

By the time Rivarol composed his essay for the Berlin Academy's prize, Britain had already lost its struggle to retain control of its thirteen American colonies. Rivarol could therefore point directly to the American Revolution and write that "Britain, witness to our successes, has no share in them. Its last war with us has left it doubly eclipsed in literature and in its preponderance, and this war has given Europe a grand spectacle. We have witnessed a free people driven by Britain into slavery, and brought back to liberty by a young monarch. The history of America can be reduced to three epochs: butchered by Spain, oppressed by Britain, and saved by France."[1] With these words Rivarol concluded his argument for the superiority of the French language. In doing so, he took a parting shot at France's commercial and imperial rival. The gloating reference by this eventual counterrevolutionary to the American Revolution shows that Rivarol had no idea his own country would soon be in the midst of its own revolutionary struggle and that this French Revolution would bring to the fore complaints about the levity of the French language that he and others had been so keen to celebrate. Some historians have argued that during the revolutionary period language assumed a "unique, magical quality."[2] In this book I have shown that, in fact, during the entire period from the late seventeenth century to the end of the eighteenth century, French and British thinkers were tremendously engaged with the implications of different languages. Although certain linguistic concerns were either new or gained a new importance during the American and French revolutions, others were continuous with discourses of the late seventeenth and eighteenth centuries.

A number of American and French revolutionaries announced that their revolutions would regenerate their respective languages and that their regenerated language would contribute to the regeneration of society. As historians have emphasized, the revolutionaries' preeminent concerns were with establishing a standard national language and with characterizing their respective revolutionary languages as facilitating communicational clarity.[3] While many British and French thinkers had through the eighteenth century argued that their own language was the best one,

---

1. Antoine de Rivarol, *L'Universalité de la langue française* (Paris: Arléa, 1991), 90–91.
2. Lynn Hunt, *Politics, Culture, and Class in the French Revolution* (Berkeley: University of California Press, 1984), 20.
3. For works on theories of language during the revolutions, see John Howe, *Language and Political Meaning in Revolutionary America* (Amherst: University of Massachusetts Press, 2004); Michael P. Kramer, *Imagining Language in America: From the Revolution to the Civil War* (Princeton: Princeton University Press, 1992); David Simpson, *The Politics of American English, 1776–1850* (Oxford: Oxford University Pres, 1986); Sophia Rosenfeld, *A Revolution in Language: The Problem of Signs in Late Eighteenth-Century France* (Stanford: Stanford University Press, 2001); David Bell, "Lingua Populi, Lingua Dei: Language, Religion, and the Origins of French Revolutionary Nationalism," *American Historical Review* 100, no. 5 (December 1995): 1403–1437; and

American and French revolutionaries frequently argued that these languages had lost any capacity to communicate serious matters with a sufficiently expressive intensity. In this respect, the revolutions represented not just a continuation of earlier concerns with linguistic transparency but also a triumph of the ideal of communicative energy that had been associated with American Indian languages and English over an ideal of levity that many had identified with the French language.

Ironically, some Americans used the very same argument that Smellie and others had developed to contrast an energetic English language with a corrupt and meaningless French language. In these American hands, however, the English language used in Britain became the corrosive polite tongue that they contrasted with a surging energetic American English. Among those who wrote about language in the wake of the American Revolution, Noah Webster (1758–1843) holds a particularly prominent place.[4] In one of his earliest works, *An American Selection of Lessons in Reading and Speaking* (1787), Webster rehearsed the British elocutionists' emphasis on the importance of expressing genuine emotion when speaking. His fourth "Rule for Reading and Speaking" was "Let the sentiment you express be accompanied with proper tones, looks and gestures."[5] Under this heading, he explained that "all these should be perfectly natural. They should be the same which we use in common conversation. A speaker should endeavor to feel what he speaks."[6] Among his *Collection of Essays and Fugitiv Writings* (1790), Webster also presented a letter purporting to be from a young lady and his reply. The young lady's letter expresses her concerns about the propriety of engaging with "a gentleman who professed an unalterable attachment for her." This young lady explains that "tho he professed himself to be an admirer of candor, and a strict adherer to the rules of honor, still I could not but doubt his sincerity from the extravagance of his

---

Michel de Certeau, Dominique Julia, and Jacques Revel, *Une Politique de la langue: La Révolution française et les patois: L'enquête de Grégoire* (Paris: Gallimard, 1975).

4. On Noah Webster's ideas about language, see among others V. P. Bynack, "Noah Webster's Linguistic Thought and the Idea of an American National Culture," *Journal of the History of Ideas* 45, no. 1 (1984): 99–114; Simpson, *The Politics of American English*, 52–90; and Kramer, *Imagining Language in America*, 35–63.

5. Noah Webster, *An American Selection of Lessons in Reading and Speaking* (Philadelphia: Printed by Young and M'Culloch, 1787), 15.

6. Ibid., 15–16.

expressions."[7] In "An Address to Yung Ladies" from the same collection, Webster wrote, "You are taught to suspect the man who flatters you. But your good sense wil very eezily distinguish between expressions of mere civility and declarations of real esteem. In general one rule holds, that the man who iz most lavish in declarations of esteem and admiration, luvs and admires you the leest. A profusion of flattery iz real ground for suspicion."[8] Together these passages suggest that Webster, like Smellie, believed that sincerity and deception manifested themselves in speech and that a language that facilitated energetic expressions would more easily discover sincerity and dissimulation. Like Smellie, Webster believed that English was more energetic than other languages; unlike Smellie, however, he argued that the language spoken in Britain was a corrupt form of English that resembled French more than did the English spoken in America.

In his *Dissertations on the English Language* (1789), Webster argued that "the people of America...speak the most *pure English* now known in the world." He argued that "Great Britain, whose children we are, and whose language we speak, should no longer be *our* standard; for the taste of her writers is already corrupted." Webster blamed corruptions in British English on the "practice of the court and stage in London." Webster's argument stood in stark contrast to Rivarol's hierarchical French speech community. According to Webster, "when a particular set of men, in exalted stations, undertake to say 'we are the standards of propriety and elegance, and if all men do not conform to our practice, they shall be accounted vulgar and ignorant,' they take a very great liberty with the rules of the language and the rights of civility." Webster presented the English language as having arrived at a state of near perfection at the beginning of the eighteenth century and argued that since then, certain British writers had contributed to its corruption. Among these writers, he blamed Samuel Johnson, David Hume, and Edward Gibbon. Webster characterized Johnson's language as "a mixture of Latin and English; an intolerable composition of

---

7. Noah Webster, *A Collection of Essays and Fugitiv Writings on Moral, Historical, Political and Literary Subjects* (Boston: Printed by I. Thomas and E. T. Andrews, 1790), 239.

8. Ibid., 407. In the collection's fifteenth essay, titled "Sketches of the Rise, Progress and Consequences of the late Revolution," Webster noted that "the deliberations of the first American Legislature were marked with wisdom, spirit and generally with candor" (204). Webster's peculiar spellings in these passages are an example of his desire to simplify and rationalize what he took to be the unnecessary complexity and irregularity of English spelling.

Latinity, affected smoothness, scholastic accuracy and roundness of periods." "Hume," he wrote, "has borrowed French idioms without number." He criticized "Gibbon's harmony of prose" for being "calculated to delight our ears" and complained that in his writing "perspicuity, the first requisite of stile, is sometimes sacrificed to melody; the mind of a reader is constantly dazzled by a glare of ornament, or charmed from the subject by the music of the language." Webster thus characterized the British English of his day in terms similar to those who either celebrated or criticized the French language for the sweetness of its sounds and the brilliance of its charming wit. Like Smellie, who complained that French facilitated disingenuous and unmeaning flattery, Webster wrote that the "taste of the age" in Britain was such that "simplicity of stile is neglected for ornament, and sense is sacrificed to sound." "The same taste," he added, "prevailed in Rome, under the Emperors, when genius was prostituted to the mean purposes of flattery" and he quoted the elocutionary movement's John Mason to the effect that "after the dissolution of the Roman republic,... Men grew excessively fond of the numerous stile, and readily sacrificed the strength and energy of their discourse to the harmony of their language."[9]

In characterizing the relationship between British and American English, Webster thus transposed a conventional British argument that contrasted an expressively energetic and sincere English to a gallantly light but shallow and insincere French. Webster, in fact, had made this clear in one of his earliest works, *Sketches of American Policy* (1785), where he wrote, "America is an independent empire, and ought to assume a national character. Nothing can be more ridiculous, than a servile imitation of the manners, the language, and the vices of foreigners." "Nothing can betray a more despicable disposition in Americans," he wrote, "than to be the apes of Europeans. An American ought not to ask what is the custom of London and Paris; but... every fashionable folly is brought from Europe and adopted without scruple in our dress, our manners and our conversation.... The *belles* and the *beaux,* with tastes too refined for a vulgar language, must, in all their discourse, mingle a spice of *sans souci* and *je ne sais quoi.*"[10]

---

9. Noah Webster, *Dissertations on the English Language, with an Essay on a Reformed Mode of Spelling* (Boston: Printed by Isaiah Thomas and Company, 1789), 288, 20, 24, 25, 32, 33, 34.

10. Noah Webster, *Sketches of American Policy* (Hartford: Printed by Hudson and Goodwin, 1785), 47.

After Webster's conversion experience during the Second Great Awakening, he began to argue that the original language spoken in the Garden of Eden must have been a Germanic one and that Americans should recover the more energetic Germanic roots of a primitive English language. According to Webster, "the Saxon words constitute our mother tongue; being words which our ancestors brought with them out of Asia."[11] Webster held that the existing Germanic languages had descended from the language spoken in Eden, which was preserved by the tribe of Japhet, one of Noah's sons who had immigrated to Europe. He tied his theory of linguistic development to the Tacitean notion that the Germanic-speaking peoples, in contrast to the Romance-language-speaking Romans and French, were republican, liberty loving, and virtuous. Webster argued that these Germanic tribes twice challenged Roman *imperium* and tyranny. The first occasion occurred when they brought about the fall of the decadent Roman Empire and the second when Germanic speakers stood up to Roman Catholicism. Webster thus put forward a linguistic version of the Norman-yoke myth.[12] According to Webster, the newly formed American republic needed to give up not only its political ties to a Latinized and therefore corrupt British political system but also its ties to a Latinized and therefore corrupt and corrupting British language. Americans, Webster insisted, should recover the energetic purity of their language.[13]

While it is difficult to say how widespread Webster's ideas were, historians have argued that Thomas Paine (1737–1809) and Thomas Jefferson (1743–1826) similarly believed in a linguistic version of the Norman-yoke myth. Olivia Smith has noted that Paine, for example, wrote, "[T]hat this vassalage idea and stile of speaking was not got rid of even at the Revolution of 1688, is evident from the declaration of Parliament to William and Mary in these words: 'We do most humbly *submit* ourselves, our heirs and prosperities, for ever.' Submission is wholly a vassalage term, repugnant to the dignity of freedom, and an echo of the language used at the

---

11. Noah Webster, introduction to *American Dictionary of the English Language* (New York: S. Converse, 1828), 4.
12. See Simpson, *The Politics of American English*, 81–90. In its more conventional political form, the phrase "Norman yoke," which gained currency in the 1640s during the English Civil War, was used to blame William the Conqueror (1027–1087) and his Norman French followers and policy for destroying an Anglo-Saxon golden age of freedom from oppression.
13. Olivia Smith, *The Politics of Language, 1791–1819* (Oxford: Clarendon, 1984), 51.

Conquest."[14] Jefferson, for his part, wrote that "English liberties are not infringements merely on the king's prerogative, extorted from our princes by taking advantage of their weaknesses; but a restitution of that antient constitution, of which our ancestors had been defrauded by the art and finess of the Norman Lawyers, rather than deprived by the force of the Norman arms."[15] Jefferson, Paine, and Webster believed that what they saw as British tyranny ultimately was caused by the corrupting influence of the overly subtle French on British English. Webster and others sought, therefore, to inoculate the new American republic against the corruptions introduced into British English by French influences.

The belief that American English was a preeminently energetic language suited to expressing with sufficient intensity the republican stuff of a grave new world also made its mark on American conceptions of oratory. Kenneth Cmiel and James Perrin Warren have both noted the rise of "Anglo-Saxonism" in antebellum American rhetorical theory.[16] In 1840, Cornelius Conway Felton (1807–1862) wrote, "It cannot be denied that the most expressive, picturesque and national parts of our complicated language are the remains of the Anglo-Saxon."[17] Cmiel presents this "Romantic eloquence" as "conjur[ing] up a democratic version of the sublime by merging the lofty with the rustic."[18] Of course, there was much in this new republican rhetorical ideal that had already been operating in both Jesuit and Puritan missionary accounts of the sublime savage eloquence of American Indians and in eighteenth-century British characterizations of an energetic English speech. And, in fact, as Carolyn Eastman has recently pointed out, the virtual obsession in postrevolutionary America with printing and performing eloquent Indian speeches encouraged Americans, particularly children, through a form of "playing Indian," to "identify as national subjects on several levels" by, for example, "articulat[ing] a unique

---

14. Thomas Paine, *The Writings of Thomas Paine,* ed. Moncure Daniel Conway (New York: G. P. Putnam's Sons, 1894), 2:331.

15. Thomas Jefferson, *The Commonplace Book of Thomas Jefferson,* ed. Gilbert Chinard (Baltimore: Johns Hopkins University Press, 1926), 192–193.

16. Kenneth Cmiel, *Democratic Eloquence: The Fight over Popular Speech in Nineteenth-Century America* (New York: Morrow, 1990); James Perrin Warren, *Culture of Eloquence: Oratory and Reform in Antebellum America* (University Park: Pennsylvania State University Press, 1999).

17. C. C. Felton, "Review of *Hyperion,*" *North American Review* 50 (1840): 148.

18. Cmiel, *Democratic Eloquence,* 95.

American history...[that] made Americans appear sharply different from their former British compatriots."[19] As I noted in chapter 6, however, the British themselves, ironically enough, had already made a similar identification. And so some American writers turned to identifying their speech not only with the eloquence of savage Indian speech but also with the linguistic energy that others had long since linked with a savage Anglo-Saxon tongue that had not yet become overly refined and soft.

George William Curtis (1824–1892), in his "Lectures and Lecturing" (1856), for example, wrote,

> Remember what a speaking style is; viz., a mind every moment forging a connecting link with other minds ...; mind touching eyes and ears every instant, and receiving, as well as awakening emotions with inconceivable rapidity. Anglo-Saxon is the style. The sharp, clean-cut words—the words that ring and echo—the words that, instead of cumbering, heighten the elasticity of the idea, are your true vocabulary. For effect—straightforward, rifle-shot effect—nothing compares with it.... If you are determined to be a real speaker, alive all through to subject and audience, you must master the language of the dogmatic will, the resolute purpose, the imperial soul—the noble, the glorious, old Anglo-Saxon.[20]

One French orator had even prophesied in April 1789 that American English would not only triumph over British English but in fact become the world's universal language. The orator was a French revolutionary minister, Jean-Marie Roland de la Platière (1734–1793), who in his inaugural discourse to the Société de Bourg-en-Bresse, delivered three short months before the storming of the Bastille, took up the old question of which language was destined to become universal. Roland replayed the usual early modern arguments about the reciprocal links between a people's circumstances and its language: "The perfection of a language and the preponderance of the people who use it, together are necessary to its universality or resolve the problem of its extension. These two causes are

---

19. Carolyn Eastman, "The Indian Censures the White Man: 'Indian Eloquence' and American Reading Audiences in the Early Republic," *William and Mary Quarterly* 65, no. 3 (July 2008): 537.

20. George William Curtis, "Lectures and Lecturing," *Harper's Monthly Magazine*, December 1856, 125.

indispensable: one without the other is insufficient." And just five years after Rivarol and Schwab shared the prize for the Berlin Academy's competition on virtually the same subject, Roland argued,

> If we consider the French tongue, which has spread into the four corners of the world..., we would be tempted to believe the issue already put to rest. The clarity...of this language, a value so apparent in an infinity of excellent works; the celebrity of many men whose genius has stamped its character onto it; the depth and the superiority of various subjects that have been treated in French; and finally, the belief held by many great persons of Europe that a study of French must be part of their children's education; all of this seems to unite to promise it the most extensive and most durable empire.

Roland argued, however, that despite the potential that the French language had to become universal, there were too many religious, political, and diplomatic circumstances that made people disdain it. Roland concluded that "jealous rivals, though they amuse themselves with our styles and look to read our good authors, they have too little esteem for our moral character, our political existence, and they dread our religious principles too much for us to ever have the degree of influence required for a language to become universal."[21]

After thus dismissing the language in which he was articulating his discourse, Roland considered the English language, "in England," to be the only modern European language that could rival the classical Greek.[22] Roland noted that "if the English language has not received from the climate a sweet insinuation that perfects harmony and subjugates the ear with charming sounds, it has received a force that imposes itself on the mind; it has received from the activity of passions and from the elevated character of its speakers, an abundance and a majesty that takes hold of the soul." As admiring as Roland was of British English, he argued that "the inhabitants of the United States, are just as proud and no less brave than the

---

21. Jean-Marie Roland de la Platière, "Apperçu des causes qui peuvent rendre une langue universelle, et observations sur celles des langues vivantes qui tend le plus à le devenir" [April 20, 1789], repr. in Anna Mandich, "Roland de la Platière et la langue universelle," *Dix-huitième Siècle* 30 (1998): 325 and 326.

22. Ibid., 326–327.

English.... [They] are more humane, more generous, and more tolerant; all of these are things suited... to speaking the language of such a people." Roland argued that the English speakers in the new American republic were by their character, policy, and principles, better suited to speaking this energetic English language, a language that he declared would "one day be universal."[23]

If one French revolutionary joined Americans in arguing that American English had greater energy than British English, most French revolutionaries who wrote about the merits and defects of language focused their attention on their own tongue. The French Revolution was at least as complicated as the American Revolution and had no fewer factions and twists. While historians have devoted much study to how revolutionaries in France worried about making communication clear and about establishing a national language, none has given any attention to the place of concerns about levity and energy in their linguistic thinking.[24] Yet just as some American revolutionaries blamed British political corruptions on the influence of French on British English, certain French revolutionaries saw themselves as engaged in a struggle against the corrosive influences of the refined and light language that so many French linguists had celebrated during France's ancien régime.

Given that a conventional eighteenth-century characterization of the French language was that it was an especially nuanced instrument that allowed speakers to manipulate apparent ambiguities to promote amusing and light forms of sociability, the French language was vulnerable to republican criticism of the aristocratic levity that Rivarol had so vehemently celebrated. As early as 1744, in fact, even Voltaire was already complaining about the disadvantages of a language that he otherwise tended to celebrate. "What one calls wit," he wrote,

> is sometimes a new comparison, sometimes a fine allusion: here it is the abuse of a word that one presents with one sense, while meaning it in another;

---

23. Ibid., 327, 328, and 329.
24. For the creation of a national tongue see David Bell, "*Lingua Populi, Lingua Dei,*" 1403–1437; and de Certeau, Julia, and Revel, *Une Politique de la langue*. For revolutionary concerns with representational clarity see Rosenfeld, *A Revolution in Language*. Much of the work on revolutionary concerns with clarity has focused on the impact of Lockean ideas, transmitted through Condillac and the Idéologues to revolutionaries.

there it is the light connection between two ideas with little in common;... it is the art of only saying half of what one is thinking and leaving the rest to be guessed at ...; but all this brilliance (and I do not mean fake brilliance) does not at all or hardly ever suit a serious work and one that must be engaging. The reason is that in such a case it is the author who becomes visible, while the audience only wants to see the heroic character. Such a hero is always either impassioned or in danger. When one is in danger and impassioned one never tries to be witty.[25]

Voltaire, who early in his literary life had frequently celebrated the French language for its promotion of cultural and intellectual refinement through witty epigrams and polite conversation, therefore also began to worry around midcentury that such forms of communication threatened to discourage the kind of energetic emotional engagement required for the dramatic and serious matters of epic historical import like politics and war.[26]

As we saw in chapter 5, this idealization of French linguistic levity began to take shape in the context of a late-seventeenth-century quarrel over whether Latin or French should be used for monumental inscriptions. Although the issue of monumental inscriptions had largely faded away by the middle of the eighteenth century, replaced as it was with the idea that French was best suited to fugitive forms of commemoration like the witty epigram, it resurfaced during the French Revolution at the very moment when the revolutionaries decided to replace the old regime's monarchical monuments with revolutionary republican monuments. Historians of the French revolutionaries' linguistic ideas have recognized the importance of the Abbé Grégoire (1750–1831), who presented his "Report on the Necessity and the Means of Annihilating Patois and of Universalizing the

---

25. Voltaire, *Oeuvres complètes de Voltaire* (Paris: Hachette, 1876), 17:446.

26. David Bell has shown that a republican critique of French légèreté became especially pronounced in the 1770s and 1780s. This critique emphasized the need for a recovery of robust energy. Bell, *The Cult of the Nation in France: Inventing Nationalism 1680–1800* (Cambridge, MA: Harvard University Press, 2001), 146–154. Elena Russo has similarly shown how certain philosophes around midcentury began to turn against the *goût moderne,* which they associated with wordplay and which they increasingly characterized as too frivolous and hollow. Their stylistic priorities therefore drifted toward the *grand goût,* an energetic style suitable for serious, momentous, and powerful ideas. Russo, *Styles of Enlightenment: Taste, Politics, and Authorship in Eighteenth-Century France* (Baltimore: Johns Hopkins University Press, 2007).

French Language," to the National Convention on June 4, 1794.[27] While these historians have extensively explored Grégoire's plan for imposing a national standard on all French citizens, they have not given any attention to another related report he made to the National Convention on January 11, 1794.

This "Report on Inscriptions for Public Monuments" took up the century-old question of whether French was the language best suited to monumental inscriptions.[28] Grégoire noted that the most significant reason for which some continued to believe that French should not be used was that, as he put it, "some writers reproach our language for its lack of energy." Grégoire's report tackled this objection by noting that, although the French language had not lacked energy to the extent its detractors had suggested, to the extent that it did lack energy, this was only because it had had to labor under the influence of despotism. Grégoire explained to the convention that the French language

> did indeed have the timidity of slavery when the corruption of the court dictated its laws.... And how could its genius have shaken off that degrading yoke...? The feudal insolence that condemns the useful professions also excludes from the language the very terms that are relevant to them.... The time is coming when the terms *cow* and *manure,* for example, will have a value in our republican language that corresponds to that which their referents have in reality, while we will condemn as characteristics of a ridiculous and abject style the words *princess* and *courtier.* The lexicon of equality will enrich itself by such subtractions and additions.[29]

Part of Grégoire's argument therefore blamed the very thing that so many before him had celebrated as the source of French légèreté: the restricted nature of the French lexicon under the old regime.

---

27. See Henri Grégoire's "Rapport sur la nécessité et les moyens d'anéantir les patois et d'universaliser la langue française (16 prairial an II)." This text is reproduced in de Certeau, Julia, and Revel, *Une Politique de la langue,* 300–317.

28. Henri Grégoire, *Rapport sur les inscriptions des monumens publics: Séance du 22 nivôse, l'an II de la République* (Paris: Imprimé par ordre de la Convention Nationale, 1794), 12 n. 5, directed readers to one of the key defenses of Latin in the querelle de l'arc de triomphe: Jean Lucas' *De monumentis publicis Latine inscribendis* (Paris: Simon Benard, 1677).

29. Ibid., 5–6.

Grégoire therefore projected a revolutionary reformation of the lexicon that would go hand in hand with a regeneration of linguistic energy for French speakers. "Our language," he wrote, "will recover its antique naïveté." "It will rejuvenate superannuated terms, and will perfect its forms; it will acquire those energetic turns of phrase that it lacks; it will have that laconic pride, which, in each word engraves a thought; it will give birth to inscriptions, such as the one on that bronze statue erected by the Romans to Cornelia. Such praise in so few words! *To the mother of the Gracchi.*" He concluded his report by announcing, "[F]or public monuments, as for monies, the French People must not admit anything but the national idiom. The walls, the marble, and the bronze, must all be made to speak to all present and future sansculottes in the language of liberty."[30] Just as some American revolutionaries conceived of an English language that would be regenerated by recovering the antique energy suited to liberated speakers, so Grégoire promised that the French revolutionaries were revivifying their all-too-gay language and turning it into a linguistic instrument worthy of the energetic actions of the sansculottes.

Despite the fact that the Thermidorean reaction, Napoleon, and the Restoration either left unfinished or wiped away many of Grégoire's and the Revolution's more radical programs, his suggestion that after the Revolution the French language could no longer be thought of principally as a language lacking in energy did seem to have been in one sense correct. Indeed, even though the reporter discussed at the end of chapter 5 could see the revolutionary crowd's laughter at the way the deflating balloon resembled a failing phallus as a sign that the Revolution had not destroyed French gaiety, and even though the Marquis de Bièvre could insist in 1799 that Parisians had not lost their taste for puns, others disagreed. None other than the champion of French linguistic levity, Rivarol, looked back on the French Revolution and declared, for example, that "France no longer laughs and French gaiety has passed away and become a shadow.... In the end, we imported England's philosophy to rescue the French nation. We have those writers who have given our language an English accent to thank for this state of ours!"[31] In Rivarol's mind, not only had French

---

30. Ibid., 6–7 and 10.
31. Antoine de Rivarol, *Le Petit Almanach de Nos Grands Hommes pour l'année 1788. Suivi d'un grand nombre de pièces inédites* (Paris: Chez Léopold Collin, 1808), 1–2. In 1790, Rivarol had complained, "[T]he enemies of the language have become all of a sudden the defenders of the nation.

speakers stopped using their language for the witty epigrammatic speech to which he had argued it was best suited, but the Revolution had even anglicized it.

And when, in 1826, the antiquarian and philologist Charles Nicolas Allou (1787–1843) read his *Essai sur l'universalité de la langue française* to the Académie des Inscriptions, he cited almost all the eighteenth-century French commentators on the language and replayed close to all of their claims about the virtues of the language, but he significantly omitted one of them. "One of the principal characteristics of this language," he insisted, "is first of all its extreme clarity." Significantly, Allou argued that this wonderful clarity "renders it less susceptible than any other language to obscurity, equivocal words, and double meanings."[32] Indeed, he even went out of his way to note that "the lack of synonyms (which are more rare in French, than at least in other modern languages) must tend also to make it easier to use and allows speakers to avoid many of those equivocations that are so disagreeable and yet so common among foreigners."[33] The French language therefore had passed curiously from being celebrated for having the most synonyms to being praised for having the fewest.

Allou's arguments about the clarity of French and George William Curtis's claims about the energy of American English, however, were those of amateur linguists speaking during a time when the domain of linguistics had long since begun the process of academic professionalization that turned attention away from many of the specific issues that had preoccupied early modern linguistic thinkers. This is not to suggest that attitudes toward different languages did not continue to influence in many significant ways the conclusions that professional linguists drew about the character of speakers and speech communities.[34] Although prejudices about different languages have persisted, many of these prejudices changed with

---

One can never be too wary in this world of such sudden metamorphoses." See Rivarol, *Petit Dictionnaire des grands hommes de la Révolution* (1790; Paris: Editions Desjonqueres, 1987), 34.

32. Charles Nicolas Allou, *Essai sur l'universalité de la language Française* (Paris: Firmin Didot, 1828), 245.

33. Ibid., 250 n. 1.

34. See, for example, Douglas A. Kibbee, "'The People' and Their Language in 19th-Century French Linguistic Thought," in *The Emergence of the Modern Language Sciences: Studies on the Transition from Historical-Comparative to Structural Linguistics in Honour of E. F. K. Koerner*, ed. Sheila Embleton, John E. Joseph, and Hans-Joseph Niederehe (Philadelphia: John Benjamins, 1999), 111–127; and Tony Crowley, *Language and History: Theories and Texts* (London: Routledge, 1996), 99–188.

the intensification of imperial and industrial expansion and the emergence of new concerns about nations, classes, and races. Also, professional linguists developed and adopted new theoretical frameworks that focused, for example, on the historical or genetic links among different language families. This newly scientific framework provided linguists with the means to justify a new set of prejudices about the comparative merits of different communities. As the previous discussion shows, the changed circumstances of the revolutionary period itself were already dramatically transforming attitudes toward the French and English languages.

BIBLIOGRAPHY

Primary Sources

Académie de Berlin. *De l'universalité Européenne de la langue française, 1784.* Textes revus par Pierre Pénisson. Paris: Librairie Arthème Fayard, 1995.

Adams, John Quincy. *Memoirs of John Quincy Adams.* Edited by Charles Francis Adams. 12 vols. Philadelphia: J. B. Lippincott and Co., 1874–1877.

Addison, Joseph, and Richard Steele. *The Spectator.* Edited by Donald F. Bond. 5 vols. Oxford: Clarendon Press, 1965.

Alleine, Joseph. *A Sure Guide to Heaven.* Edinburgh: Banner of Truth Trust, 1959.

Allou, Charles Nicolas. *Essai sur l'universalité de la language Française.* Paris: Firmin Didot, 1828.

Andrews, John. *An Account of the Character and Manners of the French.* London: Printed by C. Dilly, J. Robson, and J. Walter, 1770.

Anon. *Confédération nationale, ou Récit exact et circonstancié de tout ce qui s'est passé à Paris, le 14 juillet 1790, à la federation.* Paris: Chez Garnéry, 1790.

———. *The Dying Speeches of Several Excellent Persons Who suffered for Their Zeal against Popery; and Arbitrary Government.* London, 1689.

Aristotle. *The Basic Works of Aristotle.* Edited by Richard McKeon. New York: Random House, 1941.

Arnauld, Antoine, and Pierre Nicole. *La Logique ou l'art de penser; contenant, outre les règles communes, plusieurs observations nouvelles, propres à former le jugement.* Paris: Flammarion, 1970.

Augustine, Saint. *On Christian Doctrine.* Translated by D. W. Robertson, Jr. New York: Macmillan, 1958.

Bacon, Francis. *The Philosophical Works of Francis Bacon.* Edited by Peter Shaw. London: Printed for J. J. and P. Knapton, 1733.

Bauzée, Nicolas. *Grammaire générale ou exposition raisonnée des éléments nécessaires du langage, pour servir de fondement à l'étude de toutes les langues.* Stuttgart-Bad Cannstatt: Friedrich Frommann Verlag, 1974.

Beattie, James. *The Theory of Language.* London: A. Strahan and T. Cadell, 1788.

Bièvre, Marquis de. *Calembours et autres jeux sur les mots d'esprit.* Edited by Antoine de Baecque. Paris: Éditions Payot et Rivages, 2000.

Blackwell, Thomas. *An Enquiry into the Life and Writings of Homer.* London, 1735.

Blair, Hugh. *Lectures on Rhetoric and Belles Lettres.* Philadelphia: Troutman and Hayes, 1853.

Böhme, Jacob. *Mysterium Magnum, or an Exposition of the first book of Moses, called Genesis.* Translated by J. Sparrow and J. Ellistone. London: Printed by M. Simmons for H. Blunden, 1654.

———. *The Works of Jacob Behmen, the Teutonic Theosopher.* London: Printed for G. Robinson, 1772.

Boswell, James. *London Journal, 1762–1763.* Edited by Frederick A. Pottle. New Haven: Yale University Press, 1950.

Bougeant, Guillaume-Hyacinthe. *Amusement philosophique sur le langage des bêtes.* Edited by Hester Hastings. Genève-Lille: Droz-Giard, 1954.

———. *Amusement philosophique sur le langage des bêtes; avec le supplément, ou plutôt la critique de cet ouvrage; la lettre du P. Bougeant à M. l'abbé Savalette; et un Précis sur la vie et sur les Ouvrages de l'Auteur de l'Amusement Philosophique.* Peking: Chez Gogué et Née de la Rochelle, 1783.

———. *La Femme docteur, ou la Théologie janséniste tombée en quenouille, comédie.* Amsterdam, Chez E. Ledet, 1731.

———. *Les Quakres François, ou Les Nouveaux Trembleurs, comedie.* Utrecht: Chez Henry Khyrks le jeune, 1732.

———. *Le Saint déniché ou la Banqueroute des marchands de miracles, comedie.* The Hague: Chez Pierre l'Orloge, 1732.

———. *Voyage Merveilleux du Prince Fan-Férédin dans la Romancie; Contenant plusieurs Observations Historiques, Géographiques, Physiques, Critiques et Morales.* Edited by Jean Sgard et Geraldine Sheridan. Saint-Étienne: Publications de l'Université de St-Étienne, 1992.

Bouhours, Dominique de. *Entretiens d'Ariste et d'Eugène.* Edited by René Radouant. Paris: Editions Bossard, 1920.

Boullier, David-Renaud. *Essai philosophique sur l'âme des bêtes précédé du Traité des Vrais Principes qui Servent de Fondement à la Certitude Morale.* Amsterdam: Chez François Changuinon, 1737.

Brown, John. *An Estimate of the Manners and Principles of the Times.* London: Printed for L. Davis, and C. Reymers, 1757.

Chanet, Pierre. *De l'instinct et de la connoissance des animaux avec l'examen de ce que M. de la Chambre a escrit sur cette matière*. La Rochelle: Par Toussaincts de Govy, 1646.

Charlevoix, François-Xavier. *Histoire et Description générale de la Nouvelle-France*. 3 vols. Paris: Pierre-François Giffart, 1744.

———. *Journal d'un Voyage fait par ordre du Roy dans l'Amérique Septentrionnale*. Edited by Pierre Berthiaume. Montreal: Les Presses de l'Université de Montréal, 1994.

Charpentier, François. *Défense de la langue françoise pour l'inscription de l'Arc de triomphe*. Paris: Chez Claude Barbin, 1676.

———. *De l'excellence de la langue françoise*. Paris: Chez la Veuve Bilaine, 1683.

Chastellux, François-Jean de. *Voyages de M. le marquis de Chastellux dans l'Amérique Septentrionale, dans les années 1780, 1781 & 1782*. 2 vols. Paris: Prault, 1791.

Chaudon, Louis-Mayeul. *Bibliothèque d'un home de goût*. Avignon: J. Blery, 1772.

Clark, Michael P., ed. *The Eliot Tracts: With letters from John Eliot to Thomas Thorowgood and Richard Baxter*. Westport, CT: Praeger, 2003.

Colden, Cadwallader. *The History of the Five Indian Nations of Canada*. London: Lockyer Davis, J. Wren and J. Ward, 1755.

Colletet, Guillaume. *Traité de l'épigramme*. Paris: Antoine de Sommaville, 1658.

Condillac. *Œuvres complètes*. 16 vols. Genève: Slatkine Reprints, 1970.

———. *Traité des animaux*. Paris: Librairie J. Vrin, 1987.

Court de Gébelin, Antoine. *Monde primitif analysé et comparé avec le monde moderne*. Paris: L'auteur, 1773–82.

Cureau de la Chambre, Marin. *Traité de la connaissance des animaux*. Paris: Librairie Arthème Fayard, 1989.

Curtis, George William. "Lectures and Lecturing" *Harper's Monthly Magazine*, December 1856, 122–125.

Diderot, Denis. *Oeuvres complètes*. Paris: Garnier Frères, 1875.

Diderot, Denis, and Denis d'Alembert, eds. *Encyclopédie, ou, Dictionnaire raisonné des sciences, des arts et des métiers*. 35 vols. Stuttgart-Bad Cannstatt: Frommann, 1966.

Dixmerie, Nicolas Bricaire de la. *Le Sauvage de Taïti aux Français; avec un envoi au philosophe ami des sauvages*. London: Chez Le Jay, 1770.

Du Bos, Abbé. *Réflexions critiques sur la poésie et sur la peinture*. Translated from the Latin by Anne-Marie Lenoir, Sonia Miret, Sophie Rabau, and Michelle Rosellini. Paris: Ecole Nationale Supérieure des Beaux-Arts, 1993.

Dunbar, James. *Essays on the History of Mankind*. London: William Strahan and Thomas Cadell, 1781.

Elliot, John. *The Dying Speeches of Several Indians*. Cambridge, 1685.

———. *A Further Account of the Progress of the Gospel amongst the Indians in New England*. London: Printed by John Macock, 1660.

———. *Late and Further Manifestation of the Progress of the Gospel amongst the Indians in New England*. London: Printed by M.S., 1655.

———. *Tears of Repentance or a Further Narrative of the Progress of the Gospel amongst the Indians in New England*. London: Printed by Peter Cole in Leaden-Hall, 1653.

Felton, C. C. "Review of *Hyperion*." *North American Review* 50 (1840): 145–161.

Fenwick, John. *The Indian: A Farce*. London: Printed for West and Hughes, 1800.

Ferguson, Adam. *An Essay on the History of Civil Soceity*. Edinburgh: Printed for A. Millar and T. Caddel, 1767.

Ferguson, James, ed. *The British Essayists: With Prefaces, Biographical, Historical, and Critical*. 45 vols. London: Printed by J. Haddon for G. Offer, 1819.

Fontenelle, Bernard Le Bovier de. *Conversations on the Plurality of Worlds*. Translated by H. A. Hargreaves. Berkeley: University of California Press, 1990.

Frain du Tremblay, J. *Traité des Langues, où l'on donne des principes et des règles pour juger du mérite et de l'excellence de chaque langue, et en particulier de la langue françoise*. Paris: J.-B. Collignon, 1703.

Fréron, Élie-Catherine. "*Voltériana*," *ou éloge amphigouriques de Fr. Marie Arrouet, Sr. de Voltaire, discutés et décidés pour sa réception à l'Académie française*. Paris, 1748.

Girard, Abbé Gabriel. *La justesse de la langue françoise, ou les différentes significations des mots qui passent pour synonymes*. Paris: Laurent d'Houry, 1718.

———. *Les Vrais principes de la langue françoise*. Genève: Librairie Droz, 1982.

———. *Les Vrais principes de la langue françoise, ou la parole réduite en méthode conformément aux lois de l'usage*. Paris: Le Breton, 1747.

Godwin, William. *The Enquirer: Reflections on Education, Manners, and Literature*. London: Printed for G. G. and J. Robinson, 1797.

Goujet, Abbé Claude-Pierre. *Bibliothèque française, ou histoire de la literature française*. 18 vols. Paris: Chez P. J. Mariette and H.-L. Guerin, 1740–1756.

Grégoire, Henri. *Lettres à Grégoire sur les patois de France, documents inédits sur la langue, les moeurs et l'état des esprits dans les divers régoins de la France au début de la Révolution, suivie du rapport de Grégoire à la Convention, avec une intr. et des notes par A. Gazier*. Paris: Pedone, 1880.

———. *Rapport sur les inscriptions des monumens publics: Séance du 22 nivôse, l'an II de la République*. Paris: Imprimé par ordre de la Convention Natinoale, 1794.

Gregory, John. *A Father's Legacy to His Daughters*. London: Printed for W. Strahan, T. Cadell, and W. Creech, 1774.

Helvétius, Claude-Adrien. *De l'homme*. London: Société typographique, 1773.

———. *Notes de la main d'Helvétius*. Edited by Albert Keim. Paris: Félix Alcan, 1907.

Henley, John. *An Introduction to an English Grammar*. London: Printed by J. Roberts, J. Woodman, J. Stone and R. King, 1726.

Herries, John. *The Elements of Speech*. London: Edward and Charles Dilly, 1773.

Hobbes, Thomas. *The Correspondence of Thomas Hobbes*. Edited by Noel Malcolm. Oxford: Clarendon Press, 1994.

———. *The English Works of Thomas Hobbes*. 12 vols. London: John Bohn, 1841.

———. *Leviathan*. Edited by C. B. Macpherson. Harmondsworth, UK: Penguin, 1968.

Hooker, Thomas. *The Soules Vocation or Effectual Calling to Christ*. London: 1638.

Jefferson, Thomas. *The Commonplace Book of Thomas Jefferson*. Edited by Gilbert Chinard. Baltimore: Johns Hopkins University Press, 1926.

———. *Notes on the State of Virginia*. Edited by William Peden. London: John Stockdale, 1787; New York: Norton, 1972.

Johnson, Samuel. *Johnson's Dictionary: A Modern Selection*. Edited by E. L. McAdam and George Milne. New York: Pantheon, 1963.

Journal de Trévoux, ou, Mémoires pour servir à l'histoire des sciences et des arts. 67 vols. Genève: Slatkine Reprints, 1968–1969.

Kames, Henry Home, Lord. *Elements of Criticism.* Edited by Peter Jones. 2 vols. Indianapolis: Liberty Fund, 2005.

Lafitau, Joseph François. *Customs of the American Indians Compared with the Customs of Primitive Times.* Edited and translated by William N. Fenton and Elizabeth L. Moore. 2 vols. Toronto: Champlain Society, 1977.

LeBouvyer-Desmortiers, Urbain-René-Thomas. *Mémoire ou considération sur les sourds-muets de naissance et sur les moyens de donner l'ouïe et la parole à ceux qui sont susceptibles.* Paris: F. Buisson, 1800.

Le Roy, Tillet, Brisson, Cadet, Lavoisier, Bossut, de Condorcet and Desmarest. "Rapport fait à l'Académie des Sciences, sur la Machine aérostatique, de MM. de Mongolfier." In *Histoire de l'académie royale des sciences avec les mémoires de mathématique et de physique tirés des registres de cette Académie,* 5–23. Paris: Imprimerie Royale, 1784.

Le Sage, Alain-René, *Œuvres.* 4 vols. Paris: A.A. Renouard, 1821.

Locke, John. *An Essay concerning Human Understanding.* Edited by Alexander Campbell Fraser. 2 vols. New York: Dover, 1959.

Mandeville, Bernard. *The Fable of the Bees: Or Private Vices, Publick Benefits.* Edited by F. B. Kay. 2 vols. Oxford: Clarendon Press, 1924.

Mason, John. *An Essay on Elocution, or, Pronunciation.* London: Printed for R. Hett; J. Buckland; J. Waugh; and M. Cooper, 1748.

———. *An Essay on the Power and Harmony of Prosaic Numbers.* London: Printed by James Waugh, for M. Cooper, 1749.

Mather, Cotton. *Magnalia Christi Americana or, The Ecclesiastical History of New England; from Its First Planting, in the Year 1620, unto the Year of our Lord 1698.* Hartford, CT: Silas Andrus and Son, 1853.

Maupertuis, Pierre-Louis Moreau de. *Oeuvres.* Lyons, 1756.

Meister, Jacob Heinrich. *Souvenirs de mes voyages en Angleterre.* Zurich: Chez P. F. Aubin, 1795.

Mercier, Louis-Sebastien. *Tableau de Paris.* Amsterdam, 1782–1788.

Miege, Guy. *The English Grammar.* Menston: Scolar Press, 1969.

The Mirror. 2 vols. Dublin: Printed for T. Walker, J. Beatty, R. Burton, P. Bryne, T. Webb and J. Cash, 1779.

Monboddo, James Burnet, Lord. *Of the Origin and Progress of Language.* 6 vols. Edinburgh: A. Kincaid and W. Creech, 1773–1792.

Montesquieu. *Persian Letters.* Edited and translated by George Robert Healy. Indianapolis: Bobbs-Merrill, 1964.

Morellet, André. *De la conversation.* Paris: Éditions Payot et Rivages, 1995.

Muralt, Béat-Louis de. *Lettres sur les Anglois et les François.* Edited by C. Gould. Paris: H. Champion, 1933.

Paine, Thomas. *The Writings of Thomas Paine.* Edited by Moncure Daniel Conway. 4 vols., esp. vol. 2. New York and London: Putnam, 1894.

Parker, Samuel. *A Discourse of Ecclesiastical Politie.* London: Printed for John Martyn, 1670.

Percy, George. *Observations by Master George Percy, 1607.* New York: Scribner's, 1907. http://www.americanjourneys.org/aj-073/.

Philipon-de-la-Madelaine, Louis. *Homonymes Français, ou Mots qui dans notre langue se ressemblent par le son et diffèrent par le sens.* Paris: Capelle et Renand, 1806.

Piozzi, Hester Lynch. *British Synonymy*. 2 vols. London: Printed for G. G. and J. Robinson, 1794.
Priestley, Joseph. *A Course of Lectures on the Theory of Language and Universal Grammar*. Warrington, UK: Printed by W. Eyres, 1762.
———. *An Essay on the Gift of Tongues, Proving That It Was Not the Gift of Languages in a Letter to a Friend*. Bath, 1786.
Rapin, René. *The Whole Critical Works of Monsieur Rapin*. 2 vols. London: Printed for H. Bonwicke. T. Goodwin, M. Wotton, B. Tooke. S. Manship, 1706.
Reid, Thomas. *An Inquiry into the Human Mind, on the Principles of Common Sense*. Edinburgh: Printed for A. Millar, 1764.
———. *Philosophical Works*. Hildesheim, Ger.: G. Olms, 1983.
Rivarol, Antoine de. *Le Petit Almanach de Nos Grands Hommes pour l'année 1788. Suivi d'un grand nombre de pièces inédites*. Paris: Chez Léopold Collin, 1808.
———. *Petit Dictionnaire des grands hommes de la Révolution*. Paris: Editions Desjonqueres, 1987.
Roland de la Platière, Jean-Marie. "Apperçu des causes qui peuvent rendre une langue universelle, et observations sur celles des langues vivantes qui tend le plus à le devenir," [April 20, 1789]. Reprinted in Anna Mandich, "Roland de la Platière et la langue universelle," *Dix-huitième Siècle* 30 (1998): 317–330.
Rousseau, Jean-Jacques. *Discours sur l'origine et les fondemens de l'inegalité parmi les hommes*. Amsterdam: M. M. Rey, 1755.
———. *The First and Second Discourses together with the Replies to Critics and Essay on the Origin of Languages*. Edited by Victor Gourevitch. New York: Harper Torchbooks, 1990.
———. *Oeuvres complètes*. Paris: Pléiade, 1969.
———. *Oeuvres politiques*. Edited by Jean Roussel. Paris: Bordas, 1989.
———. *Politics and the Arts: Letter to d'Alembert on the Theatre*. Translated by Allan Bloom. Ithaca: Cornell University Press, 1968.
Saint-Evremond. *Oeuvres de Monsieur de Saint-Evremond*. Vol. 6. Londres: Chez Jacob Tonson, 1711.
Sewall, Samuel. *The Letter-Book of Samuel Sewall*. Collections of the Massachusetts Historical Society, 6th ser., vol. 1. Boston, 1888.
Shepard, Thomas. *The Clear Sunshine of the Gospel Breaking Forth upon the Indians in New-England*. London: Printed by R. Cotes for J. Bellamy, 1648.
Sheridan, Thomas. *British Education: Or, the sources of Disorders of Great Britain*. London: R. and J. Dodsley 1756.
———. *A Course of Lectures on Elocution*. London: Printed by W. Strahan, for A. Millar, R. and J. Dodsley, T. Davies, C. Henderson, J. Wilkie, and E. Dilly, 1762.
———. *A Rhetorical Grammar of the English Language*. Dublin: Printed for W. Price, 1781.
Smellie, William. *Encyclopaedia Britannica*. Edinburgh: Printed by A. Bell and C. MacFarquhar, 1771.
———. *Literary and Characteristical Lives of John Gregory, M.D. Henry Home, Lord Kames; David Hume, Esq. and Adam Smith, L.L.D., to Which Are Added a Dissertation on Public Spirit; and Three Essays*. Edited by Alexander Smellie. Edinburgh: Alex. Smellie, etc., 1800.

Smith, Adam. *Lectures on Rhetoric and Belles Lettres.* Indianapolis: Liberty Classics, 1985.

Sprat, Thomas. *History of the Royal Society of London.* London: Printed by T. R., 1667.

Stackhouse, Thomas. *Reflections on the Nature and Property of Languages.* London: Printed by J. Batley, 1731.

Steele, Joshua. *Prosodia Rationalis.* London: Printed by W. Bowyer and J. Nichols: for J. Almon, 1775.

Swift, Jonathan. *The Correspondence of Jonathan Swift 1718–1727.* Edited by F. Erlington Ball. 6 vols. London: G. Bell and Sons, 1910–1914.

———. *Gulliver's Travels.* London: Penguin, 1967.

———. *Poems.* Edited by Harold Williams. 3 vols. Oxford: Clarendon Press, 1958.

———. *A Proposal for Correcting, Improving and Ascertaining the English Tongue.* London: Printed for Benj. Tooke, 1712.

———. *The Prose Works of Jonathan Swift.* 14 vols. Oxford: Printed at the Shakespeare Head Press and Pub. for the press by B. Blackwell, 1939–1968.

———. *A Tale of a Tub, The Battle of the Books, and Other Satires.* London: Everyman's Library, 1909.

———. *The Works of Jonathan Swift, Dean of St. Patrick's Dublin, Containing Additional Letters, Tracts, and Poems Not Hitherto Published with Notes and a Life of the Author.* Edited by Sir Walter Scott. 19 vols. Boston: Houghton, Mifflin, 1883.

Swift, Jonathan, and Thomas Sheridan. *The Intelligencer.* Edited by James Woolley. Oxford: Clarendon Press, 1992.

Temple, William. *Miscellanea in Four Essays.* London: Printed by J.R. for Ri. and Ra. Simpson, 1690.

———. *The Works of Sir William Temple.* 4 vols. New York: Greenwood Press, 1968.

Thwaites, Reuben Gold, ed. *The Jesuit Relations and Allied Documents.* 73 vols. Cleveland, 1896–1901. Reprint, New York: Pageant, 1959.

Tilloston, John. *Of Sincerity towards God and Man.* London: Printed by J. and T. Dormer, 1735.

Villencour, Baret de. *Discours Public sur les langues en general, et sur la langue françoise en particulier.* Paris: Chez l'Auteur, La Veuve Duchesne, Durand, et Cellot, 1780.

Voisenon, Abbé de. *Œuvres complètes.* 5 vols. Paris: Moutard, 1781.

Voltaire. *Le Brutus de M. de Voltaire, avec un Discours sur la tragédie; Seconde édition revue et corrigée par l'auteur.* Amsterdam: J. Ledet et Jaques Desbordes, 1731.

———. *Candide, Zadig and Selected Stories.* New York: Signet Classics, 1961.

———. *Oeuvres complètes.* 52 vols. Paris: Garnier Frères, 1877–1885.

Vossius, Isaac. *De Poematum cantu et viribus rythmi.* Oxonii: E Theatro Sheldoniano; Prostant Londini: Apud Rob. Scot., 1673.

Walker, John. *The Melody of Speaking Delineated.* London: Printed for the author; and sold by G. G. J. and J. Robinson; and T. Cadell, 1787.

Ward, Seth, and J. Wilkins. *Vindiciae academiarum. Containing Some Briefe Animadversions upon Mr. Webster's Book, Stiled, The Examination of Academies.* Oxford: Printed by Leonard Lichfield... for Thomas Robinson, 1654.

Webster, John. *Academiarum Examen, or thee Examination of Academies.* London: Printed for Giles Calvert, 1653.

———. *The Vail of the Covering, Spread over All Nations.* 2nd ed. London: Printed for J. Sowle, 1713.
Webster, Noah. *An American Dictionary of the English Language.* New York: S. Converse, 1828.
———. *An American Selection of Lessons in Reading and Speaking.* Philadelphia: Printed by Young and M'Culloch, 1787.
———. *A Collection of Essays and Fugitiv Writings on Moral, Historical, Political and Literary Subjects.* Boston: I. Thomas and E.T. Andrews, 1790.
———. *Dissertations on the English Language, with an Essay on a Reformed Mode of Spelling.* Boston: Printed by Isaiah Thomas and Company, 1789.
———. *Sketches of American Policy.* Hartford, CT: Printed by Hudson and Goodwin, 1785.
Welsted, Leonard. "Dissertation Concerning the Perfection of the English Language, the State of Poetry, etc." In *Critical Essays of the Eighteenth Century,* edited by Willard Higley Durham, 355–395. New York: Russell and Russell, 1961.
Wilkins, John. *Essay Towards a Real Character and a Philosophical Language.* London: Printed for Sa. Gellibrand, and for John Martyn, 1668.
Williams, Roger. *A Key into the Language of America: Or, An Help to the Language of the Natives in That Part of America Called New-England. Together with Briefe Observations of the Customes, Manners and Worships, etc. of the Aforesaid Natives, in Peace and Warre, in Life and Death...* London: Gregory Dexter, 1643.
Wilson, Thomas. *The Many Advantages of a Good Language to Any Nation.* London: Printed for J. Knapton, 1724.
Winslow, Edward. *The Glorious Progress of the Gospel amongst the Indians of New England.* London: Printed for Hannah Allen, 1649.
Woolverton, Charles. *The Upright Lives of the Heathen and the Dying-Words of Ockanickon, an Indian King.* Philadelphia: Printed by A. and W. Bradford, 1740.

Secondary Sources

Aarsleff, Hans. *From Locke to Saussure: Essays in the Study of Language and Intellectual History.* Minneapolis: University of Minnesota Press, 1982.
Aldridge, Alfred Owen. "Shaftesbury and the Test of Truth." *Publications of the Modern Language Association of America* 60, no. 1 (1945): 129–156.
Allen, Phyllis. "Scientific Studies in the English Universities of the Seventeenth Century." *Journal of the History of Ideas* 10, no. 2 (1949): 219–253.
Axtell, James. *The Invasion Within: The Contest of Cultures in Colonial North America.* Oxford: Oxford University Press, 1985.
Beach, Adam R. "The Creation of a Classical Language in the Eighteenth Century: Standardizing English, Cultural Imperialism, and the Future of the Literary Canon." *Texas Studies in Literature and Language* 43, no. 2 (Summer 2001): 117–141.
Bell, David. *The Cult of the Nation in France: Inventing Nationalism, 1680–1800.* Cambridge, MA: Harvard University Press, 2001.
———. "*Lingua Populi, Lingua Dei:* Language, Religion, and the Origins of French Revolutionary Nationalism," *American Historical Review* 100, no. 5 (December 1995): 1403–1437.

Boas, George. *The Happy Beast in French Thought of the Seventeenth Century.* Baltimore: Johns Hopkins University Press, 1933.
Bradley, James E., and Dale K. Van Kley, eds. *Religion and Politics in Enlightenment Europe.* Notre Dame, IN: University of Notre Dame Press, 2001.
Bross, Kristina. *Dry Bones and Indian Sermons: Praying Indians in Colonial America.* Ithaca: Cornell University Press, 2004.
Brunot, Ferdinand. *Histoire de la Langue Française des origines à 1900.* 13 vols. Paris: Librairie Armand Colin, 1913.
Bynack, V. P. "Noah Webster's Linguistic Thought and the Idea of an American National Culture." *Journal of the History of Ideas* 45, no. 1 (1984): 99–114.
Caldwell, Patricia. *The Puritan Conversion Narrative: The Beginnings of American Expression.* Cambridge: Cambridge University Press, 1983.
Cmiel, Kenneth. *Democratic Eloquence: The Fight over Popular Speech in Nineteenth-Century America.* Berkeley: University of California Press, 1990.
Cohen, Charles Lloyd. "The Conversion among Puritans and Amerindians: A Theological and Cultural Perspective." In *Puritanism: Transatlantic Perspectives on a Seventeenth-Century Anglo-American Faith,* edited by Francis J. Bremer, 233–256. Boston: Massachusetts Historical Society, 1993.
———. *God's Caress: The Psychology of Puritan Religious Experience.* Oxford: Oxford University Press, 1986.
Cohen, Michèle. *Fashioning Masculinity: National Identity and Language in the Eighteenth Century.* London: Routledge, 1996.
Cohen, Murray. *Sensible Words: Linguistic Practice in England 1640–1785.* Baltimore: Johns Hopkins University Press, 1977.
Cointat, Michel. *Rivarol (1753–1801): Un écrivain controversé.* Paris: L'Harmattan, 2001.
Crowley, Tony. *Language in History: Theory and Texts.* London: Routledge, 1996.
Curtis, Mark H. *Oxford and Cambridge in Transition 1558–1642.* Oxford: Clarendon Press, 1959.
Dabezies, André. "Érudition et humour: Le Père Bougeant (1690–1743)." *Dix-Huitième Siècle* 9 (1977): 259–271.
Debus, Allen G. *Science and Education in the Seventeenth Century: The Webster-Ward Debate.* London: MacDonald, 1970.
de Rochemonteix, Camille. *Les Jésuites et la Nouvelle-France au XVIIIe siècle.* Paris: A. Picard et fils, 1906.
Doiron, Normand. *L'art de voyager: Le déplacement à l'époque classique.* Sainte-Foy, Québec: Presses de l'Université Laval, 1995.
Duncan, C. S. *The New Science and English Literature in the Classical Period.* Chicago: University of Chicago Press, 1913.
Eastman, Carolyn. "The Indian Censures the White Man: 'Indian Eloquence' and American Reading Audiences in the Early Republic." *William and Mary Quarterly* 65, no. 3 (July 2008): 535–564.
Eco, Umberto. *The Search for the Perfect Language.* Translated by James Fentress. Oxford: Blackwell, 1995.
Elmer, Peter. *The Library of Dr John Webster: The Making of a Seventeenth-Century Radical.* London: Wellcome Institute for the History of Medicine, 1986.

Eustace, Nicole. *Passion Is the Gale: Emotion, Power, and the Coming of the American Revolution*. Chapel Hill: University of North Carolina Press, 2008.
Faÿ, Bernard. *Rivarol et la Révolution*. Paris: Librairie Académique Perrin, 1978.
Fraser, Alexander Campbell. *Thomas Reid*. Edinburgh: Oliphant Anderson and Ferrier, 1898.
Friedland, Paul. *Political Actors: Representative Bodies and Theatricality in the Age of the French Revolution*. Ithaca: Cornell University Press, 2002.
Fudge, Erica. *Brutal Reasoning: Animals, Rationality, and Humanity in Early Modern England*. Ithaca: Cornell University Press, 2006.
Fumaroli, Marc. *L'âge de l'éloquence: Rhétorique et «res literaria» de la Renaissance au seuil de l'époque classique*. Genève: Librairie Droz, 1980.
Gefriaud-Rosso, Jeanette. "L'Encyclopédie, la femme et la grammaire." In *Éclectisme et cohérences des Lumières: Mélanges offerts à Jean Ehrard*, edited by Jean-Louis Jam, 79–89. Paris: Librairie Nizet, 1992.
Gillispie, Charles Coulston. *The Montgolfier Brothers and the Invention of Aviation, 1783–1784*. Princeton: Princeton University Press, 1983.
Gombrich, E. H. "The Debate on Primitivism in Ancient Rhetoric." *Journal of the Warburg and Courtauld Institutes* 29 (1966): 24–38.
Goodman, Dena. *The Republic of Letters: A Cultural History of the French Enlightenment*. Ithaca: Cornell University Press, 1994.
Gordon, Daniel. *Citizens without Sovereignty: Equality and Sociability in French Thought, 1670–1789*. Princeton: Princeton University Press, 1994.
Gravelle, Sarah Stever. "The Latin-Vernacular Question and Humanist Theory of Language and Culture." *Journal of the History of Ideas* 49, no. 3 (1988): 367–386.
Gray, Edward. *New World Babel: Languages and Nations in Early America*. Princeton: Princeton University Press, 1999.
Gray, Richard T. "Buying into Signs: Money and Semiosis in Eighteenth-Century German Language Theory." In *German Quarterly* 69, no. 1 (Winter 1996): 1–14.
Grayson, Cecil. *A Renaissance Controversy: Latin or Italian*. Oxford: Clarendon Press, 1960.
Grimsley, Ronald, ed. *Maupertuis, Turgot et Maine de Biran: Sur l'origine du langage*. Geneva: Librairie Droz, 1971.
Gustafson, Sandra M. *Eloquence Is Power: Oratory and Performance in Early America*. Chapel Hill: University of North Carolina Press, 2000.
Hall, Robert Jr. *The Italian Questione della Lingua*. Chapel Hill: University of North Carolina Press, 1942.
Hastings, Hester. *Man and Beast in French Thought of the Eighteenth Century*. Baltimore: Johns Hopkins University Press, 1936.
Healy, George R. "The French Jesuits and the Idea of the Noble Savage." *William and Mary Quarterly* 15, no. 2 (1958): 143–167.
Holifield, E. Brooks. *Era of Persuasion: American Thought and Culture, 1521–1680*. Boston: Twayne Publishers, 1989.
Hollyman, Jim. *Études sur les langues du Nord de la Nouvelle-Calédonie*. Paris: Peters, 1999.
Howe, John. *Language and Political Meaning in Revolutionary America*. Amherst: University of Massachusetts Press, 2004.

Howell, Wilbur Samuel. *Eighteenth-Century British Logic and Rhetoric*. Princeton: Princeton University Press, 1971.

Hüllen, Werner. "Good Language—Bad Language: Some Case Studies on the Criteria of Linguistic Evaluation in Three Centuries." In *History and Rationality; The Skövde Papers in the Historiography of Linguistics*, edited by Klaus D. Dutz and Kjell-Ake Forsgren, 315–334. Munster, Ger.: Nodus Publikationen, 1995.

———. *A History of Roget's Theasurus: Origins, Development, and Design*. Oxford: Oxford University Press, 2004.

———. Hundert, Edward. *The Enlightenment's Fable*. Cambridge: Cambridge University Press, 1994.

Hunt, Lynn. *Politics, Culture, and Class in the French Revolution*. Berkeley: University of California Press, 1984.

Hutton, James. *The Greek Anthology in France*. Ithaca: Cornell University Press, 1946.

Jones, Richard Foster. *Ancients and Moderns: A Study of the Rise of the Scientific Movement in Seventeenth-Century England*. Berkeley: University of California Press, 1961.

———. *The Triumph of the English Language*. Stanford: Stanford University Press, 1953.

Kafker, Frank A. "William Smellie's Edition of the *Encyclopaedia Britannica*." In *Notable Encyclopedias of the Late Eighteenth Century: Eleven Successors of the Encyclopédie*, edited by Frank A. Kafker, 145–182. Oxford: Voltaire Foundation, 1994.

Keen, Paul. "The 'Balloonomania': Science and Spectacle in 1780s England." *Eighteenth-Century Studies* 39, no. 4 (Summer 2006): 507–535.

Kelly, Anne Cline. *Swift and the English Language*. Philadelphia: University of Pennsylvania Press, 1988.

Kennedy, George A. *A New History of Classical Rhetoric*. Princeton: Princeton University Press, 1994.

Kennedy, J. H. *Jesuit and Savage in New France*. New Haven: Yale University Press, 1950.

Kerr, Robert. *Memoirs of the Life, Writings, and Correspondence of William Smellie*. Bristol: Thoemmes Press, 1996.

Kibbee, Douglas A. 'The People' and Their Language in 19th-Century French Linguistic Thought." In *The Emergence of the Modern Language Sciences: Studies on the Transition from Historical-Comparative to Structural Linguistics in Honour of E. F. K. Koerner*, edited by Sheila Embleton, John E. Joseph, and Hans-Joseph Niederehe, 111–127. Philadelphia: John Benjamins, 1999.

Klein, Lawrence. "'Politeness' as linguistic ideology in late seventeenth- and early eighteenth-century England." In *Towards a standard English: 1600–1800*, edited by Dieter Stein and Ingrid Tieken-Boon van Ostade, 31–50. Berlin: Mouton de Gruyter, 1994.

Knowlson, James R. *Universal Language Schemes in England and France 1600–1800*. Toronto: University of Toronto Press, 1975.

Kramer, Michael P. *Imagining Language in America: From the Revolution to the Civil War*. Princeton: Princeton University Press, 1992.

Land, Stephen K. *The Philosophy of Language in Britain: Major Theories from Hobbes to Thomas Reid*. New York: AMS Press, 1986.

Langford, Paul. *Englishness Identified: Manners and Character, 1650–1850*. Oxford: Oxford University Press, 2000.

Lauzon, Matthew. "*A Language More Peculiarly Circumstanced Than Any That Has Yet Appeared*: English as a *Perfect* Language in Eighteenth-Century Linguistic Thought." In *History of Linguistics 1996*, edited by David Cram, Andrew R. Linn and Elke Nowak, vol. 2, 175–182. Amsterdam; Philadelphia: John Benjamins, 1999.

———. "Savage Eloquence in America and the Linguistic Construction of a British Identity in the 18th Century." *Historiographia Linguistica* 23, nos. 1/2 (1996): 123–158.

———. "Welsh Indians and Savage Scots: History, Antiquarianism, and Indian Languages in Eighteenth-Century Britain." *History of European Ideas* 34, no. 3 (2008): 250–269.

Lewis, Rhodri. *Language, Mind and Nature: Artificial Languages in England from Bacon to Locke*. Cambridge: Cambridge University Press, 2007.

Lombard, A. *L'Abbé Du Bos: Un initiateur de la pensée moderne (1670–1742)*. Paris: Hachette, 1913.

Lovejoy, Arthur O. *Reflections on Human Nature*. Baltimore: Johns Hopkins University Press, 1961.

Lovejoy, Arthur O., and George Boas. *Primitivism and Related Ideas in Antiquity*. Baltimore: Johns Hopkins Press, 1997.

Lupton, Christina. "Sincere Performances: Franklin, Tillotson, and Steele on the Plain Style." *Eighteenth-Century Studies* 40, no. 2 (2007): 177–192.

Markley, Robert. *Fallen Languages: Crises of Representation in Newtonian England 1660–1740*. Ithaca: Cornell University Press, 1993.

McCosh, James. *The Scottish Philosophy: Biographical, Expository, Critical, from Hutcheson to Hamilton*. London, 1875; repr. Hildesheim: G. Olms, 1966.

Moore, J. L. *Tudor-Stuart Views on the Growth Status and Destiny of the English Language*. College Park, MD: McGrath, 1970.

Morgan, Edmund S. *Visible Saints: The History of a Puritan Idea*. New York: New York University Press, 1963.

Newman, Gerald. *The Rise of English Nationalism: A Cultural History 1740–1830*. New York: St. Martin's, 1987.

Ong, Walter. *Orality and Literacy: The Technologizing of the Word*. London: Methuen, 1982.

Ornmsby-Lennon, Hugh. "Rosicrucian Linguistics: Twilight of a Renaissance Tradition." In *Hermeticism and the Renaissance*, edited by Ingrid Merkel and Allen Debus, 311–341. Washington: Folger Shakespeare Library–Associated University Press, 1988.

Pagden, Anthony. *The Fall of Natural Man: The American Indian and the Origins of Comparative Ethnology*. Cambridge: Cambridge University Press, 1982.

Pearce, Roy Harvey. *Savagism and Civilization: A Study of the Indian and the American Mind*. Berkeley: University of California Press, 1988.

Peters, John Durham. *Speaking into the Air: A History of the Idea of Communication*. Chicago: University of Chicago Press, 1999.

Pettit, Philip. *Made with Words: Hobbes on Language, Mind, and Politics*. Princeton: Princeton University Press, 2008.

Proust, Jacques. *L'Encyclopédie*. Paris: Collection Armand Colin, 1965.
Rath, Richard Cullen. *How Early America Sounded*. Ithaca: Cornell University Press, 2003.
Ricken, Ulrich. *Grammaire et philosophie au siècle des lumières: Controverse sur l'ordre naturel et la clarté du français*. Lille: Publications de l'Université de Lille III, 1978.
———. *Linguistics, Anthropology and Philosophy in the French Enlightenment*. London: Routledge, 1994.
Rochemonteix, Camille de. *Les Jésuites et la Nouvelle-France au XVIIIe siècle*. Paris: A. Picard et fils, 1906.
Rosenfeld, Sophia Anne. *A Revolution in Language: The Problem of Signs in Late Eighteenth-Century France*. Stanford: Stanford University Press, 2001.
Rosenfield, L. C. *From Beast-Machine to Man-Machine: The Theme of Animal Soul in French Letters from Descartes to La Mettrie*. New York: Oxford University Press, 1941.
Russo, Elena. *Styles of Enlightenment: Taste, Politics, and Authorship in Eighteenth-Century France*. Baltimore: Johns Hopkins University Press, 2007.
Sayre, Gordon M. *Les Sauvages Américains: Representations of Native Americans in French and English Colonial Literature*. Chapel Hill: University of North Carolina Press, 1997.
Serjeantson, R. W. "The Passions and Animal Language, 1540–1700." *Journal of the History of Ideas* 62, no. 3 (2001): 425–444.
Sgard, Jean, and Françoise Weil. "Les anecdotes inédites des *Mémoires de Trévoux* (1720–1744)." *Dix-huitième siècle* 8 (1976): 193–204.
Shuger, Deborah. *Sacred Rhetoric: The Christian Grand Style in the English Renaissance*. Princeton: Princeton University Press, 1988.
Simpson, David. *The Politics of American English, 1776–1850*. Oxford: Oxford University Press, 1986
Skinner, Quentin. *Reason and Rhetoric in the Philosophy of Hobbes*. Cambridge: Cambridge University Press, 1996.
Slaughter, M. M. *Universal Language and Scientific Taxonomy in the Seventeenth Century*. Cambridge: Cambridge University Press, 1982.
Smith, Olivia. *The Politics of Language 1791–1819*. Oxford: Clarendon Press, 1984.
Sorabji, Richard. *Animal Minds and Human Morals: The Origins of the Western Debate*. Ithaca: Cornell University Press, 1993.
Sorensen, Janet. *The Grammar of Empire in Eighteenth-Century British Writing*. Cambridge: Cambridge University Press, 2000.
Sparrow, John. *Visible Words: A Study of Inscriptions in and as Books and Works of Art*. Cambridge: Cambridge University Press, 1969.
Starobinski, Jean. "Eloquence et Liberté." *Revue Suisse d'histoire* 26 (1976): 549–566.
Steensma, Robert C. *Sir William Temple*. New York: Twayne Publishers, 1970.
St. George, Robert Blair. "*Heated* Speech and Literacy in Seventeenth-Century New England." In *Seventeenth-Century New England*, edited by David D. Hall and David Grayson Allen, 275–322. Boston: Colonial Society of Massachusetts, 1984.
Stillman, Robert E. *The New Philosophy and Universal Languages in Seventeenth-Century England: Bacon, Hobbes, and Wilkins*. Lewisburg, PA: Bucknell University Press, 1995.

Struever, Nancy, ed. *Language and the History of Thought*. Rochester: University of Rochester Press, 1995.

Tolles, Frederick B. "*Of the Best Sort but Plain:* The Quaker Esthetic." *American Quarterly* 11, no. 4 (Winter 1959): 484–502.

Trilling, Lionel. *Sincerity and Authenticity*. Cambridge, MA: Harvard University Press, 1972.

Vachon, André. *Éloquence Indienne*. Montreal: Fides, 1968.

Van Kley, Dale. *The Religious Origins of the French Revolution: From Calvin to the Civil Constitution, 1560–1791*. New Haven: Yale University Press, 1996.

Vickers, Brian, and Nancy Struever. *Rhetoric and the Pursuit of Truth: Language Change in the Seventeenth and Eighteenth Centuries*. Los Angeles: William Andrews Clark Memorial Library, 1985.

Warren, James Perrin. *Culture of Eloquence: Oratory and Reform in Antebellum America*. University Park: Pennsylvania State University Press, 1999.

Weiss, Helmut. "Animal Language: A Chapter from the Controversy between Rationalism and Sensualism." In *Diversions of Galway: Papers on the History of Linguistics from ICHOLS V, Galway, Ireland, 1–6 September, 1990*, edited by Anders Ahlqvist, 203–212. Amsterdam: John Benjamins, 1992.

Williams, Kathleen. *Jonathan Swift and the Age of Compromise*. Lawrence: University of Kansas Press, 1958.

Wyrick, Deborah Baker. *Jonathan Swift and the Vested Word*. Chapel Hill: University of North Carolina Press, 1988.

Woodbridge, Homer E. *Sir William Temple: The Man and His Work*. New York: Modern Language Association of America, 1940.

Zachs, William J. "The Life and Works of Gilbert Stuart, 1743–86: A Social and Literary Study." PhD diss., University of Edinburgh, 1988.

Index

Aarsleff, Hans, 2
Abstraction
   absence in animal communication, 17–19, 31, 35–36, 57, 59
   absence in primitive languages, 107
   Aristotle on, 21
   French Revolution and, 39
   Hobbes on, 31, 32
   Locke on, 17, 19, 22–23, 105–6
   Mandeville on, 43–44
   Rousseau on, 36, 106
   socially corrosive role of, 35–38, 210
   See also Ambiguity
Adams, John Quincy, 69–70
Addison, Joseph, 40, 180–81, 183, 206
Alexander the Great, 104
Alimoueskan, Eustache, 95–96
Alleine, Joseph, 79
Allou, Charles Nicolas, 229

Ambiguity, linguistic
   animal communication and lack of, 23–24, 38, 59
   celebration of, 10, 40–65, 66
   criticism of, 16–20, 65–66
   and discord, 35–36, 66, 109
   French language and, 10, 150, 155, 178, 198, 201, 225
   Hobbes on, 31–32
   ideograms and lack of, 15–16
   Locke on, 105–6, 109
   Mandeville on, 43, 66
   primitive languages and lack of, 107
   in scripture, 71
   and sociability, 43–44
   Swift on, 45–47
   and wit/humor, 40–41, 63
   women and, 201

American English
  vs. British English, 218, 219–21, 223, 225
  energy of, 222, 229
  as universal language, 225
American Indian(s)
  and American self-concept, 222–23
  dying speeches of, 88–89, 102–3
  Houyhnhnms compared with, 70
  laughter among, 69, 88n76
  poetry of, 117
  sincerity of, 5, 104–5, 130
  smoking ceremony of, 69–70
  un-Christianized, early modern accounts of, 71, 72–73, 88n76, 95, 95n87
American Indian conversions
  eloquence as evidence for authenticity of, 74, 77–78, 80–82, 85–89, 92–94
  Jesuit accounts of, 89–101
  Puritan accounts of, 74, 77–82, 85–89
  thermal metaphors in descriptions of, 78, 83–84, 90, 96, 97–98, 98n92
American Indian eloquence
  divine source of, 77–82, 85–89, 96–99, 102–4, 115
  Jefferson on, 70–71
  language structure and, 114–17, 122–23
  as proof of authenticity of conversions, 74, 77–78, 80–82, 85–89, 92–94
American Indian languages
  Charlevoix's account of, 121–23
  early modern interest in, 71, 72–73, 106–7
  and eloquence, 114–17, 122–23
  French compared with, 144, 148
  as "mother languages," 122
  and sincerity, 5, 130
American Revolution, 216–17
  and English language, 218–23, 228
Analogous languages, 140, 192, 197
  advantages of, 193–94, 210
André, Louis, 92
Andrews, John, 199–200
Anglo-Saxon, idealization of, 221–23

Animal communication
  absence of abstraction in, 17–19, 31, 35 36, 57, 59
  absence of ambiguity in, 23–24, 38, 59
  absence of wit/humor in, 62–63
  Böhme on, 24, 25, 26, 37
  Bougeant on, 56–59, 62–63
  Boullier on, 65
  vs. conversation, 53
  Cureau de la Chambre on, 20–22, 28
  Hobbes on, 6, 29–33, 35, 37, 38
  Mandeville on, 41–43
  Monboddo on, 18
  Rousseau on, 34–35, 37
  Swift on, 6, 45–47, 54–56, 66
  Vossius on, 33, 38–39
  Webster on, 24–29, 35, 36, 37, 38
Aristotle, 20, 21, 27, 29–30, 95
Arnauld, Antoine, 8
Augustine, Saint, 75–76, 77, 84–85

Bacon, Francis, 35
Balloon
  invention of, 172, 176–77
  symbolism of, 173–75
Beattie, James, 203
Beauzée, Nicolas, 137, 140, 141, 142–44
Bell, Andrew, 208
Bell, David, 147, 148, 160, 226n26
Belot, Jean, 1
Berlin Academy Prize, 8, 138, 140, 153, 156, 158, 160, 164, 176, 216
Bièvre, Marquis de, 154, 162, 228
Blackwell, Thomas, 125
Blair, Hugh, 124, 187–89
Böhme, Jacob, 24, 25, 26, 37
Bolingbroke, Viscount, 55–56
Boswell, James, 108–9, 112
Bougeant, Guillaume-Hyacinthe, 56–65
  on animal communication, 56–59, 62–63
  wit/humor of, 59–62, 64–65, 66
Bouhours, Dominique de, 145–46, 149, 157
Boullier, David-Renaud, 65
Brébeuf, Jean de, 92

British elocutionary movement, 205–6
British Empire
  English language and, 192, 213–14
  Roman Empire compared with, 166–68
British English
  vs. American English, 218, 219–21, 223, 225
  corruption of, 221
  See also English language
British national character
  English language and, 178, 181, 187, 214
  Rivarol on, 166–67
Bross, Kristina, 78
Brown, John, 199
Brown, Stephen, 208–9
Burgh, James, 205

Caldwell, Patricia, 80–81
Chanet, Pierre, 20, 23
Charles I (King of England), 166
Charles II (King of England), 33
Charlevoix, François-Xavier, 121, 124, 126
Charpentier, François, 138–39, 142, 144–45, 149–51
Charteris, Samuel, 209
Chastel, François Thomas, 153–54, 161
Chastellux, François-Jean de, 216
Chihouatenhoua, Joseph, 96
Chinese character-writing, 15–16, 26
Chinese language, 143
Christian grand style
  Augustine on, 75–76, 77, 84–85
  converted Indians and, 77–78, 80, 84, 85–89, 99–101
  in Dubos' theory, 119
  Jesuit opposition to, 90, 91–92
Christianity
  humor used to address disputes in, 60–62, 64, 65
  language and disunity in, 29, 38
  thermal metaphors in, 83, 100, 101
  See also American Indian conversions; Jansenists; Jesuits; Puritans; Quakers

Cicero, 90, 91, 91n83, 93, 95, 211
Civilized languages
  as artificial languages, 126
  criticism of, 7, 107, 112, 129
  superiority of, arguments for, 190, 192
Clarity, linguistic
  animal communication and, 23, 33, 35
  climate and, 127
  early modern idealization of, 9–10, 13–14, 38
  English language and, 183, 185, 187, 188, 191, 194
  French language and, 136, 138–42, 165, 194, 215, 224, 229
  Locke on, 14, 109, 131
  and new language schemes, 15
  primitive languages and, 107, 108
  revolutionary languages and, 217
  Swift's parody of schemes for, 47–48
  word order and, 139, 140
Class, language and, 170–71, 172, 202–3, 211
Climate
  and eloquence, 117
  and language, 127–28, 143
Cmiel, Kenneth, 222
Cohen, Charles, 83
Cohen, Michèle, 159
Colbert, Jean-Baptiste, 137, 163
Collier, Arthur, 161
Communication
  contrasting ideals of, 9–10
  emotions and, 10, 110, 112–13
  See also Animal communication; Conversation; Language(s)
Condillac, Étienne Bonnot, 2, 17–18
Conflict(s)
  in 17th-century Europe, 2, 13, 24
  abstraction/ambiguity and, 35–36, 66, 109
  humor/wit and diffusion of, 6, 48–49, 50, 60–62, 64, 65, 174n113
  languages and, 1, 2–3, 5, 8, 13, 29–32, 35–36, 38
  levity and diffusion of, 150
Consonants, Northern languages and, 145

Conversation
  vs. animal communication, 53
  British vs. French, 160
  double entendre and, 199n50
  English language and, 168, 197, 209, 210
  French language and, 147, 157–58, 169–70
  Hume on, 209n75
  and learning, 159, 173
  Rivarol's art of, 169
  Swift on, 53–54, 55
  women and, 159–61, 159n70, 199–200
Corruption of language
  English, 182, 187, 199, 219–20, 221, 222
  French, 228–29
  luxury and, 211–13
  See also Social corruption
Crinito, Pietro Riccio, 149n39
Cripps, John, 103
Cromwell, Oliver, 29
Cureau de la Chambre, Marin, 20–22, 23–24, 28
Curtis, George William, 223, 229

Dablon, Claude, 94, 96
d'Alembert, Jean le Rond, 169n96, 171, 171n103
Deparcieux, Antoine, 171, 171n103
Descartes, René, 26
Diderot, Denis, 142, 153n51
Dindimus (Indian king), 103–4, 105
Discord/disputes. *See* Conflict(s)
Dissimulation
  civilized languages and, 129
  dramatic performances and, 111–12
  French language and, 195, 196, 198–99
  inverted word order and, 142
  women's speech and, 201
  writing and, 111
Dixmerie, Nicolas Bricaire de la. *See* La Dixmerie
Double entendre, 199, 199n50
Dramatic performances
  dissimulation in, 111–12
  English language and, 206–7

Dryden, John, 104
Dubos, Jean-Baptiste, 7, 118–21, 122, 123, 124
Dunbar, James, 13, 189–91
Du Peron, François, 92
Du Verdus, François, 41
Dying speeches, of converted Indians, 88–89, 102–3

Egyptian hieroglyphs, 15, 16
Eliot, John, 76, 78, 81–89
Eliot Tracts, 78, 84, 87–88
  Jesuit Relations compared with, 90, 91, 92, 98
Eloquence
  American conceptions of, 222
  artificial manners and corruption of, 113–14, 126
  Augustine on, 75–76
  climate and, 117
  divine inspiration and, 77–82, 85–89, 96–99, 102–4, 115
  emotions and, 116, 119
  English language and, 204–6
  government forms and, 117
  language structure and, 117, 119
  luxury and decline of, 211–13
  primitive languages and, 6–7, 108, 114–17, 122–26, 128, 130
  as proof of authenticity of Indian conversions, 74, 77–78, 80–82, 85–89, 92–94
  See also Oratory; Rhetoric
Emotions
  in American Indian conversions, 85, 99
  civilized languages' inability to communicate, 112
  effective communication of, 10, 110, 112–13
  and eloquence, 116, 119
  English language and expression of, 204–6
  French language and absence of, 142
  language of nature and, 110, 111, 113, 114

primitive languages and, 111, 126
and word order, 140n15, 141
Empire
  English language and, 192, 213–14
  French language and, 165–68, 213–14
  and linguistic corruption, 211–13
Encyclopaedia Britannica, 191, 208
  article on language in, 192–98, 202–3, 206–7, 213–14
Endecott, John, 86–87
Energy, linguistic
  American English and, 222, 229
  climate and, 127
  English language and, 136, 165, 176, 180, 185–86, 188–89, 191, 195–96, 203–6, 215
  evolution of languages and, 120
  French language and lack of, 142, 148, 157n62, 194–95, 227
  French revolutionaries' schemes to recover, 228
  vs. levity, 9, 149, 218
  primitive languages and, 108, 114–15, 120–21, 122, 126, 130n87, 149
  revolution and, 218
  word order and, 140n15, 141
English Civil Wars, 2, 24, 29, 166
English language
  American Revolution and, 218–23, 228
  and clarity, 183, 185, 187, 188, 191, 194
  classical languages compared with, 191, 193
  and conversation, 168, 197, 209, 210
  corruption of, 182, 187, 199, 219–20, 221, 222
  corruption of French language by, 228–29
  and dramatic performances, 206–7
  and Empire, 192, 213–14
  energy of, 136, 165, 176, 180, 185–86, 188–89, 191, 195–96, 203–6, 215
  French compared with, 164–65, 168–69, 178, 180–84, 191, 194–203, 215, 224

  idealization by British thinkers, 7, 10, 180, 189, 190, 192–97
  lexicon of, 184–85, 187–88
  masculine character of, 202
  and national character, 178, 181, 187, 214
  and oratory, 204–6
  primitive languages compared with, 178, 179–80, 183, 188, 195–96
  Rivarol on, 168, 169
  and sincerity, 136, 178, 181, 183, 196, 203, 204
  and social equality, 202–3, 208, 210–11
  sounds in, 195
  Swift on, 179
  as universal language, 224, 225
  Webster's simplification of, 219, 219n8
  word order in, 185, 188–89, 193–94, 202
  writing and, 204–5
  See also American English; British English
Epigrams, French language and, 162–63
Equivocation. *See* Ambiguity
Etinechkawat, Jean Baptiste, 96
Ewing, Thomas, 192n33

Felton, Cornelius Conway, 222
Fenwick, John, 102
Ferguson, Adam, 124, 210
Flattery
  American thinkers on, 219
  animal communication and absence of, 42
  British English and, 220
  French language and, 198
  See also Dissimulation
Fontenelle, Bernard Le Bovier de, 116, 146, 156n59
Foote, Daniel, 103
Frain du Tremblay, Jean, 137–38, 139–40, 141, 183, 185–86
Franklin, Benjamin, 105n10

Index

French language
  and ambiguity, 10, 150, 155, 178, 198, 201, 225
  and *bel esprit*, 155–63
  British comments on, 5, 177–78, 182
  and clarity, 136, 138–42, 165, 194, 215, 224, 229
  and conversation, 147, 157–58, 169–70
  corruption by English language, 228–29
  corruption of English language by, 182, 187, 199, 222
  and dissimulation, 195, 196, 198–99
  and Empire, 165–68, 213–14
  and energy, lack of, 142, 148, 157n62, 194–95, 227–28
  English compared with, 164–65, 168–69, 178, 180–84, 191, 194–203, 215, 224
  French Revolution and, 217, 225–29
  Greek compared with, 138
  idealization by French thinkers, 5–6, 7, 10, 136
  Latin compared with, 119, 120, 138, 139, 144, 151
  and levity, 10, 136, 147–55, 158, 162–63, 165, 184, 204, 215, 225
  lexicon of, 149, 152, 154–55, 156, 184, 227–28
  and literary styles, 161–63
  and monumental inscriptions, 137, 226–28
  and national character, 7, 149–51, 154, 156–58, 165, 175
  primitive languages compared with, 129, 144, 148
  question of relative merits of, 1, 137–39, 163
  and sociability, 151–58, 161, 178
  and social stratification, 170–71, 172
  sounds in, 142–46, 156
  synonyms in, 151–54, 229
  as universal language, 8, 168, 224
  and wit, 135, 155–56, 162–63, 174
  women and, 159–61, 159n70, 199
  word order in, 139–42

French national character
  balloon as symbol of, 174
  French language and, 7, 149–51, 154, 156–58, 165, 175
French Revolution
  abuse of abstract terms during, 39
  and French language, 217, 225–29
  Jesuit-Jansenist conflict and, 62n64
  and perceptions of language, 223–25
  Rivarol's opposition to, 171–72, 228
Friedland, Paul, 39
Fugitive writing, 161, 162, 226

Galen of Pergamum, 27
Garakontié, Daniel, 94
Garrick, David, 109, 112
Gay, John, 50
Germanic languages, 221
German language, 168, 169
Gibbon, Edward, 219, 220
Giovio, Paolo, 149n39
Girard, Gabriel, 140n15, 151–53, 192
Godwin, William, 54
Goujet, Claude-Pierre, 1, 118
goût moderne, 156n59, 226n26
Government forms, and eloquence, 117
grand goût, 156n59, 226n26
Gravity
  American Indians and, 69
  English language and, 178, 180, 186–88, 207
  false, Swift on, 49
  light and, 147
Gray, Edward, 74
Greek language, 138, 144, 191
Grégoire, Henri, 226–28
Gregory, James, 126
Gregory, John, 200
Grimm, Friedrich Melchior, 158–59
Gustafson, Sandrah, 73

Hahn, Thomas, 103
Hastings, Hester, 59
Helvétius, Claude-Adrien, 2–3
Henley, John "Orator," 205

Herries, John, 205
Hieroglyphs, Egyptian, 15, 16
Hobbes, Thomas, 2, 41
  on animal communication, 6, 29–33, 35, 37, 38
  Mandeville compared with, 41–43
Hooker, Thomas, 83
Horace, 203
Houyhnhnms *(Gulliver's Travels)*, 45, 46–47, 54–56
  American Indians compared with, 70
Hume, David, 209n75, 210, 219, 220
Humor. *See* Satire; Wit

Ideograms, Chinese, 15–16, 26
Imagination
  animals and, 20–21, 22, 33
  and communication, 110
  and humor, 50–51, 52
  in language evolution theories, 189, 191
  in Rousseau's theory of language, 33, 34
  and transpositive languages, 140n15, 141
Inverted construction
  and dissimulation, 142
  English language and, 185, 189
  passions expressed with, 140n15, 141
  primitive languages and, 139, 142
Italian language, 143, 169, 212–13

Jansenists, 60–61, 62n64, 65, 76
Jaucourt, Chevalier de, 140, 141, 155, 157, 157n62
Jefferson, Thomas, 70–71, 75, 221, 222
Jesuit Relations, 90–101
Jesuits, 62n64
  Bougeant and, 60–61, 65
  on eloquence of converted Indians, 89–101
  opposition to Christian grand style, 90, 91–92
Johnson, Samuel, 161, 187, 212, 219–20
Jones, R. F., 183
Jouvency, Joseph, 92

Kames, Henry Home, Lord, 51–53, 208
Keen, Paul, 177
Kelly, Anne Cline, 48, 53–54, 55
Kennedy, George, 211
Knowlson, James R., 23, 27, 29

La Dixmerie, Nicolas Bricaire de, 6–7, 129
Lafitau, Joseph-François, 122
Lahontan, Baron de, 107, 121n58
Lalement, Jérôme, 69, 95–98
Lancelot, Claude, 8
Language(s)
  analogous, 140, 192, 193–94, 197, 210
  and class, 170–71, 172, 202–3, 211
  climate and, 127–28, 143
  and conflict, 1, 2–3, 5, 8, 13, 29–32, 35–36, 38
  and emotions, communication of, 10, 110, 112–13
  and enlightenment, 8–9
  evolution of, theories of, 123–28, 149, 179, 189, 190
  ideal, quest for, 8–9, 15–16
  lexicon and merits of, 151–54
  luxury and corruption of, 211–13
  money and, 128, 128n83
  "mother" vs. "derived," 120, 121, 122
  and national character, 1, 135, 136–37, 138, 148–51, 159, 164
  origins of, theories of, 17, 19, 106–7
  phonotactics and merits of, 142–46
  relative merits of, 1–2, 136–46, 151–54
  revolutionary period and, 217–18, 223–25
  schemes to invent, 3–4, 15, 23, 25–26
  and sociability, 2, 4, 9, 127, 148
  and social corruption, 196, 198
  syntax and merits of, 139–42
  transpositive, 140, 192, 193, 197, 202
  women and, 199–201
  See also Civilized languages; Primitive languages; Universal language; *specific languages*

Index

Latin
  English compared with, 191, 220
  French compared with, 119, 120, 138, 139, 144, 151
  Greek compared with, 144
  luxury and decline of, 211
  vs. modern languages, 117
  phonotactic characteristics of, 143
Laughter
  American Indians and, 69, 88n76
  See also Wit/Humor
LeBouvyer-Desmortiers, Urbain-René-Thomas, 38–39
Légèreté, French, 147–51, 161
  balloon as symbol of, 174
  republican critique of, 225, 226n26, 227
  See also Levity, linguistic
Lejeune, Paul, 72, 90–92, 96, 97, 98–99
Le Mercier, Father, 96
Le Sage, Alain-René, 102
Leusden, Johannes, 87
Levity, linguistic
  vs. energy, 9, 149, 218
  French language and, 10, 136, 147–55, 158, 162–63, 165, 184, 204, 215, 225
  Puritan rejection of, 88n76
  vs. sincerity, 6
Lexicon
  of English language, 184–85, 187–88
  of French language, 149, 152, 154–55, 156, 184, 227–28
  of primitive languages, 148
  and relative merits of languages, 151–54
Light, 146–47
  See also Levity
Locke, John
  on abstraction/ambiguity, 17, 19, 22–23, 105–6, 109
  on clarity, 14, 109, 131
  and Dubos, 118
  and early modern linguistics, 2–3, 4, 107–8
  and Girard, 153, 153n51
  hostility to rhetoric, 10

  method for studying and reforming language, 14–15
  Sheridan on linguistics of, 109–10
  on wit/humor, 51
Logan, John, 70–71, 75
Louis XIV (King of France), 137, 157, 170

Macfarquhar, Colin, 208
Mandeville, Bernard, 41–44, 55, 66, 178
Mangouch, Estienne, 95
Marivaux, Pierre Carlet de Chamblain de, 156, 156n59
Marolles, Michel de, 149n39
Mason, John, 205, 220
Mather, Cotton, 72, 73, 76, 79, 87
Mather, Increase, 87
Mather, Richard, 80
Maupertuis, Pierre-Louis Moreau de, 106–7
Mayet, Etienne, 156
Mayhew, Thomas, 73, 85
Meister, Jacob Heinrich, 176, 180
Mercier, Louis-Sebastien, 163
Miege, Guy, 184
Monboddo, James Burnett, Lord, 1, 18, 69
Money, language and, 128, 128n83
Montesquieu, Charles de Secondat, Baron de, 147, 156n59
Monumental inscriptions, question of, 137, 149
  French Revolution and, 226–28
Morellet, André, 148, 158, 197
Morgan, Edmund, 78
Muralt, Béat-Louis de, 50–51
Murray, John, 192n33

Naigeon, Jacques-André, 153n51
National character
  British, Rivarol on, 166–67
  English language and, 178, 181, 187, 214
  French, balloon as symbol of, 174
  French language and, 7, 149–51, 154, 156–58, 165, 175
  language and, 1, 135, 136–37, 138, 148–51, 159, 164
Native Americans. *See* American Indians

Nature, language of
  Böhme on, 24, 25
  emotions in, 110, 111, 113, 114
  influence of writing on, 111
  Mandeville on, 44
  Rousseau on, 33–37
  and sincerity, 203
  as universal language, 26, 34, 58–59
  Webster on, 25, 26
  See also Animal communication;
    Primitive languages
Neologisms, women and invention of,
  200–201
New England Puritans. *See* Puritans
Newton, Isaac, 147

Ockanickon (Lenape Chief), 102–3
Oratory
  American conceptions of, 222
  American Indian, 70, 73–75, 91, 94,
    101, 114, 124, 198–99
  English language and, 204–6
  Roman, 119
  women and, 161
  See also Eloquence

Pagden, Anthony, 72, 104, 107
Paine, Thomas, 221
Parker, Samuel, 38
Particulars, language of
  Condillac on, 17–18
  Cureau de la Chambre on, 28
  Hobbes on, 33
  Locke on, 19, 22–23
  Rousseau on, 34
  Webster on, 27–28
Pascal, Blaise, 61
Passions. *See* Emotions
Percy, George, 72–73
Pettit, Philip, 31
Philipon-de-la-Madelaine, Louis, 155
Piozzi, Hester Lynch, 161
Poetry
  American Indian, 117
  divine inspiration and, 115
  English, 188, 195, 204

Pope, Alexander, 56
Priestley, Joseph, 82n47, 146–47, 173, 177
Primitive languages
  and character of people, 148
  and eloquence, 6–7, 108, 114–17,
    122–26, 128, 130
  and emotions, 111
  and energy, 108, 114–15, 120–21, 122,
    126, 130n87, 149
  English compared with, 178, 179–80,
    183, 188, 195–96
  idealization of, 107–8, 130–31
  lexicon of, 148
  and sincerity, 6, 125, 128, 129, 130n87,
    190, 196
  superiority of civilized languages in
    relation to, 190, 192
  word order of, 139, 142
  See also American Indian languages;
    Nature, language of
Print. *See* Writing
Pronunciation, and relative merits of
  languages, 142–46
Puns, 154, 155, 162–63, 174, 174n113
Puritans
  on American Indians as barbarians,
    72–73
  and Christian grand style, 76
  on conversion and eloquence, 77–78,
    79–82, 85–89
  on dying speeches of converted
    Indians, 88–89
  importance of rhetoric for, 76
  morphology of conversion, 78–79
  textual practices of, 73–74
  thermal metaphors in descriptions of
    Indian conversions, 78, 83–84

Quakers, 102–4
Querelle de l'arc de triomphe, 137, 149
Questione della lingua, 136–37

Ragueneau, Paul, 93, 99–101
Rapin, René, 206
Rath, Richard, 72
Reid, Thomas, 7, 124–27, 189, 190

Revolution
  and language, 217–18, 223–25
  See also American Revolution; French Revolution
Rhetoric
  absence in animal communication, 42, 58–59
  Hobbes on, 31–32
  Locke on, 10
  Mandeville on, 43
  Puritans and, 76
  See also Eloquence
Rhetorical primitivism, theory of, 75–76
Rivarol, Antoine de, 7, 10, 140–41, 164–73, 215
  on American Revolution, 216–17
  on balloons, 172
  on French Empire, 165–68, 213–14
  on French légèreté, 147
  on French pronunciation, 146
  on French Revolution, 171–72, 228
  on French vs. British conversation, 160
  on French vs. English language, 164–65, 168, 169
  on French word order, 140–41
  on fugitive writing, 162
  rise to prominence, 168–69, 169n96, 171, 173
  Smellie compared with, 203, 207, 208
Rivarol, Antoine-Roche, 168n95
Rivarol, Jean-Baptiste, 168n95
Roland de la Platière, Jean-Marie, 223–25
Roman Empire, 166–68
  See also Latin
Rosenfeld, Sophia, 4–5, 6, 35, 39, 130n87
Rousseau, Jean-Jacques
  on abstraction, 36, 106
  on language and national character, 135
  on language of nature, 33–37
  on southern vs. northern languages, 127–28
  on women and conversation, 160
  on written language, 111
Royal Society of London, 25, 38

Russo, Elena, 51, 155–56, 163, 226n26
Rymer, Thomas, 206

Saint-Évremond, Charles de, 53
Salons, Parisian, 160, 160n71, 169
Satire
  Bougeant's use of, 59–61
  Swift's use of, 54–56, 66
Savage languages. *See* Primitive languages
Schwab, Johann Christoph, 160, 161–62, 176–77
Seneca, 211
Sgard, Jean, 59
Shepard, Thomas, 81, 83, 84, 86
Sheridan, Geraldine, 59
Sheridan, Thomas, 3, 108, 109–14, 127, 203–4, 205
Sign language, 4, 26, 39, 130n87
Silent *e*, in French, 145, 146, 149n41
Sincerity
  American Indians and, 5, 104–5, 130
  American thinkers on, 218–19
  as communication ideal, 9, 10
  communication of emotions and, 110
  dramatic performances and lack of, 111–12
  and effective communication, 113–14
  English language and, 136, 178, 181, 183, 196, 203, 204
  vs. levity, 6
  natural language and, 203
  primitive languages and, 6, 125, 128, 129, 130n87, 190, 196
Skinner, Quentin, 31, 32
Smellie, William, 191–98, 200, 206–13
  and democratization of knowledge, 208–11
  on luxury and corruption of language, 212–13
  on relative merits of languages, 192–94
  rise to prominence, 207–9
  on superiority of English language, 10, 195–97, 206–7, 215
  Webster compared with, 219, 220
Smith, Adam, 19, 49, 189

Smith, John, 72
Smith, Olivia, 221
Sobrière, Samuel de, 185
Sociability
   ambiguity and, 43–44
   English language and, 210, 214
   French language and, 151–58, 161, 178
   human vs. animal, 41–42
   language and, 2, 4, 9, 127, 148
   and learning, 173
   légèreté and, 147–48
   primitive vs. civilized languages and, 129
   wit and, 52
   women and, 160
Social corruption
   abstraction and, 35–38, 210
   languages and, 196, 198
Social equality, English language and, 202–3, 208, 210–11
Social stratification
   French language and, 170–71, 172
   language and, 203
Sounds
   in English language, 195
   in French language, 142–46, 156
   in transpositive languages, 193
The Spectator, 40, 180–83, 205, 206
Sprat, Thomas, 23, 186
Stackhouse, Thomas, 183, 184–86, 206
Steele, Richard, 180, 181, 182, 205
Swift, Jonathan, 45–56
   on animal communication, 6, 45–47, 54–56, 66
   on art of conversation, 53–54, 55
   on English language, 179
   on wit/humor, 6, 48, 50, 52
Synonyms
   in French language, 151–54, 229
   real vs. apparent, 151–52, 151n46
Syntax. *See* Word order

Tahitian language, 129
Temple, Sir William, 50, 115–18
   influence on Dubos, 118, 119, 121

Theater. *See* Dramatic performances
Thermal metaphors, 71
   Christian faith and, 83, 100, 101
   in descriptions of English language, 195, 196, 215
   in Greek myth of Apollo, 116
   in Jesuit accounts of Indian conversions, 90, 96, 97–98, 98n92
   in language evolution theories, 189, 191
   in "private conversation" ideal, 197
   in Puritan accounts of Indian conversions, 78, 83–84
   in Rousseau's language theory, 127–28
Tillotson, John, 181–82
Tod, William, 209
Totiri, Estienne, 99–101
Transpositive languages, 140, 192, 202
   and conversation, 197
   energy/passion in, 140n15, 141
   sounds in, 193
Tsondatsaa, Charles, 93
Tsondihouonne, René, 99

Universal language, 223–25
   American English as, 223, 225
   English language as, 224
   French language as, 5, 7, 8, 140, 154, 161, 168, 224
   language of nature as, 26, 34, 58–59
   and religious harmony, 29
   schemes to invent, 4, 23, 25–26
Universal writing systems, 26–27

Villencour, Baret de, 135, 148, 162
Vimont, Barthélemy, 93
Voisenon, Abbé de, 60
Voltaire
   on English language, 206
   on French language, 225–26
   on Girard's dictionary of synonyms, 153n50
   and *goût moderne,* 156n59
   on polite sociability, 157
   on relative merits of languages, 2

Voltaire *(cont.)*
  on Rivarol, 171n103
  on women and linguistic refinement, 160
Vos, Gerard John, 33
Vossius, Isaac, 33, 38–39
Vowels, French, 144–46

Walker, John, 205
Walpole, Horace, 177
Ward, Seth, 25, 26, 27
Warren, James Perrin, 222
Washington, George, 69, 70
Webster, John, 24–29, 35, 36, 37, 38
Webster, Noah, 218–21
Welsted, Leonard, 179
Whitfield, Henry, 86, 88
Wilkins, John, 4, 15, 25, 26, 27
Williams, Kathleen, 47
Williams, Roger, 77, 88
Wilson, John, 87
Wit/Humor
  absence in animal communication, 62–63
  as alternative to conflict, 6, 48–49, 50, 60–62, 64, 65
  ambiguity and, 40–41, 63
  Bougeant and, 59–62, 64–65, 66
  French language and, 135, 155–56, 162–63, 174
  imagination and, 50–51, 52
  Locke on, 51
  Muralt on, 50–51
  Rivarol and, 169
  and sociability, 52
  Swift on, 6, 48, 50, 52
  Temple on, 50
  women and, British attitudes toward, 200n53
  See also Satire
Women, and language
  British attitudes toward, 199–201, 200n53
  French attitudes toward, 159–61, 159n70, 199
Woolverton, Charles, 102–4
Word order
  in English, 185, 188–89, 193–94, 202
  in French, 139–42
  See also Inverted construction
Wordplay, 154, 155, 162–63, 174, 174n113
Writing
  Chinese character-writing, 15–16, 26
  Egyptian hieroglyphs, 15, 16
  English language and, 204–5
  French language and, 161–63
  and insincerity, 111
  New England Puritans and, 73–74

Yvon, Abbé Claude, 57, 64–65